DRINKING IN DEAL

Half title Outside the Swan, Queen Street.
Frontispiece Edward Galley Grigg (*left*), landlord of the Albion.
Title page Hills' brewery yard.

DRINKING IN DEAL

BEER, PUBS AND TEMPERANCE IN AN EAST KENT TOWN 1830–1914

Andrew Sargent

BOOKSEAST

For Elizabeth

This edition is published by
BooksEast
29 Nelson Street
Deal
Kent
CT14 6DR

email BooksEast@btinternet.com

www.dealbookseast.co.uk

ISBN 978-1-908304-20-9

© Andrew Sargent 2016

All rights reserved. No part of this publication may be reproduced, stored in a retrieval system, or transmitted in any way or by any means, electronic, mechanical, photocopying, recording or otherwise, without the prior written permission of the copyright holder.

The author has asserted his moral right.

A CIP catalogue record for this book is available from the British Library.

Edited and designed by Joy Wotton

Printed and bound by the CPI Group (UK) Ltd, Croydon CR0 4YY

Contents

Introduction	9
1 The Business of Brewing	**20**
Hills and Thompson's	20
Brewers and public houses	30
Brewing and town life	38
Consolidation	49
2 Pubs and Publicans	**58**
A town full of pubs	58
The houses	70
The landlords	81
The landladies	93
3 The Users and Uses of Public Houses	**101**
Boatmen, marines, lodgers and visitors	101
Conviviality and entertainment	117
Clubs and societies	128
Civic and public functions	139
4 Disorder, Regulation and Bad Behaviour	**151**
Magistrates and police	151
Drunkenness and disorder	168
Houses of ill repute	179
Enforcing the licensing laws	187
Bad behaviour at election time	201
5 Controversies and Closures	**215**
The temperance movement in Deal	215
The licensed victuallers mobilise	228
Magistrates under pressure	242
Managing the closures	254
Deal public houses and beerhouses	272
Bibliography	276
Index	281

Illustrations

Outside the Swan, Queen Street	1
Edward Galley Grigg (*left*), landlord of the Albion, Beach Street	2
Hills' brewery yard	3
Luggers on Deal Beach	9
Richard and Ann Riley	10
Fire at the Antwerp, Beach Street	14
A Leney delivery cart	17
An early print of the Lower Street brewery	22
Walmer brewery in the early days	25
Thompson's Walmer brewery after modernisation	27
North Deal in the 1920s	32
The Endeavour, Shatterling	33
The Bowling Green, Church Walk	35
The Alma, West Street	37
Deal High Street	38
Thompson & Son employees *c.*1890	39
Brewer's house, Great Mongeham	43
Thompson steam wagon in the 1930s	44
Hills' brewery yard	45
The Fawn, Lower Street	50
Stanhope Road looking east	54
Walmer Brewery in the twentieth century	55
The India Arms, Beach Street	59
The Harp, Middle Street	63
The Five Ringers, Church Walk	64
The Magnet, Church Walk	73
The Deal fire brigade outside the Royal Hotel, Beach Street	76
Fire damage to the Antwerp, Beach Street	77
Storm-damaged sea wall outside the Castle	78
The new Sandown Castle alongside the old Castle	79
Edward Hanger, landlord of the North Star, Beach Street	82
John Tandy, landlord of the Castle	83
Frederick "Flint" Roberts outside the Rose and Crown, Beach Street	85
Edward Galley Grigg (*left*), landlord of the Albion, Beach Street	88
George "Cash" Erridge, landlord of the Prince Albert, Alfred Square	91
The Liverpool Arms and the Admiral Keppel, Upper Deal	95
The Yarmouth Packet, Beach Street	96
Sarah Licence, landlady of the Saracen's Head, Alfred Square	98
Deal pier and shipping in the Downs	103

Illustrations

Beach Street after a storm showing the Royal Exchange	105
The fleet at anchor off Deal	108
Royal Marines church parade	111
Deal beach looking north	115
The garden of the Clifton, Middle Street	121
The Hare and Hounds, Western Road	122
Inside the Five Bells, Middle Street	124
William Oatridge's restaurant and the Antwerp, Beach Street	127
Charabanc outing from the Saracen's Head, Alfred Square	129
The Rose, Lower Street	133
The Eagle, Queen Street, c1922	134
The Deal Castle, Victoria Road (formerly Prospect Place)	137
The New Inn, Lower Street	143
Outside the Swan, Queen Street	145
Stage coach outside the Walmer Castle, South Street	146
Deal Town Hall in the twentieth century	155
PC James Shelvey Cox	158
Sandwich Gaol	161
Joseph Phlipott, Town Sergeant	167
The former Paragon Music Hall, Middle Street	170
An inspection at the Walmer barracks	176
The Jolly Sailor, West Street, in the 1930s	179
The Roxburgh Castle, Broad Street	182
Advertisement for the Sir Sidney Smith, Beach Street, in the 1930s	186
The Park Tavern, Park Street, in 1944	187
The Old Victory, Middle Street, *c.*1915	190
The Railway Tavern, Queen Street, *c.*1922	196
The Rose and Crown, Beach Street in the 1920s	198
The Star and Garter, Beach Street	201
Vanity Fair cartoon of Sir Julian Goldsmid	205
John Outwin's newsagent shop	206
The coxswains of the Deal, Walmer and Kingsdown lifeboats	211
Reverend Bruce Payne, Vicar of St George's	219
Enrolling temperance seaman on board ship	221
Reverend James Bartram, Congregational Minister	222
Beach House Temperance Hotel	227
Edward Hugessen Knatchbull-Hugessen MP	235
Aretas Akers-Douglas MP	237
William Licence, landlord of the Saracen's Head, Alfred Square	240
The Brickmaker's Arms, Mill Road	246
George Cottew, Mayor of Deal	251
The Three Compasses, Beach Street, *c.*1922	252

A recent picture of the Telegraph, Hamilton Road   257
Beach Street looking north, with the Royal Hotel   260
Reverend T Stanley Treanor   263
The Crown, Beach Street   264
The Liverpool Arms, Upper Deal   266
Outside the Prince Albert, Alfred Square   268

MAPS AND FAMILY TREE

Map of the main east Kent breweries, *c.*1875   11
Family tree of the Thompsons and Matthews   26
Map of Hills' public houses and beerhouses in 1901   51
Map of the Hills' brewery site   53
Map of public houses and beerhouses in Deal, *c.*1870   66
Map of public houses and beerhouses in central Deal, *c.*1870   69

PICTURE CREDITS

Author's collection: 9, 32, 38, 63, 78, 79, 103, 167, 246, 260. From E. W. Clark, *Reminiscences of Old Deal*: 146. Richard and Opal Crocker: 98, 240. Anthony Duke (maps): 11, 51, 53, 66, 69. Deal Library: 3, 22, 35, 44, 45, 54, 105, 182, 266. Deal Maritime and Local History Museum: 2, 25, 27, 50, 55, 59, 64, 76, 83, 85, 88, 91, 108, 121, 124, 127, 158, 198, 206, 219, 222, 263, 264, 268. Deal Town Hall: 251. Dover Kent Archives: 39, 43, 95, 122, 143, 190, 227. Dover Museum Archives: 1, 17, 77, 115, 145. Steve Glover and Michael Rogers: 14, 37, 73, 129, 133, 137, 155, 170, 179, 186, 187, 201, 257. Kent History and Library Centre: 134, 196, 252. London Library: 205. Chris Murray: 33. National Portrait Gallery: 235, 237. From E. C. Pain, *The Last of Our Luggers and the Men Who Sailed Them*: 82. From J.L. Roget, *Sketches of Deal, Walmer and Sandwich*: 96. Royal Marines Museum: 111, 176. Sandwich Guildhall Museum: 161. From T. Stanley Treanor, *Heroes of the Goodwin Sands*: 211. From T. Stanley Treanor, *The Log of a Sky-Pilot*: 221.

INTRODUCTION

On 2 September 1830 Arthur Wellesley, 1st Duke of Wellington, arrived in London from Walmer Castle, his official residence as Lord Warden of the Cinque Ports. He would hold this office until his death in 1852. In contrast his service to the nation as First Lord of the Treasury – Prime Minister – came to an end less than three months later following a defeat in the House of Commons. In the domestic arena his period of office had been dominated by the issue of Catholic Emancipation and by the resurgence of popular radicalism, but had also been notable for the passage of legislation which transformed the sale of beer. The 1830 Beer Act, which came into effect in October, permitted any ratepayer to sell beer subject only to the purchase of a two-guinea licence from the Excise. In the first full year almost 32,000 licences were issued.

A mile up the coast from Walmer Castle lay the town of Deal, home to several hundred boatmen and pilots serving ships taking passage through the Downs. Beerhouses soon began to open in the town, cheek by jowl with the 39 existing public houses. Some came and went, leaving little or no trace, but others established themselves and achieved a measure of respectability. The option of purchasing a licence was particularly

Luggers on Deal beach, north of the pier. Beach Street, to the left, was reckoned in 1895 to have an average of one public house every 32 yards.

DRINKING IN DEAL

The Middle Street boatman Richard Riley and his wife Ann posing for a studio portrait. Their son William ran the nearby Prince Albert, previously a grocer's shop and beerhouse, for almost 25 years.

attractive to grocers, able then to diversify by selling beer which customers could drink on the premises or take home. One such was William Riley, who ran a shop at the corner of Middle Street and Alfred Square (and who in 1861 was the victim of serial shoplifting by an 11-year-old girl with a fancy for his Dutch and Cheshire cheeses).

Riley purchased his beer licence at some point in the 1850s. In 1864 he succeeded in obtaining a full licence from the magistrates to sell wine and spirits in addition to beer, and having thus transformed his beerhouse into a public house named it the Prince Albert. Although the premises were sold at auction that year to the Canterbury brewers George Beer, Riley remained landlord until 1888. The son and brother of boatmen, and at times suspected by the authorities of smuggling, on his death in 1897 the local paper described him as highly respected and predicted that he would be remembered by many as "one whose honesty of purpose and good-heartedness were worthy of admiration"[1]. In the 1881 census his son Richard appears as a shorthand writer and daughters Maria and Amelia as pupil teachers; for one historian of the Deal boatmen "this represents a definite move away from the traditional maritime Deal towards the new, middle-class town, and may stand as a symbol of the break up of the old community which Deal was experiencing in this period[2]". The Prince Albert however survived. Enlarged in 1956 by the incorporation of the house next door, it is now a free house and restaurant. In its 1906 manifestation it graces the cover of Steve Glover and Michael Rogers' admirable survey of public houses in Deal, Walmer, Kingsdown and Mongeham[3].

I became interested in the history of Deal's public houses many years ago after the then landlord of the Prince Albert kindly showed me the deeds of the house. My interests quickly widened – just how many public

INTRODUCTION

houses and beerhouses were there in Victorian and Edwardian Deal at any one time? Where were they and what were they like; who owned them, who ran them and who brewed the beer they served? What were they "for", and what part did they play in the life of the town and the lives of those who lived there? One question led to another. How were houses in Deal regulated and controlled and by whom, and what might this mean in practice for the landlord (or landlady) and for customers drinking not wisely but too well? On the other hand, what about the significant number of people in Deal who viewed most public houses with disapproval, and the minority who forswore all alcoholic drinks and devoutly wished others would do the same? And, finally, how did

The main east Kent breweries, c.1875, mentioned in the text.

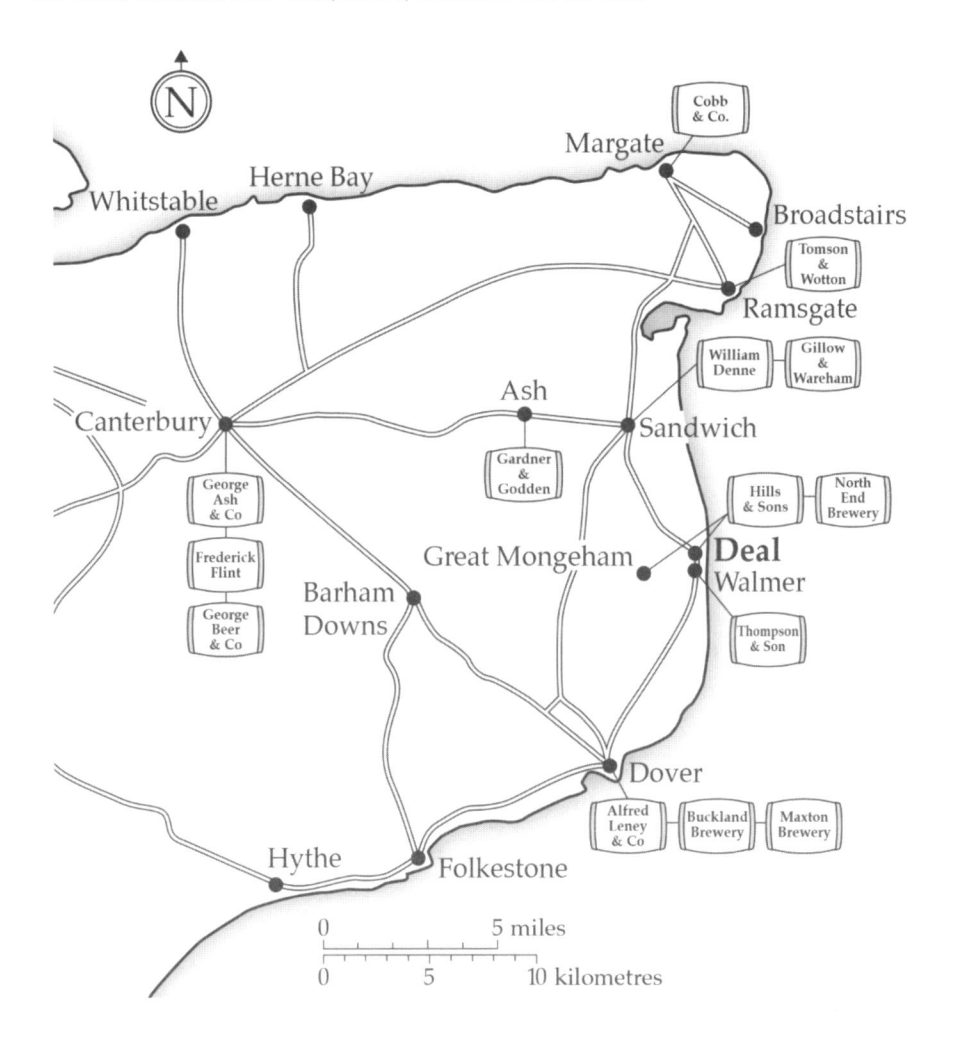

the conflicting pressures and viewpoints play out in the decisions taken by the magistrates on the opening and closing of public houses? These questions have interested me for a long time, and eventually led to the writing of this book.

Material to be found in various national and local archives, including the records of Deal Borough Council, trade directories, Parliamentary Papers and census returns, has been useful. But this book is above all an exercise in deploying evidence extracted from local newspapers. For the years between 1830 and 1858 it is difficult, in their absence, to piece together a detailed picture. But in mid-century the price of newspapers fell dramatically, following the repeal of advertisement duty, newspaper stamp tax and paper duty. A large number of new provincial weeklies soon began to appear. In Deal the Liberal-leaning *Telegram*, launched in 1858 as the *Deal, Walmer and Sandwich Telegram*, ran until 1888. The Conservative-supporting *Mercury*, initially the *Deal, Walmer and Sandwich Mercury, Downs Reporter and Cinque Ports Messenger*, was first published in 1865 and exists to this day. A third newspaper, which began life as the *Deal Chronicle, Sandwich Express and Walmer Gazette*, ran from 1875 until 1900 in various guises but had less impact.

Fortunately for the historian the Victorian editor's concept of what was newsworthy, and so deserving a good share of column inches, includes much that would today seem mundane and easily dispensable. Both the *Telegram* and the *Mercury*, in the manner of the time, carried detailed accounts of council meetings, magistrates' hearings, coroners' inquests and public meetings. Meetings of local clubs and societies were also regularly if somewhat randomly covered, though the fact that such reports were generally supplied by a participant at the event can raise doubts as to just how successful they really were. On the other hand the amount of detail that the newspapers felt it reasonable to divulge about individuals, in relation to a bankruptcy, say, or the course of a fatal illness, is surprising by today's standards. Nor did the constraints of "commercial in confidence" seem to hold as much sway, and the newspapers often published details of the tenders received by the council, for example, or by a local brewery for building work.

I have quoted extensively from both the *Telegram* and the *Mercury*. Although the apparently verbatim reports of council debates and of the proceedings at the magistrates' court published in both newspapers were clearly smoothed or improved at times by the reporter, the voices and feelings of the individual Dealites do often reach us from across the years – those of landlords and landladies, plaintiffs and defendants appearing before the bench, policemen and magistrates, councillors, brewers and temperance campaigners.

The town in which these men and women lived and worked lies on the east Kent coast eight miles north of Dover. Upper Deal, a mile or so inland, had been the original nucleus of the town. Surrounded on three sides in Victorian times by farms, market gardens, brickfields and sandhills, the town as a whole continued to have a landward as well as a seaward focus. In the seventeenth century had come the development of Lower Deal – "the only new town of any size to emerge in the county between 1600 and 1700"[4] – in streets stretching north from Deal Castle and in the lanes and alleys connecting them. These were home to hundreds of boatmen and pilots who plied a trade meeting the needs of ships taking anchor in or passage through the Downs seaway. The Goodwin Sands, shifting banks of sand several miles from the coast, gave ships at anchor in the Downs some protection, but were also a fearful and often fatal hazard. Assisting ships trapped on the Goodwins, and salvaging goods from those stuck fast, provided a significant proportion of the boatmen's collective income.

Deal did not have a harbour. Ambitions to build one came to nothing and boatmen continued to launch their vessels from the open beach throughout the nineteenth century, as they still do today. Until 1864 a navy yard occupied ground immediately north of Deal Castle, and three barracks, used first by soldiers and later by marines, stood to the south of the castle in the adjacent village of Walmer. The town thrived rumbustuously during the Revolutionary and Napoleonic Wars. It then sank into a depression with the coming of peace before beginning again to prosper, modestly, from mid-century. By 1877 the population had edged up to 8,000, but this was only a little higher than the wartime peak in 1811. Dover, in contrast, had become a major cross-Channel port, with a population in 1887 of 28,500. The opening of a new iron pier in Deal in 1864 did however help to stimulate the economy of the town, and the development on the one hand of fishing and canning, and on the other of the town as a holiday and tourist resort, offset the reducing demand for the traditional services of boatmen and pilots. By the turn of the century the population of Deal had risen to some 10,600.

Deal had enjoyed the status of a borough since the award of a royal charter in 1699. The councillors and citizens of the town were jealous of their independence and deplored the advance of central and county government into the affairs of the town as the nineteenth century wore on. The town was policed by its own force until 1889, borough magistrates met in the town hall and dispensed summary justice, and the Pavement Commission (until 1873) and the council took the lead – if not always very energetically – in developing the local infrastructure. Within the town North Deal felt itself placed rather lower in the pecking order than South Deal, which included a larger proportion of tradesmen and professional men, and Upper and Lower Deal maintained their distinctive characters. Two, and from 1850 three, Anglican churches and a Roman Catholic chapel served the town. Nonconformity had relatively strong roots, with six chapels making returns to the 1851 religious census: Wesleyan Methodist, Primitive Methodist, Congregational, Particular Baptist, United General Baptist and Strict Calvinist. It was among the non-conformist ministers and their congregations that hostility to the drink trade and to the large numbers of public houses in the town burnt most strongly.

Viewing the damage to the Antwerp, opposite Deal pier, in 1909. The smoke appears to have been added to the picture for dramatic effect.

INTRODUCTION

Despite their efforts, and the many different pressures that have born down on public houses since the late nineteenth century, there are still welcoming and convivial public houses to be found in Deal. But it is certainly sobering to realise that no fewer than nine houses, all of which appear in this book, have closed since I began my research. In July 2015 CAMRA estimated that, across the United Kingdom, an average of 29 pubs were closing every week. But at least the changes in Deal have not been entirely in one direction. To set against the many closures may be put the reopening of one old house (the Jolly Gardener), a new house created by a national pub company (the Sir Norman Wisdom) and – one of a new wave of beerhouses for the twenty-first century – Deal's first "micro-pub" (the Just Reproach).

Recent years have also seen a renaissance of brewing in Kent, at least if measured by the number of micro-breweries that have been set up. But this pales against the position in Victorian Kent, when a large number of breweries of considerable size went a long way to meeting the needs of the county's drinkers – who in the 1870s, assuming consumption matched the national average, were drinking beer at a rate of roughly six pints per head of population per week. Of these Kentish breweries only one, Shepherd Neame, now remains. The actual brewing of the beer consumed in the town of Deal is clearly where this book should begin. The focus of the first chapter is therefore on the fortunes of the two main local breweries, their ownership of public houses and beerhouses in the town, and the part they and their owners played in the life of Victorian and Edwardian Deal.

By 1914 there were 61 public houses in Deal. Seven beerhouses had also survived the course, neither closing nor being transformed into public houses. But the number of houses, of both kinds, had peaked as long ago as 1871, when there had been 79 public houses and 16 beerhouses. The total fell steadily in the decade before the outbreak of the First World War, and has done so ever since. Chapter 2 discusses how and why the number of houses rose and fell over time. It also considers their location and the kinds of establishments they were – from the small number of reasonable-sized hotels, to established neighbourhood public houses, to small public houses and beerhouses tucked away in the maze of streets in central Deal. Attention then turns to the landlords who ran the houses, and to the women who helped them or were landladies in their own right.

Chapter 3 considers the role of the town's public houses and beerhouses in meeting the needs of boatmen, marines and others before looking at the different kinds of entertainment they and other patrons might enjoy. The focus is then on the role of public houses in catering for and in many cases providing a home for the very large number of societies and clubs that came to exist in the town, and the chapter concludes by considering the public and civic functions carried out in licensed premises.

Public houses were regulated, policed and worried about in a way that would have been unthinkable for any other kind of commercial establishment. Throughout the period, and for almost a century beyond, responsibility for granting licences, in addition to dispensing summary justice to landlords and their customers, lay with the borough magistrates. Chapter 4 discusses their role, and that of the police in the town who spent so much of their time keeping a watchful eye on the goings-on in public houses. This is followed by consideration of the incidence, nature and handling of drunkenness and disorder, of houses causing particular problems and of the near obsessive attention that was paid to ensuring that publicans did not sell beer at times when they were not permitted so to do. The chapter concludes by recalling the occasion when the landlords of the town disgraced themselves spectacularly – not that they saw it that way.

I have some admiration for the nineteenth-century temperance movement; this is not simply because my maternal grandfather was employed for a short time by the Massachusetts Anti-Saloon League. The rhetoric and pious seriousness of temperance campaigners is certainly not to today's taste, and their wish to secure the closure of as many public houses as possible can only jar in an era when few would reckon the existence of public houses to be a problem in itself, and many worry about the social costs of the continuing fall in numbers. But many of the issues that concerned the temperance movement are still with us – most obviously the cost to individuals and to society of persistent excessive drinking but also the extent to which rowdy or aggressive behaviour may be fuelled or calmed by particular kinds of licensing restrictions.

The final chapter therefore begins with a survey of the temperance movement in Deal before 1914. As it gained ground, and as its spokesmen repeatedly tried to influence decisions taken by the borough magistrates, the publicans in turn banded together more effectively to defend

An advertisement for Alfred Leney & Co, showing a cart delivering to private customers. The Dover brewery delivered to Deal and owned several public houses in the town.

their interests. The impact of the different camps on the politics of the town, and on the magistrates' licensing decisions, is then discussed. By the 1890s there was in fact widespread agreement that there were too many public houses in Deal, although the magistrates' attempt to respond to this in the case of the Three Compasses came badly unstuck. The chapter concludes by discussing the way in which over 20% of the town's public houses and beerhouses were closed during the Edwardian period through enforcement, negotiation and then through a managed closure programme.

One of the houses to survive the cull was the Duke of Wellington, on the corner of Water Street and Robert Street. It owed its existence as a beerhouse to legislation passed during the Duke's time as Prime Minister, and took his name some years after his death. It survived two world wars, "by all accounts a small but lively pub, especially on a Saturday night when the pianist started playing"[5], before finally closing its doors in 1971.

Acknowledgements

Many interesting books have been written on the history of Deal. I have been fortunate to be able to draw, in particular, on the work of Jacqueline Bower, Barbara Collins, David Collyer, W H Gillespie, Steve Glover and Michael Rogers, Gregory Holyoake, John Laker, Andrew Lane, Gertrude Nunns, E C Pain, Stephen Pritchard and T Stanley Treanor. The present work has been written with the aim, above all, of adding to the sum of knowledge about the fascinating town of Deal in the nineteenth and early twentieth centuries.

I have done my best to set developments in Deal within the wider county and national contexts and so be useful, in addition, to those interested in the history of Kent as a whole, and in brewing, public houses and temperance more generally. A very large number of books, many of them excellent, have been written about public houses in different parts of the country. They usually take the form of an illustrated compendium of houses past and present. This book, however, follows Paul Jennings (writing about Bradford), Rob Donovan (Norwich) and R C Riley and Philip Eley (Portsmouth) in offering a "whole story" account of the consumption of beer and the development and functioning of public houses in a specific location[6].

Landlords and others were often inconsistent or negligent in the use of apostrophes when writing down the names of public houses. I have followed the approach taken by Geoff Brandwood et al[7], in their history of the public house, of inserting an apostrophe when a reasonable guess can be made as to the sense of the name. Some houses appeared under different variants of the same "core" name at different times (the Rose, the Rose Inn and the Rose Hotel, for example). I have plumped for whichever name seemed the simplest or most appropriate, and stuck to this throughout. Public houses and beerhouses were separate legal entities although – closing times aside – this probably mattered very little to most beer drinkers. So although tempted by the catch-all term "drinking place", I decided – except where, in particular in Chapter 2, it was important to be exact – to let the terms public house or "house" be taken to embrace beerhouses, and publican, landlord and landlady to include beerhouse keepers.

I would like to thank my excellent editor Joy Wotton, and my friend Steve Glover with whom I have spent many pleasant hours talking about Deal public houses. I should also like to remember three old

Introduction

friends who enriched present-day Deal by writing about the history of the town and helping to preserve its records: David Collyer, Gertrude Nunns and Terry Williams.

I am indebted to Sue Carey, Elizabeth Casbon, Steve Glover, Jonathan Harris and Chris Murray for reading the manuscript so carefully, and for their helpful and encouraging comments. My thanks also go to Charlotte and Isabella Robson for their valuable work on the Deal and Walmer census returns, to Steve Reece for help with the pictures, to Anthony Duke for drawing the maps and to William Jack for compiling the index.

It is a pleasure to be able to thank the many staff at Deal Library, who patiently fielded so many requests over the years for access to microfilm records and printed material, and also the staff and volunteers at the Deal Maritime and Local History Museum, Deal Town Hall, the Sandwich Guildhall Museum, the Dover Museum Archives, the Kent History and Library Centre, the former East Kent Archives Centre, the Royal Marine Museum, the National Brewing Library, the former Bass Museum, the Library and Museum of Freemasonry, the London Library and the City of London Guildhall Library.

I am also very grateful for the help received from Bob Acton, Denise Coe, Richard and Opal Crocker, Judith Davies, Mollie Field, Barry Finch, Alison Firth, Robin Green, Michael Harlick, Ray Harlow, David Harper, Jo Harper, Ray Ingelton, Nick McConnell, John Mitchell, Peter Moynihan, David Plant, Paul Skelton, Lynne Steward, Colin Varrall, Colin Vurley, Helen Wicker, Bryan Williams and Rachel Witton.

---

1. *Mercury* 1 January 1898
2. J. Bower, "Deal and the Deal Boatmen c 1840 – c 1880", Unpublished PhD thesis, University of Kent, 1990 p. 218
3. S. Glover and M. Rogers, *The Old Pubs of Deal and Walmer (with Kingsdown and Mongeham)* (Whitstable, 2010)
4. J. Whyman, "Rise and Decline: Dover and Deal in the Nineteenth Century", in *Archaeologia Cantiana*, Vol LXXXIV (1969) p 124
5. Glover and Rogers p 60
6. P. Jennings, *The Public House in Bradford, 1770–1970* (Keele, 1995); R. Donovan, "Drinking in Victorian Norwich", in *Brewery History*, No 130 pp 18–64; No 132 pp 67–133; No 134 pp 87–139; No 137 pp 73–165; R. C. Riley & P. Eley, "Public Houses and Beerhouses in Nineteenth Century Portsmouth", in *The Portsmouth Papers*, No 38 (Portsmouth, 1983)
7. G. Brandwood, A. Davison and M. Slaughter, *Licensed to Sell: The History and Heritage of the Public House* (London, 2004), p xi

Chapter 1

The Business of Brewing

Hills and Thompson's
The first modern Deal regatta was held in 1826. By Victorian times the event had become, as it still is, one of the highlights of the summer. Cheered on by large crowds, luggers, galleys and galley punts from Deal, Walmer, Kingsdown and beyond competed for handsome prizes. In 1864, to the amusement of the professional boatmen, the regatta featured a race between the men of Messrs' Hills Deal brewery and those of Mr Thompson's Walmer brewery. The six men of Walmer won easily, the *Telegram* reporting that "the rowing of the Walmer crew was very good, while, as to the other, it was very awkward"[1]. The victors, flushed with success, then accepted a challenge from six sergeants of the Depot Battalion of the Royal Marines and defeated them by a boat's length in a special race the following month. At next year's regatta a boat crewed by brewers saw off a challenge from a group of brickmakers. But by 1866 Hills' men were ready to chance their arm again against the Walmer brewers, and this time their boat "Wait for the Wagon" edged out Thompson's "Paragon". Ashore, among the beer drinkers of Deal, there was no question that Hills held the dominant position, though the Walmer brewery would soon acquire a second wind and begin to challenge strongly. The final outcome would be decided 35 years later.

In 1830 there were 1,436 common brewers in England (usually defined as a brewer producing more than 1,000 barrels a year). Deal had two: Thomas Hight's North End Brewery on Beach Street and a larger brewery in Lower Street owned by Edward Iggulden. The town was in the doldrums, the sometimes feverish activity witnessed during the Revolutionary and Napoleonic Wars having long since subsided.

Then, in contrast, the Downs had been an important naval as well as commercial anchorage, with warships supplied by a busy navy yard and vessels of all kinds supported by large numbers of Deal boatmen. In the late eighteenth century and again during the Walcheren campaign in 1809 the town also played host to large numbers of soldiers embarking on generally unsuccessful continental expeditions, and purpose built cavalry and infantry barracks were erected to the south of the town in nearby Walmer.

Soldiers and sailors, and the townspeople themselves, needed large quantities of beer, and local brewers prospered in consequence. Prominent among them was Thomas Oakley, brewer, banker, shipping agent and miller. The family had been brewing in Deal for a hundred years or more, but in 1807 his son Thomas Parker Oakley sold the brewery and moved to Ealing in Middlesex. The brewery stood at the north end of Beach Street and included in the sale were a copper, mash tun, hop-back coolers, leaden squares and four vats of 90 barrels, a two-storied malthouse and a large residence boasting "a delightful and uninterrupted view of the Downs, French Coast and Isle of Thanet"[2]. The auction particulars stressed not only the advantage of the location for supplying ships in the Downs with beer but also for providing them with fresh water, "the trade of the latter very considerable, there being an abundant supply of excellent water from a well belonging to the brewhouse and malthouse".[3]

A large proportion of the beer consumed in the town and supplied to ships at anchor in the Downs was however brewed elsewhere, and brought around the coast from Dover or Thanet. The major force was the Margate financial and brewing powerhouse created by Francis Cobb. According to Peter Mathias "much of the beer [he] brewed at Margate in the second half of the eighteenth century was sent round to Deal for the fleet"[4]. In due course Cobb bought a brewery in Deal itself and purchased or leased a good many of the town's public houses. The facilities of the navy yard to the north of Deal Castle also included a small brewery, and other small-scale brewing will have taken place in the town for both domestic and commercial purposes.

Edward Iggulden, in contrast, came from a wealthy Deal family. His father John, "another Deal agent who had his finger in many maritime pies"[5], had speculated in whaling and privateering and, on dry land, in the purchase of a brewery in Lower Street. Like Thomas Oakley's brewery, this also did good business in supplying water, as well as beer, to ships

DRINKING IN DEAL

An early print of the brewery owned by John and then Edward Iggulden and purchased by Charles Hills in 1852. On the right is the Rose, to which Hills added a third storey in 1885.

in the Downs. On John Iggulden's death in 1817 the brewery passed to his son Edward, who owned and ran it, "highly respected for the many virtues which adorned both his private and public character" as the *Kentish Gazette* dutifully put it[6], until his death in 1852.

The purchaser of his brewery was Charles Hills, a prosperous wine merchant who had moved from Canterbury to Deal in the 1820s, and Hills Brewery it now became for the rest of its existence. Aged 50, Hills had been Mayor of Deal in 1851, and served a second term of office two years later. He and his wife Ann, the daughter of a Deal solicitor, had nine children. The eldest, Daniel Mackintosh Hills, became senior partner on his father's death in 1854 and would be the town's leading brewer for almost 50 years. In due course Edwin, the youngest of the nine siblings, became junior partner. A third brother Charles, who trained as a solicitor, probably served as company secretary in the 1880s.

Daniel, his widowed mother and his large consort of brothers and sisters lived in Edward Iggulden's former residence, situated in "the best and most central part of Lower Deal"[7]. Put to auction in December 1852 by Iggulden's executors, this was a handsome Georgian house "with excellent and large dining and drawing rooms and ante rooms, office or library, large bed rooms, kitchens [and] scullery"[8], and large vaulted cellars which were later used for bottling beer. The Hills family could enjoy in addition to "lawn and flower garden… hot house and vinery"[9] extensive kitchen and fruit gardens covering over two acres of former meadow land, also purchased from the Iggulden estate, stretching back to West Street. Further up Lower Street, through an entrance a little to the north, lay the brewery itself, with its yard and outbuildings.

The brewery when fully developed was described as "18 quarter" – one in principle capable, that is, of brewing around 18,000 barrels a year. It drew its water from two deep chalk wells and later from the town waterworks. But ensuring the purity of the brewing "liquor" cannot have been straightforward; according to Stebbing, an analysis in 1869 of water from one of Hills' wells concluded from the levels of chlorine that there must be "fairly free communication with the sea", and also found "strong pollution by organic matter"[10]. A separately housed steam engine powered the machinery, and at some point the Hills brothers added a bottling plant and washing store. In 1890 the author of a town guide enthused that the increase of business had "necessitat[ed] a re-arrangement and renewal of most of the plant according to the latest improved principles, one of the most recent additions being a fine modern dome copper of large capacity"[11]. Ten years later the equipment included, in addition to this 50-barrel copper, a small (15-barrel) copper, two copper refrigerators, two malt mills, engines, grinding mills, a yeast press and a cask washing machine.

Brewers in the barley-growing counties of southern and eastern England were almost always their own maltsters, and Hills were no exception. The Lower Street complex included a 15-quarter malthouse, and a second 25-quarter malthouse, "an old and interesting Elizabethan building"[12], stood near Thomas Hight's North End Brewery on Beach Street. In the 1860s Hills expanded the business significantly by acquiring John Noakes Coleman's brewery at Great Mongeham, a village on the oustskirts of Deal. Hills modernised the six-quarter plant on the "tower" principle, and continued to brew there despite a serious fire in 1877. The Deal brewery in contrast, the praises in the town guide notwithstanding, seems increasingly to have shown its age.

The five-quarter North End Brewery was a much smaller enterprise, and by the 1870s had ceased to be viable. Thomas Hight had begun brewing in Deal during the Napoleonic Wars, having purchased Thomas Oakley's Beach Street brewery, and continued to do so for almost 60 years until his death in 1868 aged 87. In his official capacity as Receiver of Droits he was also involved on occasion in the sale of beer arriving unexpectedly in the town, such as the seven hogsheads of London porter taken from the wreck of the *Robin Hood* he put to auction in 1865. Although his brewery had been carried on under the name of Thomas Hight & Son, the son in question, Thomas Tapley Hight, was eager to be rid of it on his father's death. When sold the following year the brewery consisted of "brewing and cooling floors, fermenting and vat rooms, stores and counting-house, excellent stabling and waggon lodges"[13]. With the brewery came a quay and capstan ground on the beach, but the advantage of easy seaward access must have been offset to an extent by the disadvantages of having to pipe water from a well in Water Street, some distance away to the west of Lower Street, up to a tank at the top of the brewery building. There is no sign that either of the Deal breweries was still supplying water to ships in the Downs at this stage, but the brewing process itself required large quantities of liquor; by 1900 brewers needed 15 or 16 barrels of water for every barrel of beer they brewed.

The North End Brewery was bought in March 1869 by John Hatton, from Dover, for £200 (only slightly more than he paid at the same time for the brewery's nearby tied house, the North Star). Offering "a good article at the fair price"[14], he ran the brewery for five years. Then things began to unravel. George Elkins took over in 1874, followed next year by a W H Davies. But in 1877 Davies' business went into liquidation, and the brewery was put to auction together with the waterworks in Water Street and 800 feet of piping[15]. The *Telegram* reported that the purchasers were said to be forming a company "with a view to establishing in connection with the Brewery an aerated water company"[16]. But this came to nothing, and by July 1878 the brewery was back on the market, together with its two public houses. The following February the same paper reported optimistically that the brewery would shortly be reopened by a "thoroughly practical brewer, at present residing in a populous town in the western division of Kent"[17]. This was the last false dawn. Brewing ceased, and in due course part of the premises were put to use as a preserving factory.

Up the hill in Upper Walmer, two miles to the south, it was a very different story. Thompson & Son were now well on their way to a secure future as a profitable independent local brewery. The business even had its own founding myth: that the Thompson family fortune had been secured in Tudor times when Richard Thompson led a party of Deal boatmen in the sacking of the *San de Luis*, a Spanish galleon aground on the Goodwin Sands, and in the ransoming of rescued survivors. Whether any of this fortune found its way in time to Edmund Thompson, the son of a Deal pilot, and helped to smooth his

A cheerful image of the Walmer brewery in the early days, possibly as it was before the improvements made by Edmund Thompson in the 1820s. Edmund, the son of a Cinque Ports pilot, had served an apprenticeship in Deal as a carpenter before marrying the daughter of the owner of the brewery in 1816.

entry into the brewing business, is unclear. More to the point was that in 1816 he married Mary Holtum, whose father owned a small brewery in Walmer. Edmund was persuaded by his father-in-law John to join him in the business, with the result (as the *Telegram* saw it, at any rate) that "each succeeding year witnessed increasing success in trade, and "Thompson's brewery" eventually became a most important establishment in the village, and a source of consequence and wealth to its enterprising proprietor"[18]. Mary died in 1820, aged only 29, but in due course Edmund married her younger sister Elizabeth. His own sister Elizabeth had by now married the prosperous Deal builder George Cottew.

Edmund developed the brewery in the 1820s, but seems then to have left much of the actual business of brewing to his nephew George Holtum, preferring instead to concentrate on running the adjacent farm. A carpenter's apprentice in his youth, Edmund became, according to the *Telegram*, "a remarkably clear-headed man of business, of persevering habits and possessed of cool judgement, with calm, thoughtful, and unassuming manners"[19]. In 1855 he took his son Morris into partnership, and the business was henceforth conducted under the name of Thompson & Son. When Edmund died in 1862 full ownership duly passed to Morris, who had in practice been running the brewery during Edmund's later years. Morris gave every impression of relishing the position this gave him in local society: as Lieutenant in the 3rd Cinque Ports Artillery Volunteers, Member of the Walmer Board of Health, Poor Law Guardian, Director of the Downs Hotel Company, benefactor to the Foresters friendly society and much more besides. But in 1867, at the age of only 33, he decided to cash in his hand.

DRINKING IN DEAL

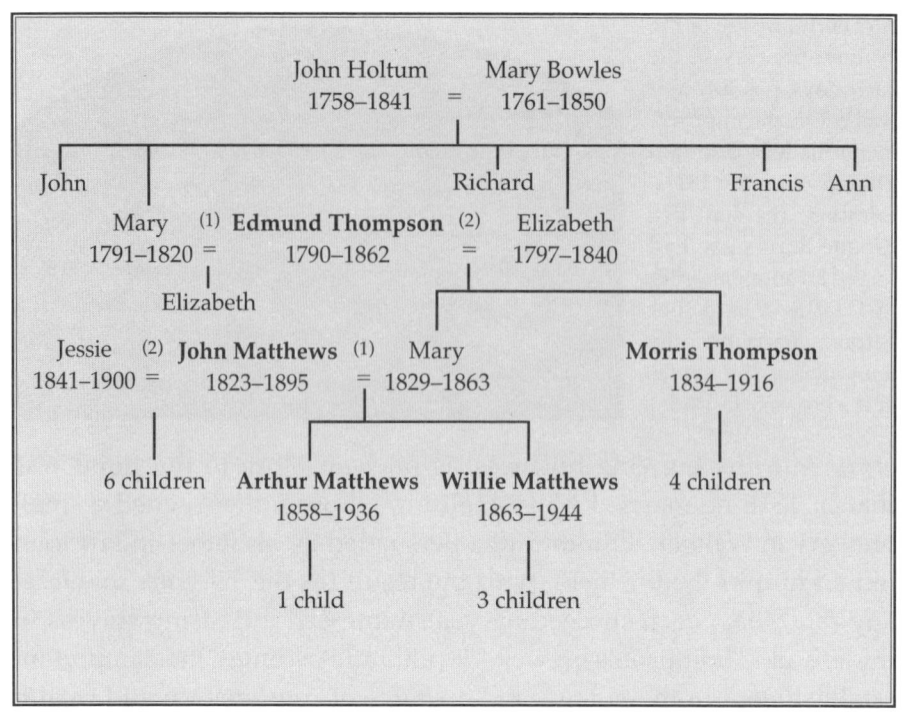

```
                    John Holtum      Mary Bowles
                    1758–1841    =   1761–1850
                              │
      ┌───────────────────────┼───────────────────┬──────┐
    John                   Richard             Francis  Ann
         Mary   (1) Edmund Thompson (2)   Elizabeth
         1791–1820 =   1790–1862     =    1797–1840
              │                              │
         Elizabeth              ┌────────────┴────────────┐
    Jessie   (2) John Matthews (1) Mary          Morris Thompson
    1841–1900 =    1823–1895    = 1829–1863        1834–1916
         │              │                                │
      6 children   Arthur Matthews  Willie Matthews   4 children
                   1858–1936        1863–1944
                        │                │
                     1 child          3 children
```

Thompsons and Matthews: Walmer brewers. The owners are shown in **bold type**.

Why he did so is not known. But the circumstances in which he was able to lay down the cares of brewery management are no mystery. Once again the fortunes of the Walmer brewery were being transformed as a result of a marriage, in this case between Morris' elder sister Mary and John Matthews, senior partner in the firm of Matthews & Canning, of the Anchor Brewery, Chelsea. The couple had married in 1853, but Mary died ten years later. Now John, in his mid-40s, decided to up sticks with his two sons and transform himself into the owner of a small east Kent brewery, and to transform the brewery itself into the bargain. The transition included building for his brother-in-law Morris Thompson a large new house opposite the rectory in the village of Temple Ewell, near Dover. Newspaper predictions that this would be a "most healthful place of abode"[20] proved sadly wide of the mark some years later, however, when Morris was attacked and severely gored by a bull "the injuries inflicted being of so grave a nature as to cause serious apprehension to his friends"[21]. He lived to tell the tale, but Temple Ewell evidently lost its charms. Morris moved soon afterwards to Great Mongeham, near the Hills brewery, where his chief claim to fame became his long and successful tenure as Master of Foxhounds for the West Street Harriers. But he continued to describe himself as a brewer until his death in 1916 at the age of 81.

John Matthews' father had been a brewer in Dorset. Now, given the chance to apply his experience of brewing in the capital to the running of his own Kent brewery, John set about things with a will. Thompson & Son's Brewery it remained, but the buildings and plant were enlarged and extensively modernised. In partnership for 12 years with Frederick Ommanney until the latter's early death in 1889, Matthews also turned his attention to the malting side of the business, first adding three new ranges alongside the existing malthouse, and then a fourth in 1886, "somewhat ornate in design"[22], constructed in red and white brick to the design of Karslake & Co of Westminster. The business also owned maltings in Deal, not far from the Hills brewery, and in 1883 leased another in Great Mongeham. In all, the maltings produced some 10,000 quarters of malt annually, for sale across Kent and beyond as well as for the brewery's own use. The Walmer brewery and malthouses covered an area of some three acres. The buildings were surrounded by a 70-acre farm, the late Edmund Thompson's pride and joy. The business also owned a 150-acre dairy farm in nearby Wingleton.

Thompson's brewery complex after being modernised and extended by John Matthews. The brewery buildings are on the right, the maltings on the left. In front are stacks of beer barrels and at least two small delivery carts.

John Matthews, first at Matthews & Canning and then as the owner of Thompson & Son, operated and prospered during an era which saw a steady increase in the national production of beer. Powered in part by rising per capita consumption, beer production in the United Kingdom rose from an average of 13,486 thousand standard barrels in 1831–4 to 29,032 thousand in 1876. There are no figures for the quantities of beer brewed by Thompson & Son in John Matthews' time. But later company accounts show that in 1911 the firm sold just over 28,000 barrels (at a time when almost three-quarters of the common brewers in the United Kingdom sold fewer than 20,000 barrels) and made a profit of 12s.9d per barrel. The size of the workforce and the number of horses needed to transport the beer they produced suggest that similar volumes were brewed during the John Matthews era.

The writer Alfred Barnard, in the course of his series of peregrinations around selected breweries in Great Britain and Ireland, journeyed down from London at some point in 1890 for a day out at the Walmer Brewery. He found a tower brewery of modern design: at the top, beneath the iron reservoir, the malt receiving store; next the mill-room, hot-liquor tanks and hop store; then the two mash tuns with a capacity of 56 quarters and a 20-horse-power horizontal engine. Next door was the copper house ("a lofty and extensive place, with an open louvred roof constructed of iron"[23]) and close by the cooling department, fermenting room and cleansing room. The last of these drew Barnard's particular attention for containing "two settling backs and 400 ponto vessels, commanded by five capacious topping tanks. It is in these utensils that the wort is cleansed. These ponto vessels are familiar enough in the London porter breweries, but we had not seen them before in the country"[24].

Barnard was at this point refreshed by what he expansively considered to be "the finest stout we had ever tasted"[25]. He was also much taken later on with the AK light bitter ("a delicious drink, clean to the palate and well flavoured with the hop"[26]), while noting that the best known of the "Walmer ales" was probably the XX beer. What strikes the modern reader and drinker is the remarkably wide range of styles and strengths of beers that small local breweries chose and were expected to brew. As Gourvish and Wilson note, "by the 1880s, most brewers of any scale were producing eight to ten beers".[27] Hills, for example, at around the time of Barnard's visit to Walmer, were brewing XXX, XX and X ales, an "especially fine bitter ale known as the "Deal Pale Ale" which has excellent tonic properties", a pale bitter ale "and the usual grades of stout, porter, table ale and table beer"[28]. Even the small North End Brewery, on its last legs in the 1870s, brewed porter, stout, mild, bitter and pale ales. On the other hand feedback from the wholesalers on the quality of the brewers' products is hard to come by. One hundred years previously, in contrast, Daniel Stoddard, opening a coffee room in the nearby village of Ash, had no qualms about expressing his ire in the *Kentish Gazette*: "he has also laid in three Butts of Mr Cantis' fine pale beer, being obliged to apply to Canterbury, as he met with such bad success with the half-anchors of Mr Oakley's Stout Ale, which he bought in Deal"[29].

Cooling equipment, like Thompson's "two vertical refrigerators of the newest pattern"[30] able to cool 50 barrels an hour, ensured that brewing could now be an all-year round process. Until the introduction of refrigeration brewing could only be carried out in the autumn, winter and early spring since higher temperatures led to uncontrollable fermentation which could ruin the whole brew. Consumers, too, had to take care. In 1858, for example, Thompson's were urging their patrons to lose no time in ordering their supplies of XXX Ale and East India Pale Ale "as its keeping Mild and Brilliant throughout the year is secured by having it before the weather gets warm"[31.] But here and across the industry the practical application of the science of brewing made significant if variable progress in the following decades, and there is little reason to doubt that Thompson's (and, probably, Hills) bore testimony to Gourvish and Wilson's later assessment that "most brewers turned out better beers in 1900 than they had fifty years earlier".[32]

Barnard does not mention the bottling of beer at the Walmer brewery. But, unlike the brewing and vatting of porter in the London style which so delighted him, this was very much a pointer to the future. Thompson's were by then bottling a range of their lighter beers in screw-top bottles. Hills' bottled beers included their No 1 and No 2 Ales and No 1 and No 2 Stouts, samples of which, finding their way to *The Anti-Adulteration Review*, prompted an outburst of approval for the gentlemen who belong to "the old stamp, and pride themselves on making beer from the old fashioned materials, viz. malt and hops"[33]. John Matthews and his sons no doubt considered themselves no less traditional in this regard. But forward looking they were, and the direction lay almost inexorably towards ties with large national brewers. By the 1890s the brewery was bottling large quantities of Bass ales in addition to its own. This partnership seems to have served the Walmer brewery well. But often the interest of a large brewery in a smaller one would have a very different outcome. Four years after John Matthews' death in 1895 his old London firm of Matthews & Canning was acquired by Whitbread, and the brewery closed in 1907. Much later, especially during the 1960s, Whitbread would extend their reach dramatically and purchase and then close down many Kentish breweries. These included the Margate brewery of Cobb & Co, a firm once so influential in the development of brewing and beer retailing in Deal.

Brewers and public houses
The practice of private brewing declined steadily after 1830, and for many common brewers the selling of beer direct to private customers formed a significant part of their business. This was true of Hills and Thompson's, both of whom routinely placed advertisements in the two local papers in the 1860s and 1870s, either prosaic ("families supplied with Casks, from four and a half gallons upwards"[34] – Hills) or promotional ("XXX Ale and East India Pale Ale now ready and in splendid condition"[35] – Thompson's). The latter still had an extensive private business in 1890, according to Barnard, but by 1900 Hills' private trade had all but withered away. By now the habit of drinking beer at home had been given fresh impetus as a consequence of technological advances in the bottling of beer. It was a sign of the times that in 1903, to augment their deliveries to licensed retailers and private individuals – and against some local opposition – Thompson's secured an "off" beer licence to sell their bottled beers at the brewery (in quantities of under three dozen).

But for Thompson's and Hills alike the sale of their beer through public houses was critical to their success. These were either "free" or "tied". By the end of the century the tied house – a licensed premise owned or leased by the brewer and selling the brewer's beer – had become the dominant form of public house ownership across the country. In many parts of southern England, and certainly in Deal, this model took hold very early. Common brewers in Deal had publican tenants by the 1730s, and part of Cobb's strategy for the expansion of trade with and in the town during the Napoleonic Wars included purchasing or leasing at least seven public houses. Whereas nationally only a minority of licensed premises were tied (in one way or another) to individual brewers in 1830, in that year 23 of the town's 39 houses belonged to the Deal brewer Edward Iggulden, with several others almost certainly owned by other east Kent brewers.

The next chapter looks at the distribution and development of public houses and beerhouses in Victorian Deal. It considers in particular the extraordinary increase in the number of houses between 1847 and 1870, and the ensuing stability, at least in terms of overall numbers, that lasted for the next 30 years. The expansion mid-century was the product of a mixed economy, the cumulative result of business ventures by individuals and groups of investors as well as by the brewers. What then took place was a steady re-concentration of public houses into the brewers' hands, and the almost complete disappearance from the town of the privately owned licensed house. By 1900 the impact of Government policy and the decisions of the local magistrates were beginning to be felt, and the overall number of houses began to decrease inexorably soon afterwards.

In terms of the ownership of public houses in Deal, Hills were unquestionably in the dominant position. As early as 1807 the brewery later bought by Charles Hills had attached to it 17 public houses "in and near the town of Deal"[36]. To these John and Edward Iggulden added perhaps a dozen more, through the purchase or lease of houses formerly tied to Cobb, or following the auction in 1828 of the land of the Manor of Chamberlain's Fee (one of Deal's three ancient manors). At the time of Charles Hills' purchase of the brewery the estate included some 25 houses in Deal, which by 1870 had been increased to 30 – almost 40% of the licensed premises in the town. This was a smaller proportion than Iggulden had owned in 1830 but was against a much higher total: Deal now had 79 public houses compared with 39 in 1830. Acquisitions by Hills during that period included the rebuilt Pelican on Beach Street, and two houses on the outskirts of the town (the Lord Warden and the Duke of York). In the 1870s several further purchases came from the sale of other brewery estates, in particular the Ship in Middle Street (from John Omer of Sandwich) and the two houses previously attached to the North End Brewery, the North Star and the Queen's Head. Thereafter, as the availability of individual houses for purchase increasingly dried up, and the willingness of the magistrates to grant new licences virtually

North Deal in the 1920s. Thompson's provoked indignation in 1869 when they built the Lifeboat close by the North End Brewery's North Star. From left to right are the North Star, the Deal lifeboat house, the former Lifeboat beerhouse, and the Forester.

disappeared, Hills' investments were largely directed towards rebuilding and refurbishment. Though here too there is a sense of declining energy and business drive as the century wore on.

The same cannot be said of Thompson's. Their first house in Deal was probably the Providence, for which Edmund Thompson held the lease in 1839, and by 1870 the number had risen to seven. Over the next ten years Thompson's more than doubled their holdings, through private sales and auctions (the White Horse, the Victoria and the Windsor Castle) and by picking up houses at auction following the failure or sale of rival breweries. The Pier Hotel and the Forester, both on Beach Street, the Druid's Arms in Market Street and the Royal Marine beerhouse came from the auction of the estate of William Denne's Sandwich brewery in April 1875, with the Park Tavern being added in 1878 from the estate of the White Post Brewery in Ash. Thompson's had previously run into opposition, however, with their decision in 1869 to build a new house, the Lifeboat, next to the North Deal Lifeboat Station but also close to the North End Brewery's North Star. The granting of a licence was strongly resisted by the new owner of the brewery, John Hatton, and by local publicans. The magistrates decided the following year to award a beer licence, on the basis that Thompson's had invested in the building of the house before the 1869 Act ended the right simply to purchase a licence from the Excise, but they refused a spirit licence. The upshot of all this enterprise was that by 1880 Thompson's owned 13 public houses and three beerhouses in the town. The activities of both Thompson's and Hills during this period give support to David Gutzke's conclusion[37] that brewers across the country were buying up sizeable numbers of public houses and beerhouses well before the reckless surge of purchases that began in the 1880s.

After the closure of the North End Brewery the only beer both brewed commercially and consumed in Deal came from Hills brewery. It is very striking, and another example of how the town was in the forefront of trends in southern England which took very much longer to work through in other parts of the country, that there is no evidence that any of the town's public houses still brewed their own beer by this period. This had been common enough in the previous century; the Five Bells "and brewhouse", for example, went to auction in 1730, and when the Swan on Beach Street was let in 1744 it came "with a good brewhouse adjoining for brewing their own beer"[38]. One or two public houses in Walmer may have continued to brew into Victorian times (in 1867 the

The Endeavour was a Hills beerhouse in the hamlet of Shatterling to the north west of Deal. On the ground floor was a bar, tap room, sitting room, kitchen and pantry. The house had a large garden and orchard.

Lord Warden offered a 250 gallon "nearly new" brewing copper for sale[39]) but there is no evidence of this for Deal. The 50-gallon copper stolen from the Star in 1854 may have been used to brew beer in earlier days but by then it was the property of Charles Hills and the house was at that point untenanted. Nationally, in contrast, an estimated 45% of all beer sold in 1830 had been brewed by publicans, and the practice continued to be widespread in the Midlands and parts of the North for many years. Private brewing, on the other hand, which had accounted for around a fifth of all beer brewed in 1830, had become a tiny part of total national output by 1870. The last trace of private brewing in Deal may have been the "brew house with coppers" included in the sale of the old Admiralty House in Queen Street in 1864[40].

Most small town brewers depended, like Hills, on a strong home base. But they usually also owned or leased a sprinkling of public houses in villages and nearby towns accessible to their drays – in practice a radius of 15 miles or so. By 1900 Hills' estate included 21 public houses and six beerhouses outside of Deal, of which five public houses and a beerhouse were in next-door Walmer. Some brewers extended their reach by establishing depots in nearby towns; part of Thompson's strategy for extending sales in Thanet was the establishment of a branch office and ale store in Ramsgate. In much the same way a significant number of east Kent breweries had a presence in Deal at one time or another. In the 1870s 11 east Kent breweries held almost 30% of the houses in Deal: four brewed in Canterbury, three in Sandwich, three in Dover and one in Ramsgate.

The most successful of these came to be the Canterbury brewer George Beer, notwithstanding the boast of its owner Alfred Beer in 1875 that the business did not need to resort to any large extent on tied houses. The bulk of their estate in Deal, including the Albion on Beach Street and the Bowling Green in Upper Deal, came from the purchase of the Buckland Brewery in Dover in 1888, but they had also bought the Prince Albert at auction in 1864 and the Port Arms, another Beach Street house, at about the same time. By the turn of the century George Beer were comfortably in third place in terms of the ownership of houses in the town, with a total of eight public houses and three beerhouses. They and other out-of-town brewers had maintained their overall share of the houses in the town, although the number of Kent breweries with a stake had fallen from eleven to seven.

Aspects of the relationship between brewers and their tenants, particularly at the point of transfer or when problems arose, will emerge in later chapters. But the chance survival of a George Beer letter book from 1906 gives a flavour of the routine exchanges between a medium-sized county brewer and its tenants. In January, for example, George Erridge (landlord of the Deal Lugger) was complaining about the quality of some of his beer; the brewery, rather affronted, suggested refining it and if necessary speaking to their agent during his next Friday visit. In the same month Walter Carter (the Crown) was being ticked off for not sending cash with his latest order – a frequent grumble – and in March had to be issued with a "timely and friendly warning"[41] after a complaint from the police. In May there were problems with a staved barrel delivered to the Prince Albert, and a disagreement with John Roberts (the Fox) about the return of waste beer in a porter barrel. But also that month came the company's latest sales push, with all tenants invited to take a 4½ gallon sample of the new XX Strong Ale. ("We find many of our customers are taking it up, and it has already gained the name "Canterbury Barley Wine"...we are sending you today a card advertising same for your Bar and no doubt this will cause enquiries to be made by your customers"[42].)

George Beer acquired the Bowling Green when they purchased the Buckland Brewery in Dover in 1888. It offered a variety of outdoor summer activities. For some reason, until Herbert Sayers took over in 1901, there were frequent changes of landlord.

DRINKING IN DEAL

Beer, even strong ale, is a high volume/low value product. In Victorian times the difficulties of transporting it imposed natural limits on the growth of breweries without extensive local markets. Although the burgeoning railway network and the later development of efficient steam- and petrol- driven road transport steadily broke down the old "tariff of bad road"[43], and so enabled the expansion among others of the mighty Burton brewers, patterns of small town public house ownership overwhelmingly reflected the dynamics of the local and regional brewing industries until well into the twentieth century. So it is surprising to find the presence in Deal of a medium-sized Surrey brewer. This was Nalder & Collyer of Croydon. The brewery had made a point of acquiring or building premises in Surrey and Kent as the railway began to open up the countryside, and they owned many "railway houses". By the 1860s they had reached Folkestone, and in due course came a foothold in Dover. The building of the line between Dover and Deal, which opened in 1881, was the signal for Nalder & Collyer to move onwards to Deal itself with the purchase of the Alma in West Street and the Greyhound in Middle Street. To these were later added the Clifton, a Middle Street house boasting a good-sized garden and a tennis court.

Signage, in large letters, on the Alma, the Greyhound and the Clifton put the name of Nalder & Collyer in the public eye. The products of the major London and Burton brewers were of course well known, and arrived for sale in some public houses and in wine merchants' shops in barrels and increasingly in bottles. An important retailer of bottled beer in the town was the wine merchant A F S Bird, whose wine vaults were in the India Arms on Beach Street. As well as retailing Bass and Guinness bottled beer, Bird moved into the "own brand" market in 1873 by offering beer "brewed expressly for AFSB at one of the first breweries in the County"[44] and sold in bottles with labels of his own design. A similar tie with a large London brewer enabled him to offer Bird's London Cooper Stout, which he described in 1888 as "almost equal to Stout but less heady and very strengthening"[45]. Bottled beer was also increasingly available from licensed grocers' shops, much to the irritation of the publicans. In 1885 this included, from a shop in Walmer, "Anglo-Lager Beer"[46] brewed by Mackeson & Co of Hythe – a small trickle that would become a torrent 100 years later.

Bird's India Arms soon ceased to operate other than as a wine, spirits and beer store, the *Mercury* noting in 1905 that the only value of its

The Alma was built in 1855, a year after the Crimean War battle from which it took its name, and in its early years was home to the Deal Horticultural Society. In the 1880s it was one of three houses owned by the Croydon brewers Nalder & Collyer – the only non-Kentish brewer to have pubs in the town.

licence was to sell wines and spirits in less than full bottles. Certainly by the end of the nineteenth century Hills, Thompson's, George Beer and the rest had virtually squeezed the privately owned public house out of existence. Roughly half of the new spirit licences taken out between 1845 and 1870 had been granted to private individuals, with the result that a quarter of Deal licensed premises were then in private hands. But by 1900 there were only four such: the India Arms itself, the Royal Hotel, the Star and Garter and (not really a pub) the Pier Refreshment Rooms.

The brewers' success in gathering up almost all of the licensed premises in Deal, and within their ranks the dominance in the town of a single owner, is very striking even in contrast to other areas of east Kent. Parliamentary returns in 1892 showed that at that point less than 4% of houses in Deal were owner occupied, an appreciably lower proportion than in Dover (10%) or Sandwich and its liberties (7%). At that point Hills owned 45% of the houses in Deal. In Dover, a larger town with several competing brewers, the firm with the largest number of houses (George Beer, having bought and dismantled the Buckland Brewery) owned 28% of the total. Tomson & Wotton of Ramsgate owned 25% of houses in the Sandwich licensing district, the East Kent Brewery Company in Sandwich owning only 5%. The returns also show that Thompson's, with ten houses, had made much more headway in Dover than Hills (with only two houses). In the Sandwich licensing area, which included Walmer, Hills owned ten houses and Thompson's eight.

The transfer of licensed premises to brewery ownership was often the result of a disposal by executors after the death of the owner. A viable house was a very desirable commodity and, unlike today, the existence of a licence to sell beer, wine and spirits was itself a valuable asset. That was certainly the experience of the boatman and boat owner Onesiphorus

Sneller. In 1853 he bought a plot of ground on the seaward side of Beach Street from Edward Iggulden's trustees. With the help of a mortgage from the local building society he then built and ran a beerhouse which he named the Napier Tavern. A full licence was granted by the magistrates in 1859. When Sneller sold the house to the Dover brewers Alfred Leney in 1873 he did so for £125 plus an annuity for him and his wife of 25 shillings a week, though only – Leney were taking no chances – on the strength of an undertaking that they would never again "directly or indirectly sell Beer, Ale or Porter in Deal"[47].

Brewing and town life

Hills and Thompson's had a significant physical presence, Hills in the centre of Deal with their two tall brewery chimneys visible for miles, and Thompson's "on the brow of a gentle hill rising above the village .. a prominent, and we may add" – this is Barnard again – "a graceful object in the landscape of which [the brewery] forms a part"[48]. The bustle, noise and smell of their brewing and malting helped shape the urban and rural environment of this corner of east Kent. But the presence of the breweries was felt in other ways too, for example as a source of employment, in the movements of their drays and wagons and through their community and philanthropic activities. And the brewery owners – the Igguldens, Hills, Thompsons and Matthews – were men of

Smartly dressed townsmen and women, probably returning from worship at St George's church, pass Hills brewery on the left. The High Street entrance to the brewery is in the middle of the picture.

consequence in the small town social, commercial and political circles which sustained Victorian and Edwardian Deal and Walmer.

The nineteenth-century brewing industry was capital intensive. But in contrast to many other units of production, breweries were not major employers of labour. Bass in Burton-on-Trent employed 2,560 men and boys and 200 clerks in 1887, but such giants were the exception. Medium-sized London and regional brewers operated with a workforce of 200 or so, and small local breweries made do with just a handful of permanent employees; Thomas Richardson, running the Great Mongeham brewery for Hills, had only two staff in 1871. Employment was often part-time or seasonal. The same was true for many agricultural workers and was one reason why, for the employer, running a farm as well as a brewery made good sense whether or not the former grew barley for the firm's own malthouses. When Thompson's were looking for a new drayman in 1866, for example, their advertisement took care to make clear that some work on the adjoining farm would also be expected.

Thompson employees – all male – around 1890. By this time summer outings, dinners and cricket matches were regular events. In 1887 John Matthews and his sons extended their hospitality to all the inhabitants of Walmer in lavish celebration of Queen Victoria's Golden Jubilee.

In 1851, according to the census, Edmund Thompson was employing 19 men, of whom six worked on his farm. In that year Edward Iggulden in Deal employed 11 men, suggesting that the two breweries were then roughly the same size. In Deal the position was much the same 30 years later, Edwin Hills reckoning in 1880 that he and his brother had 13 or 14 employees. At Walmer, on the other hand, John Matthews' development of his brewery and maltings had increased employment significantly. The 1881 census listed him as the employer of 41 men and three boys, a picture broadly corroborated ten years later by Barnard, who reported that 27 men were employed at the brewery (excluding "brewers, clerks and other officials"[49]) with a further 16 at the maltings. When Arthur Matthews, John's eldest son, held a supper for staff in 1897 to celebrate his forthcoming marriage this was attended by 70 employees from the brewery, maltings and two farms. Fellow feeling at such events was no doubt reinforced by the fact that, whereas Hills' employees were dotted around the town, in Walmer many of the brewers' labourers, brewers' servants, draymen, maltsters, cellarmen and (brewery) engine drivers lived in a compact cluster near the brewery.

It was a matter of pride to brewers across the country, demonstrating as they saw it loyal commitment to considerate and esteemed employers, that some employees remained with them through most or all of their working lives. Hills and Thompson's certainly did not buck the trend. William Spinner, for example, had served Iggulden and Hills for 37 years on his death in 1872 aged 56. Thomas Knight, who died four years later aged 78, had been "for over 50 years a faithful servant to Messrs Thompson and Son"[50] while Edward Halliday, in his youth a member of the Cinque Ports Volunteers serving under his employer Morris Thompson, died in 1912 having worked at the Walmer brewery for some 40 years. Even if, to a modern historian, "under closer scrutiny, the stability of many English brewery workforces proves to be somewhat illusory"[51], Alfred Barnard, having visited the brewery in 1890, could of course be relied upon to see things in the right way:

> "the best proof of the esteem in which [Mr Matthews] is held, and the good feeling that exists with regard to the firm, lies in the fact that, as we understand, there is hardly ever a change in the staff or tenants of the brewery. We should mention that the chief cashier, Mr A Morton, has now been with the firm for upwards of twenty-three years, and Messrs. Marley and Flood, the collector and ledger clerk respectively, for almost an equally long period"[52].

As for Matthews' father-in-law, Edmund Thompson, "his goodness and leniency to his tenants is proverbial", said the *Telegram* on his death. "He was never known to distrain for rent – preferring loss to coercion and the appearance of unkindness to his inferiors and dependents".[53] Brewing was a quintessentially paternalist industry, and Thompson's were no exception. Almost 100 years later the brewery could still be found proudly boasting of "the 'family' atmosphere that pervades the Walmer Brewery, where every employee is personally known to the management, and works in the happy assurance that should ill-health or misfortune come his way, he will be certain of the most sympathetic and helpful treatment. Many of the staff have been in the employ of the Brewery for a quarter of a century, and some for a great deal longer..."[54].

The most public demonstrations of mutual goodwill fostered by benevolent management were the holding of regular celebratory dinners for employees, and sometimes their families. This was certainly de rigueur for both Hills and Thompson's, whether at Christmas or harvest festival, or to celebrate a birth, marriage or anniversary or a royal jubilee. Outings of various kinds became popular later in the century, and the enthusiasms of individual employers showed through in different ways: the cricket match between married and single Thompson's employees, for instance, organised in 1893 by the brothers Arthur and Willie Matthews which rounded off with a dinner in one of the firm's malt-houses. More lastingly, their father John had some years before converted a building across the road from the brewery into "a spacious reading and recreation room for the amusement, comfort and well-being of the men in [his] employ"[55]. He also constructed "neat dwelling-houses" for the head brewer, clerks, foremen and others, not to mention "a charming Gothic cottage" for his sons[56].

Matthews and his sons seem to have run a pretty tight ship. That is not the impression given of Daniel Hills, from the glimpses to be had in the local papers. When the son of one of his long-serving employees was caught pilfering barley Hills explained that "the younger prisoner White used to work for me some three or four years ago. [But] I did not know he was [now] doing odd jobs for me. The elder White has had the privilege of selecting his own mate, and also allowed to employ people for odd jobs, and I used to pay him any money he had spent on such labour. The younger White may have been employed at the malt-house, but I did not know of it..."[57]. A pleasing impression of working life at the Hills brewery, on the other hand, appears in the recollections of a local resident, Frank Simmons, who in 1952 could still recall the tasselled red caps[58] that the men at the brewery wore at work.

Daniel Hills seems to have managed most of the business of the brewery himself (and to have been the only signatory for cheques). For help in managing his tenants and liaising with the council and the magistrates he turned to local auctioneers and estate agents, in particular Morris Langley and, later, William Hayman: it no doubt helped that both had long spells on the town council. Thompson's, in contrast, seemed to have depended from mid-century on salaried employees: men like George Marley, the long-serving "collector", and later Edward Lidbury. In 1912 the *Mercury* carried the obituary of Benjamin Turner, who had joined the firm 20 years before "to attend to the collecting and outside part of the business. In this capacity he was brought into contact with a wide clientèle in all parts of east Kent, and won not only the fullest confidence of the firm, but the respect of all those with whom he had dealings"[59]. His younger son was also employed at the brewery. The work of trusted employees might include running a public house for a time to avoid closure between tenants, while Edward Redsull (then keeping the Jolly Gardener beerhouse) may not have been the only licensee who – by dint of leaving his wife in charge of the house – was able to combine this with working at Hills' brewery for a time.

The work of those who actually malted the barley or brewed the beer involved periods of hard physical labour, and accidents were not uncommon. In 1882, for example, a workman in one of the Walmer malthouses was badly hurt when he fell through a hatchway on to the concrete floor below. The brewery yard could also be a dangerous place for the unwary, as the Walmer postman found when he tripped into a brewery cesspool one Saturday afternoon. Morris Thompson organised the rescue, and although the mail survived the immersion thanks to a stout letter bag the postman himself was said to have been "strangely altered in his personal appearance"[60]. Most minor accidents probably went unrecorded. On the other hand – rather distastefully to present-day sensibilities – the newspapers did not hesitate to give details of the suicides of those who chose an empty malthouse or brewery building for their final moments: men such as Edwin White, found by his father hanging in one of Hills' malt stores in 1876 "dressed in his working apparel and with his brewer's apron on"[61], or William Halliday, an engine driver at Thompson's overcome by domestic worries, who took his life in a boiler room in 1909.

To judge from reports in the local papers, the work of the draymen was particularly hazardous, either in controlling their large vehicles or when manoeuvring unwieldy 36-gallon barrels. The accounts make painful reading. In 1871 a Hills drayman delivering to Sandwich suffered serious internal injuries when his horse started and jammed him between the wheel of his cart and a wall. Nine years later another Hills drayman, Henry White, fell from his dray which then ran over his legs. In 1894 a third, by the name of Spicer, was unloading barrels at the Liverpool Arms when "his horse suddenly gave the dray a jerk, with the result that the cask rolled and fell on his leg, breaking it"[62]. Lowering barrels into the cellars of public houses was particularly tricky. In the same year John Church (Thompson's) caught his leg in a pulley when delivering beer in Dover and broke his leg just above the ankle. Several other examples of broken limbs and internal injuries sustained by draymen in moving or lowering their barrels can be found. Not that working on one of Thompson's farms was necessarily a safe option: in November 1862 the *Telegram* reported that a collection was being made for the widow and children of a labourer killed working a steam threshing machine at the farm adjoining the brewery.

Hills purchased the Great Mongeham brewery in the 1860s. The handsome brewer's house survived the fire in 1877 during which, said the *Mercury*, "a considerable part of the premises [were] destroyed, the store houses [were] gutted, and nearly the whole of the barrelled ales in stock entirely lost".

Fire was always a risk. Hills invested in their own fire engine at an early stage, and Thompson's were reported in 1881 to be following suit. Both the Deal and Walmer breweries seem to have escaped without serious incident, though the latter was occasionally threatened by straw fires in the surrounding fields. The main casualty was Hills' Great Mongeham brewery. In October 1877 sparks from a nearby chimney ignited the thatch on a grain barn. There was considerable damage to the brewery, though with the help of the Deal fire brigade and engines from the marine barracks the fire was contained and did not reach the machinery house or the brewer's house. The loss of most of the barrelled beer left the *Mercury*'s reporter unable to resist some heavy-handed humour: "... the ground literally flowed with beer, and great was the apparent thirst of men working among it, and many the dips which a

A Thompson's steam wagon in the 1930s. Like many Kent brewers, Thompson's invested in steam wagons before the First World War to replace its lumbering traction-engines and horse-drawn drays.

certain tin measure made to alleviate it. We have been assured that that tin measure got neither burnt nor singed during the whole course of the fiery proceedings"[63].

For the people of Deal, and certainly for the substantial minority who rarely if ever ventured into licensed houses, the most visible sign of the industry of the two breweries would have been the movements through the town of their drays and delivery carts. The Deal brewery compound included four stalls and two loose boxes, together with wagon and cart sheds, and according to the 1890 town guide Hills' wagons were "easily distinguishable by their uniformly red colour, and, let us say also, by the good quality and excellent condition of the cattle [ie the horses]"[64]. By that time the larger Walmer brewery had 13 stalls and two loose boxes, with 15 horses and (according to Barnard) nearly the same number of vans, drays, and other vehicles[65]. Some time after that the firm began to make use of traction engines to pull the larger wagons. It subsequently invested in three Foden five-ton steam wagons between 1907 and 1915, two of which saw service until 1934.

The drays, and later Thompson's steam engines, were some of the largest vehicles on the road. In the narrow streets of Deal they caused regular inconvenience and occasional damage, to the anger of the Town Sergeant and the Inspector of Nuisances. Sometimes the culprits were drays or lorries from elsewhere in Kent. Leney's delivered from Dover to Deal and district on Thursdays and Saturdays, and two deliveries a week seems to have been the pattern for most out-of-town breweries. By-laws dating from the eighteenth century stipulated that tradesmen must not let drays stand in a street for any longer than necessary, and the Town Sergeant did his best to ensure compliance. When he brought before the magistrates the driver of a lorry belonging to the East Kent Brewery who had blocked most of the width of the High Street for almost an hour the latter tried to shift the blame: his vehicle "was not loaded to the best advantage for unloading...he wished they would not load him up with such a big load."[66] But perhaps inevitably, what is most visible in the newspapers is the fairly steady stream of accidents causing injury and sometimes death to passers-by: to the unwary or unlucky, the young or the inebriate.

Transport before the steam age had a mind of its own. In January 1874 the driver of one of Leney's drays, returning to Dover after a delivery, was found dead on the turnpike road between Deal and Walmer but the horses had dutifully continued on their homeward journey. In 1889 George Wraight, one of Thompson's draymen, was injured after falling under the hooves of his two horses, and three years later

Hills' yard looking east towards the brewery, with two of the red drays praised in the 1890 town guide. The premises as a whole covered an acre and a half between West Street and the High Street (previously called Lower Street).

was charged with manslaughter after having allowed his dray, returning from Margate with a load of empty barrels, to snag a perambulator and drag the baby inside to her death. Wraight denied he was asleep but the coroner concluded otherwise. Nor were very low speeds a guarantee of safety. In November 1909 an inquest heard that John Erridge, an inmate of Eastry Workhouse (and "never known to have any occupation, except that he sometimes helped heave up boats"[67]) was run over by a Thompson's lorry for all that it had been travelling at only 4 mph. In this case the driver was exonerated.

Off duty, wagons were sometimes put to pleasing use. Here in contrast is the Hills' "car" at the 1895 regatta trades procession:

"[it was] strikingly attractive, and called forth frequent rounds of applause. In the car was a pile of barrels, with coloured ends and letters representing the quality of the contents, PA, XXX, etc. In relief between the barrels at their ends, were miniature sheaves of barley, while the whole car was bedecked with flowers, and had an upper and lower row of fairy lamps with holders, the finest and best in the show, while at each corner was an old-fashioned mashing bat used before the invention of steam."[68]

The part played by the two breweries in the life of their local communities went well beyond participation in processions and festivals. Water from one of Hills' wells was used to flush the High Street sewer, and yeast from the brewery was sold to domestic bread makers and commercial bakers. Until 1874, when the town acquired its own machine, the most practical contribution was probably made by Hills' fire engine. This was frequently pressed into service, as for example when a fire broke out in January 1868 at an ironmongers in St George's Place and "doubtless would have soon spread to the adjacent property but for the speedy arrival of the fire engine belonging to Messrs Hills and Sons, brewers, in [the] charge of several of their workmen"[69]. Malthouses could also be put to community use, for instance to dry the clothes of shipwrecked seamen. Thompson's newly erected malthouse provided sterling service in 1887 as the venue for a Jubilee tea party for the children of Walmer and, next day, for a "thoroughly good old English repast"[70] for almost 700 adults. And both Hills and Thompson's could always be relied upon to contribute generously (and publicly) to appeals of every kind, whether for the families of boatmen lost at sea or by donating prizes, sometimes in the form of barrels of beer, for regatta races or shooting competitions of the Cinque Ports Artillery Volunteers.

The brewers themselves were men of substance, significant figures in the life of Deal and Walmer. Edward Iggulden, like Thomas Oakley and other local brewers before him, was a merchant and shipping agent as well as a brewer. At various times he also served as Vice Consul to the United States, Denmark, Prussia, Spain and Sweden, among others. Thomas Hight, owner of the North End Brewery, also held the lucrative post of deputy sergeant to the Cinque Ports. Daniel Hills followed in their footsteps – possibly to the detriment of his brewery – in pursuing a wide range of other business interests in the town: at various times he could be found chairing or serving on the boards of the Deal & Walmer Printing Company, the Walmer Building Company, the Deal & Walmer Trading Bank, the wine merchants Nethersole & Son, the Kent Provident Manufacturing Society ("for the purpose of buying, processing, canning and selling fish, fruit and vegetables etc"[71]) and the South Eastern Hotel. John Matthews, in contrast, seems to have focused his business energies more squarely on promoting the success of Thompson & Son.

The Matthews, father and sons, like the Thompsons before them, were big fish in small ponds. Virtually all served as Justices of the Peace, and Edmund Thompson was also Deputy Mayor of Sandwich (which at that time still retained its jurisdiction over Walmer). Morris Thompson served on the Walmer Local Board, as later did Frederick Ommanney, and his brother-in-law John Matthews chaired the Board for several years. In due course both Arthur and Willie Matthews became members of Walmer District Council, Arthur serving as Chairman between 1896 and 1912. In 1888 John Matthews had been elected to serve on the new Kent County Council, one of an estimated 10% of councillors involved in the brewing and wine and spirits trades. He retained a connection with London as a governor of Christ's Hospital School and, nearer to home, followed Edmund Thompson in taking a close interest in agricultural matters. Both Matthews and his partner Frederick Ommanney were also leading lights in the campaign to raise funds to build the new church of St Mary's in Walmer, Matthews acting as treasurer and personally contributing £500. Both served as churchwardens. The energetic and popular Ommanney received a particularly fulsome obituary from the *Mercury* on his early death in 1889, not least for his determination "to improve and advance the place [ie Walmer] as a seaside resort, being fully convinced in his own mind that [its] future prosperity depended absolutely and entirely upon the progress made in that direction"[72].

Edward Iggulden and Charles Hills both held office as Mayor of Deal. Daniel Hills, on the other hand, though he served on the Deal Pavement Commission for some years, did not in the event follow in his father's footsteps and play a significant part in the politics of the town. Although a consistent supporter of charities and community activities (serving on the committee of the Deal Catch Club, for example, and as trustee for Hockley's Charity) he was heavily defeated in 1858 when he stood in the North Ward for election to the town council, and did not try again for elected office. On his death the *Mercury* noted that "he did not take an active part in public affairs [but] was always ready to support any good object that would tend to the benefit of the town... He was a very liberal-minded gentleman, and to mention any deserving cause to him was to secure for it a ready helper and one who would take an interest in it as well as become a subscriber to its funds"[73].

Edward Iggulden was a Liberal. So too were the Hills, though Edwin Hills probably wished he had been rather less active when the 1880 by-election scandal – discussed in Chapter 4 – washed to his door. Edmund Thompson, from a strict non-conformist background, was "a firm and consistent liberal", and on his death in 1862 "the Whig party in the Borough... lost a true friend"[74]. Ten years before, in proposing the Liberal candidate for the vacant Parliamentary seat, he had identified three national priorities: the maintenance of free trade, the further extension of the franchise and – no doubt very conscious of his own non-conformist background – the ending of the ban on Jews entering Parliament ("the one remnant remaining of religious intolerance")[75]. Morris followed in his father's footsteps as an active speaker and benefactor in the Liberal cause until he parted company on the issue of Home Rule. Proposing Edward Knatchbull-Hugessen for the seat in 1865 he recalled fondly that his father had done likewise in 1857.

Nationally however, as the century wore on, there was a growing commonality and identification of interest between brewers and the Conservative Party, and certainly the sale of Thompson's to John Matthews brought a sharp local about-face. Matthews was a staunch

Conservative, his stated intention in standing for the Kent County Council being to oppose "any measures calculated to add to the burdens of my Constituents, and while promoting your interests to the utmost of my ability [to] strenuously endeavour to prevent any expenditure which is not consistent with true economy".[76] His partner Frederick Ommanney, though said by the Dover Express to have been "one of the most genial and liberal of men to those of a contrary opinion"[77], was equally committed to the Conservative Party. The two younger Matthews in turn soon became dominant figures in the local party organisation.

Consolidation

Daniel Mackintosh Hills, a bachelor, died on 9 October 1900 aged 71. His brother Edwin had no wish to run the business on his own. Early the following year he and his two surviving sisters put the entire Hills estate up for auction. This consisted not only of the Deal and Great Mongeham breweries, brewers' residences and malthouses and 63 licensed houses "all within a radius of about twelve miles from the Brewery"[78], but also six shops, eighteen cottages and three capstan grounds. The auction particulars, however, in presenting what it claimed would be an "opportunity almost unique"[79] for the ambitious investor, pulled few punches in describing the state of the business that Daniel Hills had left behind. There was no doubt that "the business having been carried on upon old lines...with the adoption of modern practices the Trade of the Houses can be doubled, and a large Private Trade (now practically nil) added. There is also every facility for carrying on the Wine and Spirit Trade, which with 63 tied houses would at once form a lucrative branch". As for the tenants of the public houses and beerhouses "the Rents paid...are all low, and in most cases quite inadequate"[80].

The auction took place at the Park Street Sale Rooms on 1 August 1901. The *Mercury* reported "a very large attendance, with many genuine bidders". The latter included representatives of the Dartford Brewery Company, who helped take the bidding well beyond the reserve price, and of Cobb & Co of Margate (who went to £91,000). A Mr W H Duttson of Sydenham then took the bidding to £92,000. The estate was eventually knocked down to Thompson & Son for £93,000. "The result was evidently viewed with favour by those present, as there was great cheering when the announcement was made"[81].

By this time, Edmund Thompson's grandsons Arthur and William (Willie) Matthews were at the helm, Frederick Ommanney having died in 1889 at the age of 42 and their father six years later. A year before his death John Matthews had converted the business "as a matter of family arrangements"[82] into a private limited company, stealing a march on the second wave of "frenzied floatations"[83] which swept across the brewing industry between 1895 and 1899. By 1900 no fewer than 42 Kent brewers had taken this route. The new company of Thompson & Son had capital of £105,000, most of the £10 shares being taken by members of the Matthews family; John Matthews naturally became Chairman of Directors. His first wife Mary, Edmund Thompson's daughter, had died in 1863, but Matthews had married again and left a further six children by his second wife Jessie. On his death in 1895 his estate was valued at £28,635.6.8d. Following public subscription a memorial to him was erected in St Mary's church, near the stained-glass windows he and his sons had previously dedicated to his partner Ommanney.

The Fawn was a Hills beerhouse to the north of Alfred Square. On the wall is a poster announcing the auction in August 1901 of the brewery and its tied estate of 63 houses.

His elder sons and their fellow Directors had no interest in the Deal brewery as such. This might have survived for a while longer had either Cobb or the Dartford Brewing Company been successful in their bids. But as it was the writing was immediately on the wall. Thompson's wanted not only to reduce local capacity and competition but more especially to safeguard continuing demand for their own beer through an extension of their tied estate. Nationally, beer production had stagnated –

The distribution of Hills' public houses and beerhouses purchased by Thompson's in 1901.

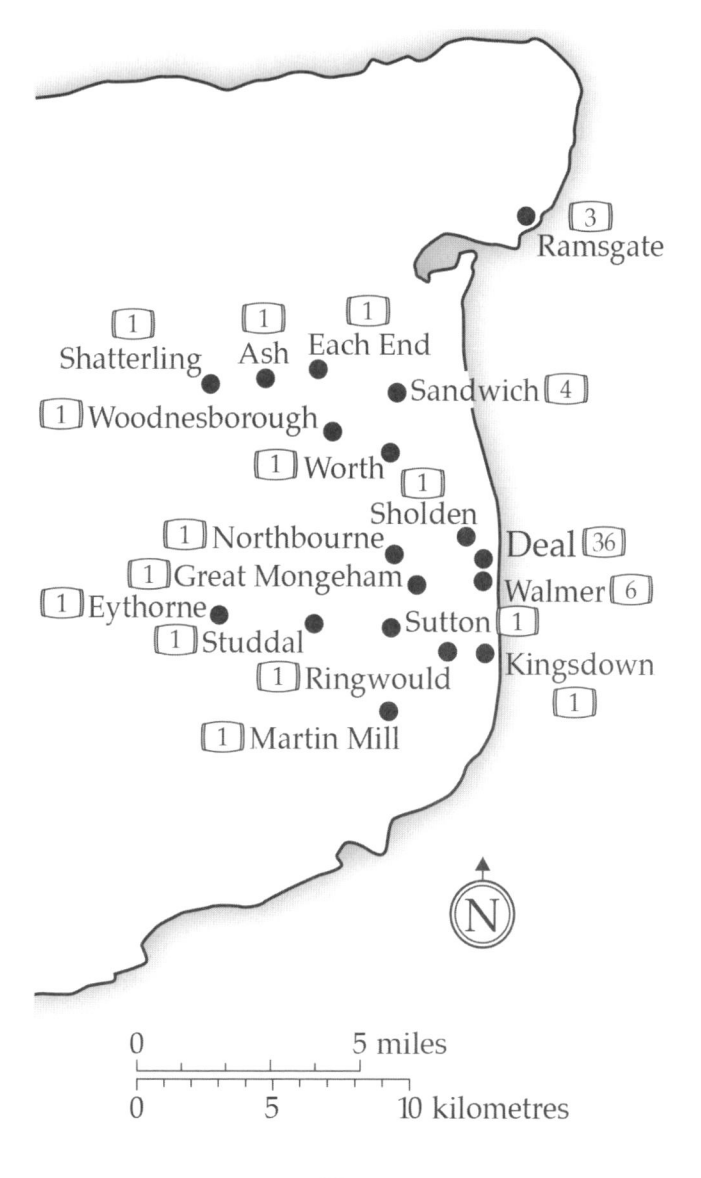

in England and Wales as a whole annual average production in the period 1900–4 was only 8% higher than it had been in 1875–79 – and investment by Thompson's to modernise and maintain the Deal brewery was probably never on the cards. The public houses, however, were another matter, and soon the prominent Thompson's signage was to be seen on the majority of houses in the town. The day before the auction Thompson's owned 14 of Deal's 73 public houses, the day after 46 (together with 6 of the town's 13 beerhouses).

The wheel had therefore turned full circle since 1830. In that year a single brewery – Edward Iggulden's – had owned 59% of the public houses in Deal; Thompson's now owned virtually the same proportion (63%). In 1913 an old resident of Walmer would look back in some amazement: "the originator of Thompson and Son was the village brewer in my early days, and I must have sampled his productions in the forties. The firm has made enormous progress in the last sixty years or so, and appears almost to have taken possession of Deal..."[84].

Over the next few months Thompson's steadily disposed of property in which it had no interest, auctioned the contents of the brewery (including – the last of the Hills' line – "a quantity of old ale in vats and bottles"[85]) and began to demolish the Deal brewery itself. According to Barbara Collins "the crashing down of the largest of the old chimneys was a sight long remembered by pupils in the nearby old St George's Central School"[86]. In October 1902 Thompson's put the site up for auction, together with plans for a new street to run through it, Daniel Hills' former residence and three other adjacent High Street properties. These were knocked down as a single lot for £6,500 to Joshua Philpott, the Town Sergeant, acting as agent for an anonymous purchaser – who then, no doubt to the sergeant's consternation, failed to appear. A week later the *Mercury* reported that the gentleman in question had still "not yet turned up... Mr Philpott is using his endeavours to dispose of his bargain. May he" – said the paper, keeping a straight face – "be amply rewarded for his enterprise"[87].

In November the purchasers of the site were revealed to be Thomas Steed Bayly, a local ironmonger and china dealer and a future Mayor, and his partner Arthur Wise. According to a later report Bayly had tried unsuccessfully to persuade the council to buy the land; the partners' plans now were said to include erecting 60 houses "at moderate rental" along the new street, and eight sets of business premises on the High

The Business of Brewing

Street in front of the existing houses. The *Mercury* rejoiced that the redevelopment would be undertaken by two Dealites "and that the advantages of this development of the old town will not go to outsiders"[88]. Thompson's also put several public houses from their newly expanded portfolio up for auction. These included the Walmer Castle and the Black Horse, two of Hills' larger inns. But these did not find buyers, and remained with the company.

Nationally the demise of Hills' brewery was part of a process of contraction, consolidation and closure which saw the number of common brewers fall from a peak of 2,192 in 1871 to 1,520 in 1901. For Thompson's the challenge was both to integrate their newly acquired houses into their business – which presumably included deciding what to do about the "quite inadequate" rents previously enjoyed by Hills' tenants – and developing and modernising their estate against the backdrop of a statutory programme to reduce the total number of houses across the country. An important part over the next few years was played by Edwin Dawes, an experienced brewer from Lincolnshire who had

The Hills brewery site following the building of Stanhope Road. The brewer's house and the former malthouse survived and were put to new use.

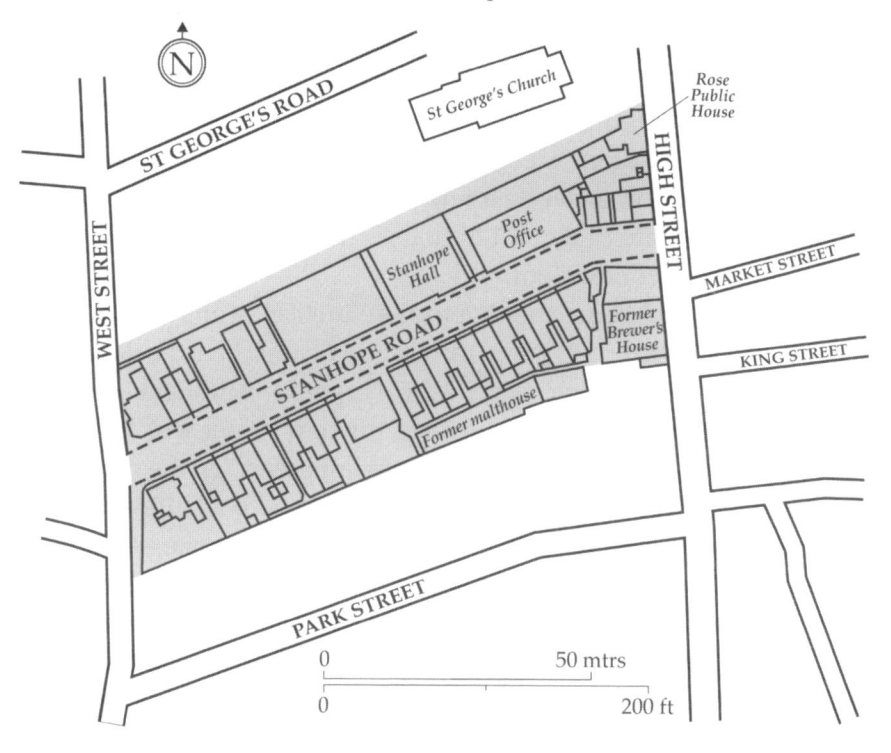

Stanhope Road after the First World War looking east towards the High Street. On the left, where Hills brewery had stood, are Stanhope Hall (now the Astor Community Theatre), the central post office and the Queen's Cinema.

owned and run the Diamond Brewery in Dover in the 1890s. Dawes became a director of Thompson & Son in 1902 and was soon playing a leading role in arguing the company's case before the borough magistrates when attempting to preserve existing licences or acquire new ones. By 1914, after a considerable number of closures under the 1904 Licensing Act offset by a few purchases and new licences, the brewery had an estate of some 120 houses in Deal, Walmer and other towns and villages of east Kent.

Early in 1903 had come the disposal at auction of the remnants of Hills' brewery: "quartering, joists, rafters and beams, boards, doors and frames, sashes, and frames, pantiles, corrugated iron, firewood and other useful materials"[89]. In due course the new street was built and given the name Stanhope Road, and houses appeared. On the north side the Queen's Hall Picture Palace (1912), the new head post office (1903–4; "a jolly affair of three small Dutch gables and one huge one, faced with all sorts of materials"[90]) and Stanhope Hall (1906, now the Astor Community Theatre) were constructed on the site of the old brewery buildings, while the last piece of vacant land on the south side of Stanhope Road became the site of a telephone exchange which opened in 1929.

The malthouse near the High Street, however, had quickly found a new role as a covered range for the Deal and District Rifle Club, and stands to this day. The brewer's house also survived, and for many years provided a home for the Deal and Walmer (Carter) Institute.

Hills had failed to keep pace with changing business practices and with the challenges of more intensive competition. The purchase and modernisation of Thompson & Son by John Matthews, on the other hand, and the acquisition by his sons of the Hills estate, had given the Walmer brewery the hope of a secure future. The company continued to trade during the inter-war period, and although Arthur Matthews died in 1936 it remained in business during the Second World War and seemed set to prosper for a while longer. In 1947 Thompson's registered as a new private limited company with capital of £650,000, and made fresh investment in the brewing and bottling plant. In a celebratory guide to the brewery and its houses published in 1950 the company congratulated itself on "still flourishing and prospering amidst the tremendous competition of modern business, and despite the all-embracing ramifications of the big combines..."[91]. Only a year later, 50 years after the purchase of the Hills estate, the firm was taken over by one of those self-same combines, the London brewers Charrington & Co.

The Walmer brewery, not long before it was bought by Charrington & Co in 1951. Thompson's had recently invested significantly in new bottling plant, and this continued to be used until 1964.

Brewing in Walmer ceased in 1953, although malting and bottling continued until 1964. The premises were used by Charrington's as a depot until 1974, and then became derelict. The old brewery buildings were finally demolished in 1981 and in due course housing took their place. Today virtually the only sign that a prosperous brewery had ever existed in Walmer are a few street names and a public house, previously the George and Dragon but renamed in 1973 the Thompson's Bell.

1. *Telegram* 27 August 1864
2. *Kentish Gazette* 23 June 1807
3. Ibid
4. P. Mathias, *The Brewing Industry in England, 1700 – 1830* (Cambridge, 1959) p 199
5. A. Armstrong (ed), *The Economy of Kent, 1640–1914* (Woodbridge, 1995) p. 182
6. *Kentish Gazette* 10 August 1852
7. *Kentish Gazette* 7 December 1852
8. Ibid
9. *Particulars and Conditions of Sale, Valuable Freehold Estate* (1901) p 1
10. W. P. D. Stebbing, *The Invader's Shore: Some Observations on the Physiography, Archaeology, History and Sociology of Deal and Walmer* (Deal, 1937) p 47
11. *Deal, Walmer and Sandwich, Illustrated and Historical* (1890) p 43
12. Ibid
13. *Telegram* 20 February 1869
14. *Mercury* 30 April 1870
15. *Mercury* 5 May 1877
16. *Telegram* 12 May 1877
17. *Telegram* 22 February 1879
18. *Telegram* 5 April 1862
19. Ibid
20. *Telegram* 8 February 1868
21. *Telegram* 1 June 1872
22. A. Barnard, *The Noted Breweries of Great Britain and Ireland* Vol 4 (London, 1889–90) p 523
23. Barnard p 521
24. Barnard pp 521–2
25. Barnard p 522
26. Ibid
27. T. R. Gourvish and R. G. Wilson, *The British Brewing Industry 1830–1980* (Cambridge, 1994) p 46
28. *Illustrated and Historical* ...(1890) p 43
29. *Kentish Gazette* 19 November 1771
30. Barnard p 521
31. *Telegram* 3 February – 28 April 1858
32. Gourvish and Wilson p 63
33. Quoted in *Mercury* 18 April 1885
34. *Mercury* 2 June 1865
35. *Telegram* 13 June 1860
36. *Kentish Gazette* 2 June 1807
37. D. W. Gutzke, *Protecting the Pub: Brewers and Publicans Against Temperance* (Woodbridge, 1989) p 5
38. P. Moynihan, *Kentish Brewers and the Brewers of Kent* (Longfield, 2011) pp 66–7
39. *Mercury* 9 March 1867
40. G. Nunns, *A History of Deal* (Canterbury, 2006) p 111
41. Letter dated 31 March 1906 in Kent History and Library Centre (KHLC) 281/1/154
42. Round robin letters of 2 and 4 May

1906 in KHLC 281/1/154
43. Quoted in M. J. Bellamy, "Steaming into the Age of Rail and Pale Ale: John Labatt and the Transformation of Canadian Brewing 1855–1877", *Brewery History* (No 146) p 16
44. *Telegram* 9 August 1873
45. *Mercury* 21 April 1888
46. *Mercury* 16 May 1885
47. Undertaking dated 7 January 1873 Dover District Council (DDC) 66, Title Deeds: Beach Street, Deal
48. Barnard p 519
49. Barnard p 524
50. *Telegram* 18 November 1876
51. J. Reinarz "A social history of a Midland business: Flower and Sons Brewery, 1870–1914. Part IV", in *Brewery History* (No 149) p 41
52. Barnard pp 524–5
53. *Telegram* 5 April 1862
54. Thompson & Son, Ltd *The Walmer Brewery, Kent: A Guide to the Brewery and to the District where Walmer Ales are Sold* (London, 1950) p 4
55. *Mercury* 16 December 1893
56. Barnard p 524
57. *Telegram* 31 March 1888
58. Frank Simmons "Note on the Brewery Bell" 28 November 1952, in Deal Maritime and Local History Museum
59. *Mercury* 21 December 1912
60. *Kentish Chronicle* 26 January 1867
61. *Deal Chronicle* 18 February 1876
62. *Mercury* 24 March 1894
63. *Mercury* 13 October 1877
64. *Illustrated and Historical...* (1890) p 43
65. Barnard p 523
66. *Mercury* 24 August 1907
67. *Mercury* 13 November 1909
68. *Mercury* 24 August 1895
69. *Telegram* 1 February 1868
70. *Mercury* 18 June 1887
71. *Telegram* 21 January 1888
72. *Mercury* 8 June 1889
73. *Mercury* 13 October 1900
74. *Telegram* 5 April 1862.
75. *Kentish Gazette* 1 June 1852
76. *Mercury* 3 November 1888
77. *Dover Express* 14 June 1889
78. *Particulars of Sale...*(1901), front page
79. *Particulars of Sale...*(1901) p 16
80. Ibid
81. *Mercury* 3 August 1901
82. *Mercury* 24 February 1894
83. Gourvish and Wilson p 256
84. *Mercury* 27 December 1913
85. *Mercury* 7 December 1901
86. B. Collins, *Discovering Deal (Historic Guide)* (Deal, 1969) p 56
87. *Mercury* 11 October 1902
88. *Mercury* 22 November 1902
89. *Mercury* 3 January 1903
90. J. Newman, *The Buildings of England: North East and East Kent* (London, 1969) p 283
91. Thompson & Son (1950) p 3

Chapter 2

Pubs and Publicans

A town full of pubs

Victorian Deal had a very large number of public houses, even by the standards of the time. In 1893 the town had an official "density indicator" – derived from the number of licensed houses and the size of the population – of 1,057. This was far higher than those for Canterbury (881), Dover (646), Ramsgate (615) and Folkestone (556). For the temperance lobby this was of course a shocking state of affairs. But by this time the view that Deal had far too many public houses was also held by many councillors and magistrates who otherwise had little truck with temperance arguments. Just what should be done about this was much less clear, as will be seen in due course. First, however, this chapter examines how it came about that the town had quite so many public houses. It then considers where they were to be found, what kinds of establishments they were and how they evolved. The focus is then on the men and women who sought to earn a livelihood, in whole or in part, running these houses.

To be allowed to sell beer, wine and spirits – to turn a private dwelling into a "public house" – the individual concerned needed to obtain a licence from the local magistrates, and to renew it annually. The magistrates could refuse the application, so removing the person's right to trade from that house. A more suitable applicant might then come forward, or the house might have to close down. Nationally there were 50,442 licensed premises in 1829 – fewer than there had been a hundred years before, and giving a much lower ratio of premises per head of population. At that point Deal had 39 public houses. Although the national total had increased somewhat over the previous decade, no new licences had been granted in Deal for many years and the number did not begin to rise until 1847. (One house, the Pelican, had closed in 1838, to be replaced further up Beach Street by the North Star.) The town bore witness to Sidney and Beatrice Webb's later observation that, during this period, "where the population was stationary, it was customary for the old-established public houses in the small boroughs to remain, decade after decade, undisturbed, with the number of licences being neither increased or diminished"[1].

The India Arms was an old-established house on Beach Street. Bought in 1855 by Alexander Bird, a wine and spirits merchant, it ceased to function as a public house in the 1860s although the licence was kept up.

The houses in Deal included several good-sized hotels and inns, in particular the Royal Hotel, the Walmer Castle, the India Arms and the Black Horse, as well as a spread of smaller houses offering some limited accommodation for lodgers and visitors. Many had a long history, the Black Horse, holding pride of place in the magistrates' list, being reckoned to date from the reign of Queen Anne. Together they formed the core of the licensed estate throughout the Victorian period, and were a substantial presence in the architectural, social and civic landscape of Deal. In 1900 32 of the 39 houses were still open (though some had been substantially rebuilt).

The remarkable stability in the early period is partly explained by the depression which had settled on the town following the boom times of the Revolutionary and Napoleonic Wars. Indeed it was not until 1861 that Deal's population finally passed the figure of 7,351 reached in 1811. A House of Commons Select Committee in 1833 found great hardship among the many Deal boatmen, and the Parliamentary Commissioners reporting on the corporation the following year noted with dispiriting brevity that:

"The town is in a very depressed state. There is no manufactory of any kind; nearly the whole support of the town is derived from the shipping in the roads [i.e. the Downs]. House rent is extremely low, and many of the best houses are vacant. There is little or no import of anything except coals"[2].

The historian Stephen Pritchard was scarcely more cheerful 30 years later:

"It is next to an impossibility for any just arriving at middle age fully to estimate the extreme depression that followed the arrival of peace... Deal has never recovered itself since...there exists in Deal no staple articles of manufacture or no constant source of employment for the youth shooting up into manhood, as is the case in other towns"[3].

Pritchard was too disparaging about the state of the town in his own time. Deal was more prosperous than it had been in the 1830s, albeit from a low base, and in 1864 came the opening to great celebration of a new iron pier. It is certainly the case that the years between 1847 and 1869 saw a remarkable surge in the number of public houses in the town. During this period the magistrates granted an average of two new licences a year. They tended, for some reason, to do so in batches. These included four in 1848, seven in 1855, four in 1859, six in 1864 and 13 between 1867 and 1869. In 1860 the town had 60 public houses and by 1869, at the end of the period of expansion, the number had peaked at 79. Part of the explanation lies in the town's slow return to prosperity and population growth. But understanding the reasons for the prolonged steady state before 1847 in the number of public houses and for the striking increase that followed over the next 20 years must take into account the existence since 1830 of a completely new kind of drinking establishment: the beerhouse.

The creation of beerhouses was the product, as Gourvish and Wilson see it, of "a curious mixture of up-to-date political economy and old-fashioned Georgian indifference to the social consequences of legislation"[4]. Partly in an attempt to stimulate the demand for barley, the country then being in the grip of an agricultural depression, the 1830 Beer Act permitted any ratepayer to sell beer on or off the premises in exchange for an annual payment of two guineas to the Excise. The licence then granted did not extend to the sale of wine or spirits, but nor was there a need to secure the magistrates' agreement, or show why another outlet selling beer was necessary to meet the needs of local people, travellers or visitors. Within three months over 26,000 beer licences had been issued in England and Wales. By 1860 there were some 41,000 "on" licences, and a further 3,000 "off" licences. Many beerhouses operated out of or developed from existing grocers' shops. Others simply consisted of a barrel or two in a front parlour or cellar. Less than two weeks after the Act came into force the wit Sydney Smith, with a good dose of hyperbole, memorably complained that "everybody is drunk. Those who are not singing are sprawling. The sovereign people are in a beastly state"[5]. "It is hard", wrote the Webbs sternly 70 years later, "to find a redeeming feature of this débâcle"[6]. A more charitable recent assessment is that the reform was, for good or ill, a genuine attempt through "free licensing" to substitute "for the arbitrary decisions of the magistracy and the baneful effects of tied houses...the "rational" forces of consumer demand"[7].

In any event the impact in Deal does not seem to have been especially Bacchanalian. It is not clear how many beerhouses there were in the early years, but in 1847 there were said to be 30. Some managed to achieve permanence, transferring from one beerseller to another, but others had a much more transitory existence. Around 30 different beerhouses can be identified which traded in the town for a while but which had gone by the early 1870s, in many cases long before that; there were probably a good many more that left no trace. At least 16 of these 30 had been given names, though this was an optional embellishment.

Some of these acquired an unsavoury reputation, and perhaps inevitably beerhouses as a whole were held in low regard by those not actually running or frequenting them. The landlords of public houses were inclined to maintain a certain distance. In August 1873 members of the town's newly formed Licensed Victuallers Protection Society, after a vigorous discussion, decided that beerhouse keepers, "although a very respectable body of tradesmen", should not be allowed to join their society.[8] Nationally, among the middle classes, the existence of beerhouses was widely considered to be a prime cause of intemperance, poverty and disorder. As one clergyman succinctly put it, "I would sooner see a dozen Public-Houses in a parish than one Beer-Shop"[9]. It was a source of irritation to beersellers in their turn that the opening hours they had to observe were stricter than those applying to their public house competitors, and that from 1834 they – but not the publicans – had to obtain a certificate of good character signed by six local ratepayers.

Many Deal beerhouses contrived a secure future nonetheless. George Hammond ran the Saracen's Head beerhouse next door to the family coal business in Alfred Square before gaining a spirit licence in 1848 in the first main tranche of approvals. Hammond remained as landlord for twenty years and by 1870 the house, very much a going concern, had been purchased by Thompson's. Across the square the grocer William Riley, mentioned in the introduction, purchased his beer licence in the 1850s, secured a spirit licence in 1864, named his public house the Prince Albert, and, after the house had been bought by the brewers George Beer, continued there as landlord until 1888. Sometimes a beer licence was purchased with the clear intention of upgrading to the status of public house as soon as possible after that. John Hills, for example, opened the Railway Tavern near the station in 1847 – the year the railway arrived in Deal – and secured a spirit licence the following year.

It was certainly not true, however, that all public houses newly licensed during this period had served apprenticeships as beerhouses. Prior possession of a beer licence was certainly not a pre-requisite, and some new establishments made the leap to a full licence in one bound. Henry Shipley's Alma opened fully licensed from the outset. This was a new hotel, built in 1855 with "visitors to the neighbourhood [and] commercial gentlemen"[10] in mind, and the magistrates probably did not hesitate. Charles Denne, for eight years licensee of the Crown in Beach Street, bought a nearby property in 1862, opened it as the Star and Garter with a full licence in 1864 and owned and ran it until 1881. His widow then held the licence until 1921. Successful commercial ventures like those of Shipley and Denne are further evidence that, notwithstanding Pritchard's pessimism, efforts to develop the town were at last achieving some momentum.

However it was certainly the case that of the 40 or so new full licences granted by the magistrates between 1847 and 1869 the majority were to old or more recently established beerhouses. In each case the magistrates made a judgement about the need for such a licence, and considered the size and suitability of the premises, but they were clearly inclined to be helpful. They were also ready to consider prompt re-applications. The Napier Tavern, the Park Tavern and the Redan were all refused in 1858 but were successful the following year. Rejections could provoke indignation; why, asked a correspondent to the *Telegram* in 1866, had the Waterman's Arms in Beach Street been licensed, but not

The Harp in Middle Street, visible to the right, was owned by the East Kent Brewery in Sandwich. Thomas Desormeaux, hairdresser and landlord between 1878 and 1897, was said to offer a pint of beer, a twist of tobacco and a haircut for 4d.

its neighbour the Three Compasses notwithstanding "14 beds, two modern water closets, urinals and a supply of water commensurate with the wants of the inmates"[11] ? (This was rectified the following year.) And there were exceptions. George Norris of the Deal Lugger could not understand why he was refused in 1867 and again in 1869 – "in all cases of ship-wrecked crews being brought ashore, the men were taken to his house, and he wanted a spirit licence more than anything"[12] – and the house remained a beerhouse throughout its existence.

But it is clear that, Norris' disappointment notwithstanding, the borough magistrates had since 1847 operated a policy of allowing as many beerhouses as they reasonably could to become fully licensed. In some cases this was to help good-sized houses provide a better service to visitors and other respectable patrons. It was also useful, in encouraging owners to improve their properties and to offer a higher standard of accommodation, to hold out the possible reward of a spirit licence. It is possible that, as in other parts of the country, the magistrates went further and made specific improvements a pre-requisite for the award of one of these coveted licences, but there is no direct evidence for this. Above all, it would seem, was the simple wish to bring as many houses as possible fully under the control of the borough police and of themselves as magistrates for the town. Indeed in some towns and cities, and possibly in Deal, magistrates did not simply await applications but did their level best to persuade beerhouse owners to see the advantages of applying for a spirit licence.

The thatched Five Ringers was a Hills pub in Church Walk. On the right, with his family, is Thomas Kemp, landlord between 1872 and 1904. The house burnt down after Kemp left, but was rebuilt nearby.

It is certainly no coincidence that the final surge of approvals in Deal ended in 1869. In that year legislation brought the licensing of new beerhouses under the control of the magistrates, so ending the era of "free licensing" for those wishing to sell beer and removing the incentive for magistrates to award spirit licences in order to bring houses under their control. Although there were only four grounds on which magistrates could refuse to renew the licence of an existing ("ante 1869") beerhouse, including where they considered it to be of a "disorderly character, or frequented by thieves, prostitutes or persons of bad character"[13], magistrates in areas of the country with a large number of beerhouses were still able to undertake a significant cull in their numbers. This did not happen in Deal, for the simple reasons that by 1869 the licensing policy of the borough magistrates over the previous two decades had meant that relatively few beerhouses remained in the town.

This was in sharp contrast to the average across the country as a whole, where by 1869 roughly five out of every twelve licensed drinking places were beerhouses. But the proportion varied enormously from place to place. Rising demand fuelled by a growing population might sustain large numbers of beerhouses unlikely or as yet unable to make the grade as public houses. The dockyard town of Sheerness on the north Kent coast had around 30 houses of each kind, for example, while in Portsmouth public houses now constituted less than 40% of the total number of houses. In Bradford, even more strikingly, there were three times as many beerhouses as public houses and the former had become "a ubiquitous and characteristic feature of Bradford's working-class neighbourhoods"[14]. But the picture could be very different in towns and cities where one or more other factors had been in play: slow population growth, for example, a large existing stock of public houses, or (as for instance in Newcastle) magistrates notably willing to award full licences.

The last of these factors seems to have determined the outcome in Deal. The result was that although the population of the town grew by only 10% between 1831 and 1869 the number of houses with full licences doubled. The national increase over that period was only 37.5%. In 1869 there was one licence for every 192 people in England and Wales. In contrast, Bower[15] calculates from the 1871 census that the ratio in Deal had then risen to 1:101. This was up from 1:142 in 1841 and the highest it would ever be. It is true that beerhouses had not been opened in Deal at the rate experienced in many other parts of the country, and that a good many of those that did open had closed before 1849. Yet they had appeared and continued to appear over the next 20 years in sufficient numbers to transform the stock of fully licensed premises once the magistrates adopted a policy of steadily and sometimes very quickly "upgrading" viable beerhouses. The number of such houses fell from 30 in 1847 to 22 in 1860, and by 1870 there were only 16 beerhouses plying their trade alongside 79 public houses. The few that remained were well established for the most part, and were probably content to function as they always had. Thirteen beerhouses were still in business in 1900.

The town of Deal had originally developed on higher ground a mile or so inland. Two old-established public houses, the Admiral Keppel and the Liverpool Arms, stood close to the parish church of St Leonard's in Upper Deal. But in the seventeenth century the centre of gravity shifted to Lower Deal. Three parallel streets – Beach Street, Middle Street and Lower Street – ran from Alfred Square in the north to South Street and beyond, and a network of streets and passageways connected all three. Although the wartime growth in population had been reflected

Drinking in Deal

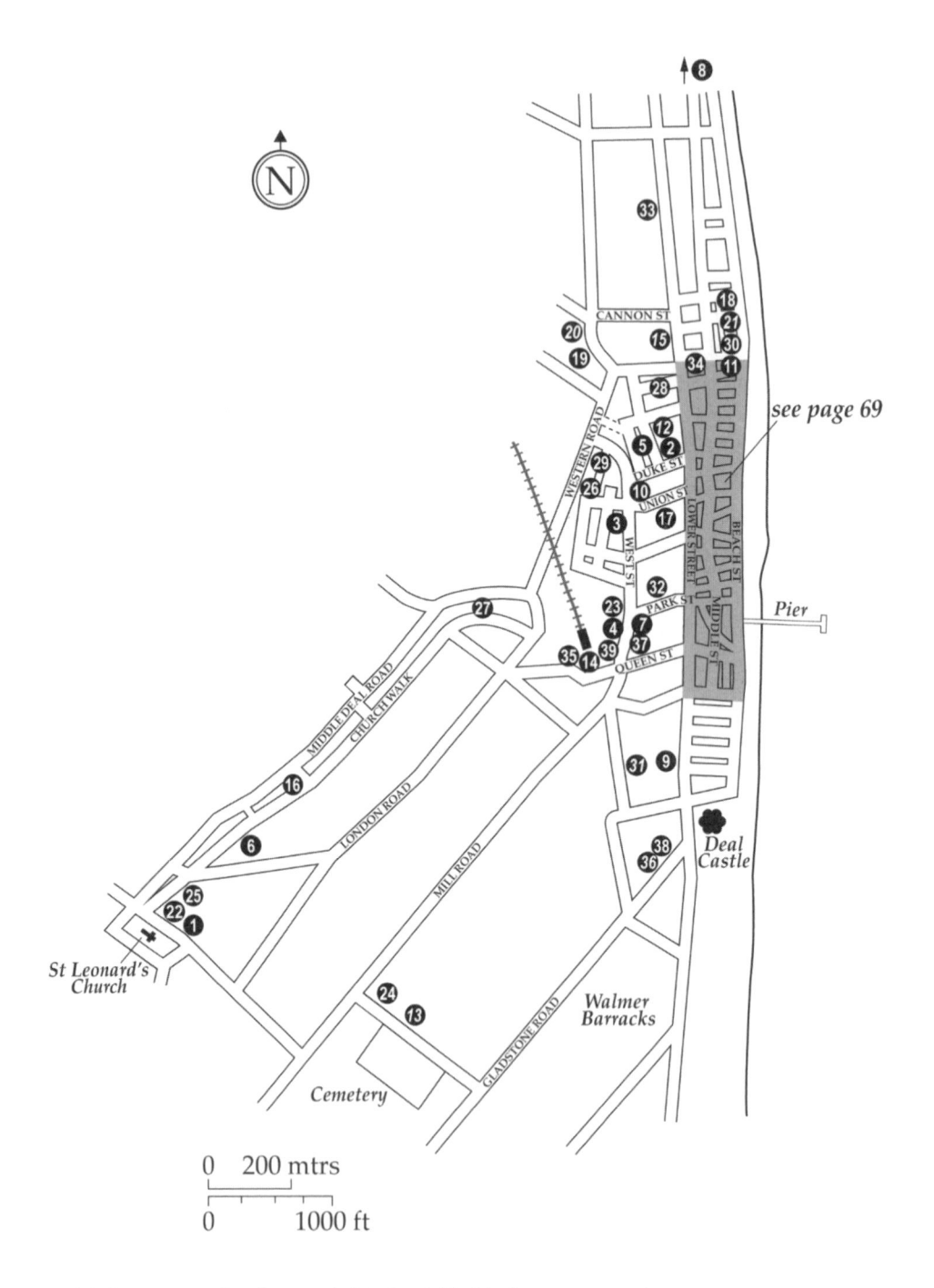

Public houses and beerhouses in Deal, c.1870. For key see opposite.

1. Admiral Keppel	14. Eagle	27. New Plough
2. Alhambra	15. *Fawn*	28. Noah's Ark
3. Alma	16. Five Ringers	29. Norfolk Arms
4. Anchor	17. Fleur de Lis	30. North Star
5. Bell	18. Forester	31. *Oak and Ivy*
6. Bowling Green	19. Hare and Hounds	32. Park Tavern
7. *Bricklayer's Arms*	20. *Jolly Gardener*	33. Prince Alfred
8. Castle	21. *Lifeboat*	34. Queen's Head
9. Deal Castle	22. Liverpool Arms	35. Railway Tavern
10. Deal Hoy	23. Locomotive	36. *Royal Marine*
11. *Deal Lugger*	24. Lord Warden	37. Swan
12. *Duke of Wellington*	25. Magnet	38. Wheatsheaf
13. Duke of York	26. Maxton Arms	39. White Horse

Public houses and beerhouses in Deal, c.1870.
Beerhouses are in *italic* type and pub names in roman.

in the laying out of new streets to the west of Lower Street, and some expansion to the north and south, in 1830 the majority of the 39 public houses were still to be found on Beach Street (14) or Lower Street (9).

It is striking that Beach Street retained much of its dominance throughout the period of expansion in the number of houses. This was despite the fact that, through clearance and redevelopment, the street steadily lost properties on its eastern side backing on to the sea; a writer to the *Telegram* in 1869 reckoned that out of 79 houses "that once obstructed the view to the sea" only 42 now remained[16]. In 1830 36% of all public houses in Deal were to be found on Beach Street. Although by 1872, taking public houses and beerhouses together, the proportion had fallen to 29%, the number of houses had actually risen to 26. In 1895 there was thought to be on average one fully licensed house every 32 yards. Both the number and the proportion of houses selling beer on Middle Street (13%) and on the streets between Beach Street and Lower Street (11%) had increased. On the other hand the number of houses on Lower Street itself was unchanged, the proportion of the whole falling sharply from 23% to 11%. This reflected the evolution of Lower Street into the central shopping and commercial street of the town, and High Street it duly became in 1879.

We have now seen how the period between 1830 and 1847 saw on the one hand no change at all in the number of public houses in Deal but on the other the birth and evolution of a volatile beerhouse sector, and also how over the next two decades the entrepreneurial energies of individual businessmen and local brewers, operating within a deliberately

1. Albion	21. King's Arms	41. Royal Oak
2. Antwerp	22. King's Head	42. Saracen's Head
3. Black Bull	23. Laurel Tree	43. Scarborough Cat
4. Black Horse	24. *Lord Nelson*	44. Seven Stars
5. *Chequers*	25. Napier Tavern	45. *Shah*
6. Clarendon Hotel	26. New Inn	46. Ship
7. Clarendon Tap	27. Pelican	47. Ship and Castle
8. *Crispin*	28. Pier Hotel	48. Sir Sidney Smith
9. Crown	29. Port Arms	49. Star
10. Deal Cutter	30. Prince Albert	50. Star and Garter
11. Druid's Arms	31. Prince of Wales	51. Sun
12. Five Bells	32. Providence	52. *Tally Ho*
13. Fountain	33. Queen's Arms	53. Three Compasses
14. *Fox*	34. Redan	54. Walmer Castle
15. *Friendly Port*	35. Rose	55. Waterman's Arms
16. Harp	36. Rose and Crown	56. Windsor Castle
17. Hope	37. *Roxburgh Castle*	57. Yarmouth Packet
18. Horse and Farrier	38. Royal Exchange	58. *19 Farrier Street*
19. India Arms	39. Royal George	
20. *Jolly Butcher*	40. Royal Hotel	

Public houses and beerhouses in Central Deal, c.1870.
Beerhouses are in *italic* type and pub names in roman.

accommodating licensing regime, brought about a transformation. Then, from 1870 until 1906, the number of public houses stabilised at the new much higher level. A few houses did close down during this period, including the King's Arms, the Alhambra and the Prince of Wales, usually having lost their licence after being shut for a year or more. But the overall number of public houses fell only slightly, from 79 to 74. (Canterbury, in contrast, lost 41 public houses between 1869 and 1900, 22% of the total.) The number of beerhouses contracted proportionally rather more, from 16 in 1871 to 11 in 1906 (two of the number by having secured spirit licenses).

This return to numerical stability between 1869 and 1906 belies the fact that this was a period of increasingly heated arguments about the number and licensing of public houses in Deal. The local temperance movement became steadily more combative, and the publicans more organised in defence of their trade. The major expansion in the number of houses before 1870 had occurred at the back of the town – west of Lower Street, north of Alfred Square, south of South Street and in the area between Upper and Lower Deal. In 1830 10 houses had served these areas, but by 1872 the number had risen to 33 (rising from 26% to 37% of the

Pubs and Publicans

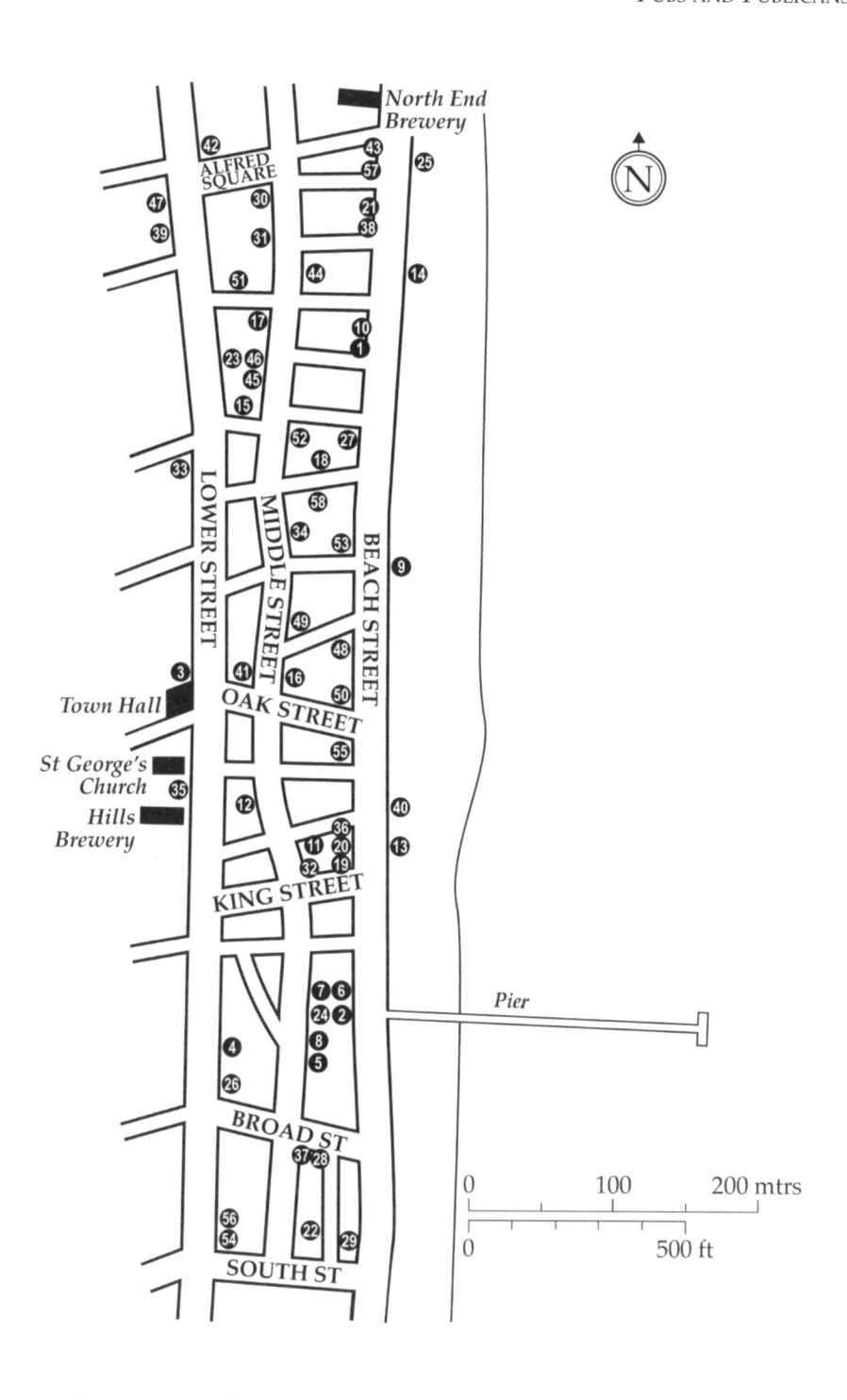

Public houses and beerhouses in central Deal, c.1870. For key see opposite.

69

total). The expansion of the town in these areas, and the relative decline in the demographic importance of the central area, continued steadily thereafter. But the era of the easy availability of new licences had long gone, and brewers now had a fight on their hands to develop their tied estates in the areas of town where customers were increasingly to be found. Applications to the bench for new on-licences or spirit licences were strongly contested, and the magistrates began to set their sights on securing, somehow, a reduction in the total number of houses.

From 1870, as the population of the town increased, so the "density" of public houses and beerhouses slowly declined. But as many of its leading citizens saw it, the town still had an unnecessarily large number of houses in absolute terms. The turning point came in 1906, with the start of a managed programme – discussed in Chapter 5 – to reduce the number of licensed premises. By 1914 the number of public houses in the town had fallen to 61, and beerhouses to 7. The trajectory was now set for the rest of the century and beyond. In the 1950s there were some 50 houses, and by 2014 roughly half that number.

The houses
To be a public house meant having a name, preferably one not used by any other house in the local area, and by 1869 almost all of the surviving beerhouses in Deal had followed suit. Some names were shared with houses in towns and villages across the country: King's Arms and King's Head, Queen's Arms and Queen's Head, Black Horse, White Horse and Black Bull, Rose, Crown and Rose and Crown. Others contributed a substantial nautical ballast appropriate to a maritime town: Fishing Boat, Hovelling Boat, Lifeboat, Ship, Scarborough Cat and Yarmouth Packet. Admirals Keith, Keppel, Nelson, Rodney and Sidney Smith were all remembered, and at least three names were particular to the town: Deal Lugger, Deal Cutter and Deal Hoy. The mid-Victorian expansion in numbers brought with it the Victoria and the Prince Albert, two Crimean War battles (Alma and Redan) and a successful general (Napier Tavern). With the arrival of the railway came the Locomotive and the Railway Tavern. The one exception to the rule that a house should have a name was "the beer shop without a sign" at 19 Farrier Street. Unsuccessful in the 1880s in gaining an on-licence, "19 Farrier Street" it remained until finally christened the Deal Lugger – the second of that name – some time after the First World War.

New licensees almost always retained the existing name of the house, but they did not have to. Approximately 20 houses experienced a change of name between 1830 and 1914, the majority in the 1860s and 1870s. The change might signal rising aspirations (from the Sandwich Arms to the Pier Hotel in 1871) or help advertise a function (from the Star to the Paragon Music Hall in 1876) or follow a thorough refurbishment, as when James Parrett bought the Redan in 1879 and refaced the front wall, laid out the garden and renamed it the Clifton. George Hayward's Cinque Port Arms became the Druid's Arms in 1867 to mark the re-founding in that house of the Deal lodge of the Ancient Order of Druids, and the rebranding of the Friendly Port beerhouse as the Oddfellow's Arms was no doubt prompted by the founding a few years earlier of an Oddfellows lodge in the town. But new names did not always stick. The Oddfellow's Arms became the Friendly Port again three years later, and in March 1884, only two months after the landlord of the Tally Ho beerhouse in Middle Street had changed the name of the house to the Frederick William, his successor changed it back again.

In some cases the new landlord was very anxious to wipe the slate clean. The Jolly Sailor became the Norfolk Arms in the wake of a cholera outbreak in 1866 (though reverted in 1889). Charles Evans, on taking the Seven Stars in 1876 and becoming "very much upset at having been told how it was formerly conducted"[17], changed its name to the Greyhound. But changes could sometimes create friction. When in 1867 John Outwin of the Clarendon Hotel added the word "Royal" to the hotel sign, Robert Allen of the nearby Royal Hotel was outraged, claiming that visitors were now confusing the two places. The magistrates were unmoved, and duly made out a licence to the Royal Clarendon Hotel, though in the event the prefix was quietly abandoned when Outwin left the house a few years later.

Pubs and hotels today tend to be different kinds of establishment, even though the former may offer accommodation and the latter will almost certainly have a bar. In the Victorian period all fell within the category of public house for licensing purposes. Beerhouses had a different legal status, but "inn" had lost its particular meaning as a public house offering both refreshment and accommodation. There was nonetheless a world of difference between the Walmer Castle, say, centrally located and offering good quality accommodation for visitors (not to mention a "commodious and light billiard room"[18]) and a small house like the

Sun, tucked away in a cul-de-sac in the network of streets which clustered around Middle Street and frequented almost exclusively by boatmen and other working men living close by.

The annual rating valuations shed light on the distribution of houses of various size and type. In 1877, and throughout the period, the Royal Hotel stood at the head of the list, with a dozen or more bedrooms and a rateable value in that year of £80. It was followed, at some distance, by the Walmer Castle (£65), the India Arms (£60), the Black Horse (£50), the Rose (£38), the Star and Garter (£35) and the New Inn (£32). Within the £21 – £30 range came 15 medium-sized public houses: considered respectable, and generally offering a reasonable standard of accommodation for lodgers and visitors. The King's Arms on Beach Street, rated at £25, was typical of this type. When put up for auction in 1876 it had:

> "in the Basement, large beer cellar; on the Ground Floor, bar, bar parlour, two sitting rooms and kitchen; on the First Floor, large cheerful sitting room and two bedrooms; and on the Second Floor, five bedrooms. In the rear is a good Garden and Outhouses comprising of a two stall stable and coal shed, with two rooms over, also a large warehouse with loft over".[19]

But most public houses – 52 out of 75 at that point – and all of the beerhouses were a good deal smaller than this, and were rated between £11 and £20. The predominance in Deal of such small, less valuable houses was particularly pronounced. In 1874–5, taking the Sandwich parliamentary constituency as a whole (of which Deal constituted the major part) 56% of houses fell within the lower band. In Canterbury City the proportion was 46%, and in Dover only 27%. By contrast 21% of Dover's houses were rated at £50 or more, and 8% of those in Canterbury. In Deal, neither an important civic centre nor a major transport hub, the proportion was only 4%.

The particulars of Hills' tied estate in 1901 are illuminating. To meet the basic needs of their clients, all 36 of the public houses and beerhouses they owned in Deal had a bar and either a bar parlour (in 15 of the larger establishments), a parlour (in 6) or a tap room (in 16 of the small houses). Four houses, including the Napier Tavern and the Castle, had all three such rooms; it would be many years yet before the fashion

The Magnet, on the right, was purchased by Cobb & Co in 1896 at great expense. Although the Margate brewers had owned or leased many Deal houses during the Napoleonic Wars, the Magnet was their only house in late Victorian Deal.

for knocking through and creating single open-plan drinking areas took hold. Smoking rooms could be found in 11 of the hotels and larger public houses, common rooms or lounges in seven, coffee rooms in the four large hotels, and billiard rooms in two. Sitting rooms and kitchens, sometimes used by residents as well as by the landlord's family, were almost universal, and most houses had a cellar. Thirteen offered stabling, with ten possessing a coach house of one kind or another. The Lord Nelson had a herring hang in the yard, to the displeasure of some near-by residents, and the Five Ringers a fowl house. The "usual conveniences" were also usually to be found in the yard or in an outbuilding: only 20 of the houses are shown as having indoor water closets, and in most cases these would have been for the use of residents or the family rather than the bar room customers.

In the 1860s significant numbers of public houses came on the market, and could be bought for £200 – £300. The Prince Albert fetched £270 at auction in 1864, as did the Cinque Port Arms in 1867. The Ship went for £290 in 1866, the Jolly Gardener for £285 in 1862 (though for only £200 in 1879) and the King's Arms for £235 in 1870. In contrast the Crispin, a small beerhouse in Middle Street, cost Thompson's only £110 in 1865. But by the 1890s the market had changed out of all recognition. Most houses were already in the brewers' hands, and the few houses offered for sale commanded huge prices as east Kent brewers (like so many brewers across the country) scrambled to expand their tied estates at almost any cost. The Canterbury brewers George Beer paid £1,050 for the New Plough in Middle Deal, albeit together with a baker's shop, cottage and stables, and when the nearby Magnet was auctioned in 1896, "representatives from almost all the brewing firms in the neighbourhood, and practically of east Kent, being present"[20], it was purchased by Cobb of Margate for a remarkable £1,060.

Brewers also spent considerable sums, as their balance sheets allowed, on refurbishing and rebuilding their existing properties. Hills rebuilt the Pelican on Beach Street in 1868, the previous building having become very dilapidated, and renovated the Scarborough Cat the following year. Growing prosperity and the steady if unspectacular development of the town as a seaside resort prompted investment to improve the capacity and facilities of several of Hills' larger inns: the Walmer Castle was given a new wing in 1871, the Swan an extension in 1874, the Rose an extra storey in 1885, and the Black Horse a new wing with a 40-foot dining room in 1887. The brewers did not follow through on their plans to add a "gin palace" to the south side of the Deal Castle in 1866, but blazed a trail with the Roxburgh Castle later in the century: according to their lawyer, arguing the case before the magistrates, "its special character differentiated it from any of the other houses in the neighbourhood, that it was of a modern style, and that as it was fitted up and conducted in the same manner as houses of refreshment frequented by City men…"[21]. Such cosmopolitan thinking, not to mention the support of a petition in favour signed by 100 residents, finally persuaded the magistrates to grant the house a spirit licence.

Twenty years earlier Hills had spent over £300 on rebuilding the Roxburgh Castle but here things had not gone well. When pulling down part of the old building a chimney collapsed and took with it a portion of the back wall. The landlord and his family had refused to move out of the house, and "extraordinary to relate, the landlady (Mrs S Watts) was being attended by Mr Hulke in her confinement and a child was born at the time the accident occurred."[22] The rebuilding went no more smoothly. The following January "a smell of gas was observed when one of the workmen struck a Lucifer to test the pipes which had recently been laid, when a loud report sufficient to alarm the neighbourhood ensued, inflicting serious damage to the premises…some of the floor being torn up, and the ceiling blown down, and most of the windows blown out".[23]

Thompson's, by then the owner of the majority of tied houses in the town, rebuilt the Castle (renamed the Sandown Castle) in 1904. Magistrates were generally much in favour of rebuilding and refurbishment. When Leney's, the Dover brewers, submitted plans to rebuild the Hare and Hounds in 1903 the magistrates were delighted: "the house at present was very bad for police supervision, being like a rabbit warren".[24] Where the town's hotels were concerned, although decisions rested with the owner, the catalyst was often the energy and ambition of the new licensee. Robert Allen drove the thorough renovation of the Royal Hotel in 1865, and William Collins, the "new and spirited proprietor",[25] did likewise at the Clarendon Hotel in 1886 – the *Telegram* particularly admired the taste he displayed in decorating the hall and veranda of the hotel with Chinese lanterns on the evening of the regatta.

But fire, whether from lanterns, gas lights or chimneys, was a constant hazard. When the closure of the navy yard was announced in 1863 the Pavement Commissioners tried to acquire the redundant fire engine but were not prepared to meet the asking price of £100. There the matter rested, and it was not until 1874 that the town had its own modern fire brigade. Until then it depended on the availability of engines from the Walmer barracks and, conveniently housed in the centre of town, Hills' brewery engine.

In 1862 fire had threatened the India Arms but the house was saved with the help of soldiers from the barracks. Five years later the Walmer Castle had no such luck. A fire thought to have been started in the wine cellar, or by a smoker lighting their pipe at the gas, completely destroyed the hotel. Hills' engine, and the engine of the 6th Depot Battalion, helped fight the blaze but the hotel was gutted. Spectators had an exciting time of it. At one stage "the large glass dome over the billiard table was observed to fall on to the table, which then fell through into the dining-room, and from there into the cellar beneath"[26]. The following day "a large double chest of drawers, full of linen, was uncovered, but immediately the air got to it it blazed up…one or two of the billiard balls have also been picked up, having the exact appearance of balls of charcoal".[27] The landlord William Jewitt, who had taken out insurance, tried to continue a wine and spirits business elsewhere but left town soon afterwards. Hills, the owners, were uninsured. They nonetheless rebuilt the house in a classical style at the cost of some £1,700 and reopened it in 1870. In 1896 the property was converted into a branch of Lloyds Bank. A new house, "[to] be conducted under the old title, but on entirely new and up to date principles"[28] was built on the other side of South Street on a portion of the old skating rink.

The limitations of the town's fire fighting capacity were again exposed in June 1869 when the Royal George in Lower Street caught fire. The landlord, looking for some brandy in the early hours, upset the spirit lamp he was attempting to light and failed to extinguish the resulting blaze by using his beer engine. The police quickly arrived but their newly purchased apparatus did not have sufficient length of hose, and the water pressure was deficient. The public house was completely destroyed, and never rebuilt. The inflammable nature of many of the houses compounded the risk. When tobacco ashes dropped into the skittle alley of the Deal Hoy, a fire quickly took hold as the building (probably an outbuilding to the main structure) was "composed entirely of wood, which is coal tarred".[29] George Norris, landlord there in the 1890s, had the distinction when a young apprentice ironmonger of causing the destruction of his employer's newly built store and workshop. Spillage from his lamp ignited spirits and then a gunpowder store. The resulting explosions blew in the windows of the nearby Providence (concussing the landlord in the process) and of the Druid's Arms.

At last, in July 1874, a meeting held at the Deal Castle resolved to form a town fire brigade. Enthusiastic volunteers were then to be seen throwing themselves into a canvas trough attached to the balcony of the Clarendon Hotel, and the brigade soon took delivery of a fire escape provided by the Society for the Protection of Life from Fire. The council

The Deal fire brigade outside the Royal Hotel. Before 1874 the town had relied on engines and manpower from Hills' brewery and the Walmer barracks.

In 1909 the Antwerp, by then owned by Thompson's, was badly damaged by fire after hot coals fell from a grate in a back room. The house was completely rebuilt.

declined to meet the cost of a (pumping) engine but public subscription did the trick. In November 1875 a brand new fire engine arrived by train from London, and was immediately put through its paces. The result was highly satisfactory to all concerned, with the probable exception of the butcher William Conley "who had one of his windows broken by the water being turned in that direction".[30] The rules of the brigade included a strict ban on the consumption on duty of "spiritous liquor...experience having shown that it causes men to be reckless not only of their own lives but also the lives of others"[31].

Happily injuries and loss of life from fire seem to have been rare, though the unfortunate John Clements, landlord of the Clarendon Tap, died in 1884 having set himself alight with a benzoline lamp. The Queen's Arms escaped in 1875 when tar being heated on a stove boiled over, and quick action by a group of boatmen saved the Yarmouth Packet two years later when soot in a chimney ignited. But modern machines could only do so much when a fire took hold. Fire gutted the Queen's Head in 1892, the thatch-roofed Five Ringers was lost in 1906 and the Antwerp on Beach Street was largely destroyed in 1909. All three were rebuilt. The previous landlord of the Antwerp, Charles Evans, had himself served with the fire brigade, but died after helping to put out a fire in Middle Street: "on returning home, he changed his uniform, but neglected to change his underclothing. Having previously been suffering from a cold, this no doubt accelerated his illness".[32]

Flooding was another hazard repeatedly faced by the town and many of its public houses. In October 1877 a high tide combined with strong winds from the north west "lashed the sea into a seething cauldron,

The Good Intent, renamed the Castle in 1863, was particularly vulnerable to flooding. The picture shows the damage done to the sea wall by a storm in 1889.

while the waves rushing inwards dashed over the Esplanades, sending showers of stones across the road"[33]. The bar rooms of the Crown and the Clarendon Hotel were partially swamped and the sea wall in front of the Royal Hotel collapsed, while the door of the Castle was beaten in and stones and seawater filled the bar room. The Castle, laying half a mile north of the town next to Sandown Castle, was particularly vulnerable. In December 1862 a north westerly gale drove waves up to the doorway, "smashing the slates (with which the front of the house is covered) with heavy boulders that were washed up by the tide"[34]. Seven years later it escaped the worst effects of the storm, which hastened the destruction of the castle itself, thanks to the efforts of its landlord Thomas Cattermole "who a few days previously had driven a quantity of wooden piles in front for its protection" though the house was nonetheless once again completely surrounded by seawater. The *Telegram* reckoned that the Castle "appears sooner or later to be doomed to destruction"[35] but in the event it managed to survive repeated batterings for the rest of the century. In 1904 Thompson's finally closed the old house having built a replacement set back further from the sea.

The involvement of the Pavement Commissioners and the town council, as distinct from the magistrates in discharging their regulatory functions, was largely focused on the opportunities that the closure or rebuilding of houses gave for road widening and extending the promenade. In 1836 the commissioners bought the old Admiral Rodney public house, which had closed some eight years before, for £300, and in 1863 considered buying the South Foreland beerhouse as part of a programme to widen South Street. They were able to agree with Hills that the new

Walmer Castle, rebuilt after the fire in 1867, should be set back to improve access along Lower Street but were criticised two years later when the brewers were allowed to rebuild the Scarborough Cat on Beach Street to the same footprint though standing at the "worst corner in the whole town"[36]. In 1909 the Mayor found himself in hot water having purchased the latter house, by then renamed the Globe, as a private individual, evidently in the (unfulfilled) expectation that the council would reimburse him and finally pursue their plans to demolish the property and widen the Beach Street junction with North Street. Some council members were still ruing the failure of their predecessors some 40 years before to purchase and pull down the Royal Hotel, on offer then for £1,250. Today the hotel is the only surviving building to the east side of Beach Street. The Napier Tavern, Fox, Crown and Fountain, which once kept it company on the seaward side, were all closed and demolished by 1924.

The council was also interested in more modest improvements where these offered the chance to widen a pavement, and were sometimes prepared to make payments or purchase small portions of land to that end. In 1881, for instance, the council paid the brewers owning the Sir John Falstaff £15 to remove an old-fashioned flight of steps projecting out on to the High Street pavement. Some street improvements could over time have an unintended effect. In 1909 the Anchor was described as "old-fashioned with steps down from the street into the bar"[37] in consequence

In 1904 Thompson's built a new house set back further from the sea wall (left), named it the Sandown Castle Hotel, and then demolished the old Castle public house (right).

of the raising of the level of West Street. (The same effect may indirectly have brought about the death of the marine Henry Hall who died in 1882 having fallen down eight steps at the Friendly Port beerhouse.) Thompson's had in fact intended to rebuild the Anchor, one of the oldest houses in Deal, but changed their plans out of sympathy for the landlady, Emily Hall. She had been widowed in 1905 when her husband Edward died after a motoring accident and successfully appealed to the brewers not to rebuild the house since she could get a living from the house as it stood, "and could not get it in any other way"[38]. Thompson's accordingly broke their contract with the builder at a cost of £100, and spent £115 on repairs instead – an instance of a sympathetic treatment which they found helpful to deploy when the magistrates came in 1909 to consider the case for enforcing closure.

By this time modifications to individual public houses might also be forced upon the owners by the borough magistrates. Since 1874 magistrates had had the power to look at the plans of proposed new premises – not that there were many of these – and the 1902 Licensing Act gave magistrates the right to require alterations as a condition of the renewal of a licence. The county police, urged on by the Chief Constable, were also pro-active. When they let it be known in the run up to the 1899 annual licensing meeting that they would oppose the renewal of licences for six houses which had side or back entrances "more or less concealed from public view and inconvenient for police supervision"[39] the threat was sufficient to persuade the brewers to make the necessary changes. When the time came for the magistrates to consider closures under the 1904 Licensing Act the configurations of different premises, as they impacted on police enforcement of the licensing laws, was one of the factors taken into account.

By now the appearance of many houses had changed considerably since the mid-Victorian period, not only following renovation and rebuilding but also because of the more conspicuous use of brewery signage. Hills had been reasonably restrained, but Thompson's and George Beer were more colourful and insistent. In 1911 Thompson's lawyer enjoyed teasing the magistrates during deliberations on possible closures for affecting not to know which houses belonged to his clients despite "a certain green paint and gilded lettering which indicated very plainly to whom they belonged"[40]. Pub names were sometimes prominently written on the sides of buildings, though suspended or free standing signs seem to have been relatively rare.

Individual landlords, like John Fisher while licensee of the Crown, might also choose to display their name in large letters on an outside wall. Complete anonymity was in any event no longer an option for any licensee. Beerhouses had from the outset been required to display a sign carrying the beerseller's name and the words "Licensed to sell Beer by Retail", and since 1872 every publican had to "affix his name and nature of business...to some conspicuous part of his premises, the letters to be distinct, and not less than an inch in height, so as to be legible to persons passing along the thoroughfare"[41]. It is to the people whose names were to be found above the doors of public houses and beerhouses in Deal that attention now turns.

The landlords

Running a public house is today a full-time job for most landlords. But in Victorian England it was common for licensed victuallers to have an additional trade or occupation. In Norwich, for example, a quarter of landlords were recorded as having a second occupation in 1851 and again in 1881. Jacqueline Bower calculates from the census returns that the proportion in Deal in 1861 was also around a quarter, falling to some 13% in 1871 and 1881.[42] But these are probably underestimates, for often clues only emerge from chance reports in local newspapers rather than from census returns. This was particularly true in the case of Deal landlords who were also boatmen or, as the case may be, Deal boatmen who were also the licensees of public houses.

The dozens of luggers, galleys and punts that gave Deal its claim to fame were launched directly from the beach. Boatmen naturally frequented the public houses and beerhouses that lined either side of Beach Street, mixing together in the evenings, planning their activities, taking refreshment before setting sail or having returned, or simply waiting there for any opportunity that might appear, if only for a few hours work helping with a launch or a landing. It was not surprising that some boatmen and boat owners chose to run such houses themselves, and to divide their time between the business of the sea and the bar counter.

At the top of the tree were men like Onesiphorus Sneller, who built the Napier Tavern in 1855, George Porter (licensee of the Fountain between 1872 and 1876) who had "shares in three boats, and was the owner of four others"[43] and, later, Harry Meakins, the prosperous boatman landlord of the Port Arms from 1897 until 1940. But ownership or part ownership of a boat was widespread among seafront landlords: men like John Tandy of the Castle, whose boat was stolen by marines in 1883 and later turned up in Ramsgate, or William Spears, "master mariner and pleasure boat owner", who ran the Antwerp for a time. Edward Trott was holding the licence of the King's Arms when he lost his life in the wreck of the lugger *Reform*, which overturned after colliding with the pier in 1871 with the loss of eight lives. Thomas Finnis, successively at the Prince of Wales, the Fox and the Deal Cutter, had better luck. "Nearly drowned three times"[44], his escapes included surviving the sinking of the lugger *Success*. Robert Wilds was both coxswain of the North Deal lifeboat and landlord of the North Star for over 20 years, and in due course Edward Hanger, second coxswain, followed him as landlord.

There was also a good fit between holding the licence of a public house and working in the building trades. Throughout the nineteenth century builders, carpenters, joiners, paper hangers and plumbers could regularly be found running public houses in Deal. These were generally located in the area around Lower Street, or towards the back of the town. For a builder like George Burton, who held the licence of the Liverpool Arms in Upper Deal between 1884 and 1898, or William Pettet (wheelwright and landlord of the Deal Castle), or Simon Marsh (blacksmith and landlord of the Anchor), yard and outhouse space was clearly important. For such men, as for carpenters like Bethel Wyborn (Five Ringers) or painters like Robert Mackie (Horse and Farrier), running a public house was a useful backstop when trade was poor, and the premises were a convenient venue for promoting and negotiating their services.

Edward Hanger, for many years second coxswain of the North Deal lifeboat, was also landlord of the North Star from 1886 to 1900. The public house stood next to the lifeboat station.

Other occupations twinned with the running of a public house included those of wood and coal dealer, sail maker, fly proprietor, picture framer, china dealer, furniture dealer and, in the case of several of the town's hoteliers, wine and spirits merchant. Winstanley has noted that in rural east Kent, "some publicans performed such a diversity of trades that it would be impossible to classify them accurately, they were by all account "mixed up with about damn near everything""[45], and much the same could have been said about some of Deal's long established landlords. The disputatious Thomas Cattermole for a time combined his bathing-machine business with running the Castle, while Thomas Desormeaux was both a hairdresser and landlord of the Harp in Middle Street for almost 20 years – a combination which inevitably led the magistrates to suspect that those receiving a trim might also be consuming beer at times when they should not have been. As already observed, some Hills' tenants, like Edward Redsull, landlord of the Jolly Gardener in the 1870s, also worked at the brewery. On the other hand cordwainers and shoemakers, one of the major occupational groupings in the town, were very under-represented among the landlords (and do not feature in Winstanley's list of occupations undertaken by landlords in rural areas). The fit in terms of working patterns, space utilisation and capital investment was clearly much less helpful here.

John Tandy was landlord of the Castle from 1885 until 1904, when he left fearing that the house, soon to be demolished, was no longer safe to live in. Tandy was also a boat owner, and had previously worked as foreman bricklayer for the builder George Cottew.

The temperance lobby, for its part, saw the fact that so many landlords had second occupations as compelling evidence that the town had far too many public houses. In 1882, according to the lawyer acting for the teetotallers in Deal, "one half of the present licensed houses were not producing a living to their occupants, who were compelled to follow some other occupation to make up a living"[46]. The issue of whether a particular house, properly conducted, could ever make a living for its landlord under its own steam would become a critical one 20 years later as the magistrates struggled to decide which houses to propose for closure.

Landlords varied a great deal in age – in 1851 from 23 to 88 – but most tended to be middle aged. At any one time roughly a third of all licensees were under 40, with around a half aged between 40 and 60. When asked by the coroner if he considered that William Browning, aged 67, and his wife had still been capable of running the Druid's Arms in the months before the former took his own life, Thompson's agent was clear that they had been up to the task (though added discouragingly that "people won't come in to see old people"[47]). The age pattern as a whole did not alter significantly over the period. But what did change, slowly but surely, was the proportion of landlords who were Deal men born and bred. In 1851 two-thirds of licensees had been born in the town. By 1891 this had fallen to only a third. The proportion born elsewhere in Kent, including in nearby Walmer, Kingsdown and Sholden, remained steady at around 30%. But the proportion born outside the county rose from 8% in 1851 to 35% in 1891.

It was certainly common, throughout the period, for licensees of hotels or the larger inns to have had experience of running similar establishments in London and the south east. George Curling sold the India Arms to Robert Neale of Twickenham in 1832 (agreeing, as part of the deal, not to open another house) and in 1860 Thompson's considered it worth advertising in *The Times* for a new tenant for the Clarendon Hotel ("to a young couple about to enter business offers advantages rarely met with"[48]). Thomas Lovegrove took the Royal Exchange in 1876 having previously held the Green Man in Covent Garden, while Arthur Banfield came to the Black Horse in 1888 fresh from running the Stoke Hotel in Guildford. Many of these new arrivals moved on after a short time – Lovegrove was gone within the year – and there was clearly a complex pattern of networks and connections linking hoteliers in London and the south east. The steady rise of a new kind of professional publican is also discernible across the period: someone who might choose to ply his trade in Deal for a time, but be ready to move on if the need or better opportunity arose – men like Richard Holness, who moved from the Rose Inn in Broadstairs to (coincidentally) the Rose in Deal in 1911, though living at the time in Ramsgate. This was his seventh house, and his second stint in Deal.

But it was certainly possible for new arrivals to put down roots and become significant figures in the community. A good example was Robert Allen, who took over and renovated the Royal Hotel in 1865 having

Frederick "Flint" Roberts, son of the previous landlord, took over the Rose and Crown in 1910 aged 21. The house had been bought by the Canterbury brewers Flint & Co in 1887.

moved to Deal from the Three Jolly Butchers in Tottenham. He was soon to be found running winter soup kitchens, organising rowing matches (including a race between employees of the Royal Hotel and the Clarendon Hotel in honour of the Queen's birthday), promoting a new omnibus route to Ramsgate and serving on the town council. Or things could go badly wrong. Up the road at the Crown William Clayton faced a succession of complaints from neighbours and was soon in trouble with the magistrates. Within a year he was disclaiming any responsibility for his wife's debts and offering a two-guinea reward for the identity of an insulting letter writer. By May 1872 he had had enough: "he had been annoyed ever since he had been in Deal. He was glad to say that he was about to leave the town and should not have to endure the arrogance to which he had been subjected much longer"[49]. Clayton lost his life two years later when the steamship on which he was serving as a boatswain and storekeeper went down. Families often suffered every bit as much. Thomas Bingham, a boatman, left "a comfortable house"[50] in Kingsdown in 1870 to chance his arm running the Scarborough Cat. Within months he was in serious debt, and had been sentenced to three months' hard labour for neglecting his wife and children.

For some licensees the life of a publican was a clean break with their former employment. Bower calculates that of the 181 men ceasing to be boatmen between 1841 and 1881 "the most popular alternative occupation…was licensed victualler or publican, with eight men turning to it immediately and two more coming to it later after spending some time working at other trades".[51] Towards the end of the century, in contrast, an increasing number of landlords were retired soldiers and marines:

men like Henry Taylor (Clarendon Tap), previously a sergeant in the Royal Marine Artillery, George Marsh (Maxton Arms), a soldier for 21 years with testimonials of exemplary conduct, Arthur Skinner (Liverpool Arms), a retired Royal Artillery Company Sergeant Major, and Albert Andrews (Waterman's Arms) wounded at Ladysmith while serving with the Rifle Brigade. Some other previous occupations lacked the same cachet: Henry Burville, for example, who took the Prince Albert in 1903, was previously a lavatory attendant in Margate.

From 1893 the council received an annual return of the number of licences transferred during the previous year. The first showed that nearly a third had changed hands but over the next 20 years the proportion was usually around one fifth. Many landlords held their licence for only a year or two, or sometimes less. In some cases the individual had been put into the house by the brewer on a temporary basis until a permanent tenant could be found. But that aside there is rarely any clue as to why particular tenures were so short-lived. No doubt in some cases the licensee, perhaps a newcomer to the trade, simply found the work less congenial or less profitable than he had expected. Ernest Steed, previously a billiard marker and porter at the King's Head, Dover (and so presumably with some idea of what he might be taking on) arrived at the Druid's Arms in 1903 with excellent references but stuck it out for only five days. Edwin Dawes, on behalf of Thompson's, could not really explain why: "it is of course unfortunate for us ...he simply cannot settle to the business. I told him if that were the case I would find someone else. I have made arrangements for a successor. He manages his house nicely, and I am sorry, but he will go out as he came in"[52].

Others simply could not cope. Earlier in 1903 Thompson's felt obliged to give William Stacey notice, after less than a year as tenant of the Crispin, for failing to curtail drunken behaviour. ("If I may be allowed to form an opinion", said PC Chapman to the magistrates, "the landlord was afraid to go into the room. The room was in a disgraceful state, and anybody with old boots would have got wet feet"[53].) The police concluded that Stacey "tries to do his best , but he is not fit for this kind of house. He would be all right for a country house"[54] When his successor Harry Jones was asked why he had left his previous house his explanation was straightforward – "because I could not make it pay, sir". ("The Clerk: "a very good reason"".)[55] George Ramsden claimed in 1874 to have taken the Castle "for pastime"[56], but quickly got into trouble and absconded within a year. Edward Pain found a more unusual way of coming to grief. His mistake was to take over the White Horse before his wife had seen it, "and when she came to that house she took an objection to it. She thought it was larger than it really was"[57]. The hapless Mr Pain held the licence for only two weeks.

What worried the magistrates was the way that some houses were particularly prone to show a rapid turnover of landlord. When the time came to decide on closures under the 1904 Licensing Act this was taken as prima facie evidence that the house had insufficient trade to provide a living and to justify its continuing existence. Sometimes the house was clearly in decline, with the landlord struggling to make ends meet. But in other cases the explanation for the rapid departures of successive landlords is less obvious. The Bowling Green, for example, had at least 18 different landlords in the 38 years between Richard Verrier, who sold the house and moved out in 1863, and the start of Herbert Sayers' long tenure in 1901. Among the larger houses the Walmer Castle showed a particularly steady turnover of landlords throughout the period.

But then of course there were the landlords and hoteliers who established themselves securely and retained their licences over a long period: men like Henry West (Yarmouth Packet 1840–72), Thomas Kidner (New Inn 1847–81), Stephen Pritchard (Eagle *c.*1855–81), David Almond (Rose 1862–85) and William Licence (Saracen's Head 1869–96). They would probably have agreed with the brewer's agent who observed to the magistrates that "the trade of a licence depended to a very great extent on the tenant. Like in the grocery, or drapery, one man might make a fortune, while another might lose one in the same business"[58] (though they might have queried the word "fortune"). Certainly men like Kidner, Almond and Licence were men of some substance and standing, and played important parts in the commercial and social networks of Victorian Deal. This was not simply in their role as landlords, but in the organisation of friendly and fraternal societies, recreational and savings clubs, trade and philanthropic associations and sometimes as members of the town council.

Continuity was often maintained through the transfer of the licence between members of the same family. The boatman Edward Galley Grigg held the licence of the Albion on Beach Street from 1862 until 1877, at which point he handed over to his son-in-law John Roberts, brother of the coxswain of the North Deal lifeboat. On Roberts' death six years later

Edward Galley Grigg (left) was landlord of the Albion on Beach Street for most of the period between 1862 until 1903. His grandson Philip (rear) then held the licence until the Second World War.

Grigg took the licence once again. Often called as an expert witness when disputes relating to the customs of the beach resulted in lawsuits, when in 1898 the magistrates, by a majority, dismissed charges of serving beer during prohibited hours, "there was a decided expression of approval in the court when the decision was announced."[59] Edward Grigg died in 1903, after which his grandson Philip ran the house for another 25 years. Edward's brother John Galley Grigg had been successively landlord of the Shah and, from 1879 until his death, of the adjacent Ship. The licence of the Fawn was held in turn by several different members of the Redsull family. Redsulls also ruled the roost at the New Plough in Middle Deal. Edward Redsull, a rare example of a publican who was also a shoemaker, held the licence for over 20 years until his death in 1880. His brother Robert then took over, followed in 1884 by Elizabeth, Robert's widow, and from 1899 until 1921 by their son William.

Most landlords who were tenants of brewers, which is to say virtually all by the turn of the century, were charged an annual rent of between £15 (for the South Foreland in 1861 and the Forester in 1875, for example) and £20. In 1880 the Maxton Brewery in Dover let the Maxton Arms for £12, and Hills the Norfolk Arms for £18; most rents seem to have fallen within that range. Twenty years later the rents from roughly half of Hills' houses in Deal were still between £15 and £20, with around a quarter in the £21 – £30 range. At the top of the scale came the Walmer Castle (£200) and the Black Horse (£220). As already noted, the agents selling the Hills estate in 1901 reckoned the rents charged were by then for the most part "quite inadequate", and certainly the £8 paid for the Admiral Keppel seems remarkably low. But it is not known how quickly

Thompson's set about raising them. The son of the landlord of the Queen's Arms remembers the rent in Edwardian times being £16; this is actually £1 less than Hills were said to have charged.

It is more difficult to be clear about the income different kinds of houses might generate, and the profit a landlord might hope to make. When Hills advertised for a tenant for the Star in 1858 they estimated the likely income at £50; for the Sir Sidney Smith in 1874, £130. In 1881 the trade of the good-sized and well-situated Railway Tavern was reckoned to be 155 barrels a year. At a profit of 12s a barrel, the usual margin according to Hills' agent in 1892, this implied a profit of £93 a year from beer sales. But according to the lawyer acting in 1893 for the Brickmaker's Arms off-licence, whose landlord claimed sales of up to six barrels a week in the summer, "there were dozens of public-houses in the town where a barrel or two a week was as much as was done"[60].

He may well have been right. The publican George Weller, arriving in Deal from Dover in 1887 burdened with debt and on the brink of bankruptcy, could only manage a barrel and a half during his first month at the Greyhound in Middle Street. In 1906 customers at the Maxton Arms were consuming only around 60 barrels of beer a year, though admittedly 16 barrels of spirits in addition. The beerhouse keeper who begged the indulgence of the bench in 1870 for his failure to pay the poor rate "on the grounds that he had not taken a shilling for the last three months"[61] was no doubt telling a tale but presumably not to the extent of risking being laughed out of court. The overall impression is that landlords of medium-sized, well-established houses, particularly if they had a second parallel source of income, could generally make an adequate or even comfortable living. Difficulties were more often experienced by landlords of the small houses and beerhouses, on the one hand, but also by hoteliers on the other.

It was certainly the case that among the steady stream of hoteliers arriving from out of town to try their luck were many whose fortunes singularly failed to revive. Thomas Gould, late of the Bush Hotel, Southsea, opened the rebuilt Walmer Castle in April 1870 but had to petition for bankruptcy only a few months later. Proprietors seem to have found it very hard to make this fine new house pay: John Bishop went into liquidation in 1879 leading to the auction of the entire contents of the hotel and when Philip Gunter, formerly of Seething Lane, London, tried his hand in 1881 he reached bankruptcy after only short time in charge.

Bankruptcy was often the culmination of a series of mistakes and misfortunes. When Herman Whitlaw of the Royal Hotel petitioned in 1865 having amassed a large number of local creditors, he attributed his failure to "losses on business, bad debts [and] domestic afflictions".[62] For Arthur Brassington, taking the New Inn in 1894 may have been the last throw of the dice. He had started business as an auctioneer and estate agent in Portman Square, London, on the basis of a £500 loan. Over the next ten years he worked his way through a large legacy, exacerbated by the failure of a speculative investment in South Africa. By the time of his bankruptcy in 1895 he had unsecured liabilities of £225.9s and assets of only £26.15s.3d. The court noted sadly that "the only book kept by him is a cash takings book"[63].

For some a sojourn in Deal was simply a stage in the road to insolvency. William Collins was another Londoner. He had begun his business career as caterer to the Officers' Mess at the Royal Naval College, Greenwich, and arrived in Deal in 1886 to take the Clarendon Hotel after a stint as manager of the Bank of England Club. He began energetically but left five years later in debt, which he then compounded while running the Trafalgar Hotel in Ramsgate. By 1895, after 17 unhappy months at that house, his debts amounted to £2,111.4s.2d.

Others, often born and bred in Deal, tried their hand at the public house trade for a while to supplement their income but still hit the rocks. John Goldup, carpenter and builder, held the licence of the Greyhound for a time before reaching bankruptcy ten years later as a High Street grocer and draper. The boatman Thomas Finnis failed to restore the fortunes of the Deal Cutter and went down on account of "bad fishing seasons and want of trade"[64]. William Goodchild went bankrupt in 1865 running a carriage business at the Anchor, and Alexander Harvey went the same way two years later as cattle dealer and landlord of the Jolly Sailor. James Graves began business as a North End coal dealer and carrier on the strength of a £75 loan from his mother. He moved to Middle Street in 1883, where he owned a stable and store, and took the licence of the Crispin beerhouse next door two years later. He was probably in trouble even then. In 1890 he was caught, drunk and belligerent, serving out of hours. ("I know what it will be. I will get three months notice to clear out. The brewers can hang their —- house round their neck if they like. I can live without it".[65]) In the event the brewers, Thompson's, stayed their hand, but in his final years as landlord Graves received "upwards of twenty County Court summons"[66] and when finally hitting bankruptcy in 1892 his liabilities exceeded his assets by £200.

John Outwin, in contrast, had a largely successful career in Deal and for many years could claim to be the town's leading hotelier. A wine and spirits merchant born in Doncaster, he took over the Clarendon Hotel in 1860 and three years later also took the licence of the Black Horse. In 1870 he opened a new establishment ("Wine Shades") next door to the Clarendon Hotel. During the 1860s Outwin also built a reputation for providing catering for civic functions, for example the grand breakfast which followed the opening of the new public rooms in Park Street. He was also one of the promoters of the new Deal pier, and when this opened in November 1864 to great fanfare provided the celebratory dinner. Outwin then proceeded to add the new licensed refreshment rooms at the end of the pier to his considerable portfolio, retaining the licence until 1879.

But he probably over-extended himself. In 1870 Outwin vacated the Clarendon Hotel, having tangled in the courts with the brewers and the landlord of the Clarendon Tap, and the following year handed in the licence of the Black Horse. For the next four years he took his turn trying to make a go of Hills' ill-starred Walmer Castle, from where he ran his wine and spirits operation specialising in Hungarian wines, before leaving the hotel business altogether for a time. He nonetheless remained a man of some consequence, brother-in-law of the brewer Edwin Hills and in 1875 elected to the town council. But when after a gap of ten years, no longer a councillor and with the "Wine Shades" venture also behind him, he decided to resume

The boatman George "Cash" Erridge was briefly landlord of the Deal Lugger before running the Prince Albert from 1907 until 1940. His brother Ralph was landlord of the North Star on Beach Street between 1913 and 1933.

his career as a hotelier it was as landlord of the more modest Three Compasses, a George Beer house on Beach Street. In 1890 he finally hit the rocks, and was obliged to file for bankruptcy with debts of £212.13s and no assets; the house very nearly closed permanently in consequence. Energetic, combative and disliked by many in the town for his radical politics, there were probably many who took pleasure in his fall from grace. Outwin nonetheless bounced back, and successfully reinvented himself as a Beach Street newsagent and bookseller until his death in 1911 at the age of 86.

Then, as now, solvency and modest prosperity generally passed by unnoticed in the local press while bankruptcies and other misfortunes were often reported at length. The death of a landlord rarely prompted comment – unless that is, the cause of death was murder or suicide. In 1856 Samuel Baker, the landlord of the Ship on Beach Street (which, rebuilt a few years later, became the Clarendon Hotel) bludgeoned 19-year-old Lieutenant McCarroll to death in the street with a poker; the latter, having evidently lost his money playing billiards at the Royal Oak attempted to gain entry to the Ship and obtain beer on credit, and in so doing insulted Baker's wife. The hot-tempered landlord was transported for life. In 1905, in only the second murder in the town since McCarroll's death, the victim was the landlord of the Fountain, Robert Pearce, and the perpetrator his 21-year-old potman Percy Murray. In a scuffle following allegations that the latter had been spying on the landlord's wife through a hole in her bedroom wall, Murray stabbed Pearce with a kitchen knife and was duly sentenced to death. A petition in the town for a reprieve attracted some 550 signatures, and the sentence was commuted to penal servitude having regard to Murray's relatively young age.

To modern eyes the reporting of inquests following a suicide seems mercilessly detailed. Publicans and other dealers in beer, wine and spirits had nearly the highest occupational suicide rates in Victorian England, second only to soldiers, and Kent had among the highest county rates for men. Nationally there was often a clear link between landlord suicides and the consequences of the ready availability of drink (with the result that mortality from alcoholism among landlords was five times higher than the general rates for males). Whether excessive drinking was a factor in the case of Deal publicans who took their own lives is not clear; men like William Piercy, a 41-year-old former marine sergeant who committed suicide in 1892 borne down by health and money worries shortly after taking the licence of the Providence, or William Browning, one time ginger beer manufacturer and landlord of the Druid's Arms for over 30 years who took his life in 1901 fearing he could no longer cope. Similar fears afflicted Edward Chandler, who had run the Duke of Wellington for six and a half years. He then worked in Ashford and managed the Cambridge Arms in Walmer for a time before returning to Deal in 1906 to take the Bell (a stone's throw from the Duke of Wellington). But this time, for whatever reason, he "could not stick it"[67] and cut his throat ten months later. In all three cases their widows were left to take on the licence, and to carry on as best they could.

The landladies
Women were often to be found as licensees in nineteenth-century Deal. But this was almost always following the death of their husband. It was standard practice for the magistrates then to agree the transfer of the licence to the widow. In many cases this proved to be a temporary arrangement, although the woman might not necessarily leave the house. Remarriage was one possibility. Sarah Trott, for example, widowed in 1871 when her husband lost his life in the sinking of the lugger *Reform*, married again the following year and the licence of the King's Head was transferred to her new husband William Lambert. Tragically William in turn lost his life at sea two years later aged 25, when the lugger *Galatea*'s punt capsized in the Channel, and the licence reverted to Sarah for a second time. She continued to run the house for another three years.

It was not in fact uncommon for widows to continue to run public houses under their own name for several years, or more, after their husband's death. Elizabeth Boakes, for instance, was widowed in 1863 but kept the King's Arms herself until the licence was lost in 1877. There were also several notable success stories. Susannah Marsh took the licence of the Admiral Keppel, opposite St Leonard's Church in Upper Deal, following the death of her husband in 1864. She held this until her own death 38 years later, aged 80, after which the licence passed to her married daughter. The house had long since become known as "Mrs Marsh's Admiral Keppel". Equally celebrated was "Mrs Kemp's Yarmouth Packet" on Beach Street. Amelia, the landlady, had previously been married to Mariner Kemp, landlord of the Crown, but from 1874 until around 1908 held the licence of the Yarmouth Packet in her own right. More humble beerhouses, many of which in the early period had an address but no name, might also be identified by the woman in charge: "Mrs Barnes' beerhouse" in Lower Street, for instance, was the venue in 1859 for a heavy drinking session which culminated in the prosecution of two men for assault.

Women could also be found running some of the town's hotels. Alice Allen, a "highly respected landlady"[68], took over the licence of the Royal Hotel on the death of her husband Robert in 1871 and continued there until her own death seven years later. Charlotte Donoghue ran the Royal Exchange for the same length of time after being widowed in 1868. On her death the licence passed to her daughter. The same mother to daughter transfer occurred five years later at the Black Bull; Mary Castle then held the licence for another eight years.

Transfers other than to widows were not usually sought or sanctioned but might be allowed if the woman already had practical experience of being in charge. When Horace Young, having run the Swan for ten years and feeling his age, applied to transfer the licence to his daughter Caroline the magistrates were in two minds, but agreed after Alderman Hayman explained that he had known the house for a long time, "and really the daughter managed the business"[69]. But a licence was hardly ever granted to a woman who had no previous connection with the house. A rare exception came in 1909 when, despite their "general objection to widows holding licences other than those carried on by the deceased husband"[70], the bench agreed that Mary Jennings, having run the Druid's Arms during her husband's protracted illness, would not be refused a licence elsewhere. She subsequently became licensee of the Fountain.

If anything, views on the suitability of women as licensees seem to have hardened over the period. When an application was made in 1902 to transfer the licence of the Brickmaker's Arms to Eliza Everett, the magistrates only agreed "on the understanding that the house in question was to be transferred to the husband on his completing his service in the marines, it being pointed out that the Bench did not care to grant licences to ladies"[71]. Later in the year the bench refused to allow Isabella Pettet to take on the licence of the Lord Nelson, a beerhouse once again in the magistrates' bad books, the police arguing that, among other factors, her age (56) meant that she was not a fit and proper person. The Lord Nelson "was used by a rough class very much...it wanted a good man to manage this house"[72].

Upper Deal in 1860, showing the Liverpool Arms and, further down on the left, the Admiral Keppel. Susannah Marsh ran the Admiral Keppel following her husband James' death in 1864 until her own death in 1902.

In mid-century Mary Finnis, unmarried but Deal born and bred and with an extended family network, brought up four nephews and nieces while running the Deal Cutter in Beach Street with the help of a succession of young female domestic servants. But for some the challenge of running a house as a single woman was simply too great. Emma Gunner tried to keep the Brickmaker's Arms off-licence and grocer's shop going after the death of her husband in 1895. But she had "very great difficulty conducting the house without offence"[73], fell foul of the magistrates several times for serving on the premises, and finally had to call it a day.

Esther Sparkes seems to have led a peripatetic and difficult life. In 1883 she and her husband Alfred were living with her widowed daughter, the licensee of the Pelican in Beach Street. In July Alfred, who violently resisted arrest, was convicted of ill-treating his wife. Esther and her daughter moved on soon afterwards, with or without Alfred, leaving the Dover Brewery Company to pursue them through the courts for failing to pay for a delivery of beer. In 1892, rather surprisingly on the face of it, Esther was granted the licence of the Greyhound, a small house in Middle Street, but stayed there for only a short time before moving to the King's Head on Beach Street. She secured a singing and music licence, but the following year was prosecuted by the Inland Revenue for neglecting to renew the licence of the house itself. Business was poor – according to Hills' solicitor the main reason was that "the new promenade greatly diverted the trade from the house"[74]. Esther moved on once again and in April 1894, by then a widow, was forced to apply for an administration order. Her debts, amounting to £48.10s., had been largely incurred, however, not in Deal but from her time as landlady of the Old Crown Inn in Canterbury.

In 1893 the lawyer prosecuting on behalf of the Licensed Victuallers Association a marine who had threatened Annie Diggerson, landlady of the Horse and Farrier, reminded the bench that "many of the public houses in Deal were managed by women ...it was of very considerable importance in the eyes of the Association, and no doubt the bench would share the same opinion, that women should be protected in their trade of licensed victuallers"[75]. Overall the census returns indicate that – as seems to have been the case in other parts of the country, and indeed in Kent over a very long period – between 10% and 20% of licences in the town were held by women at any one time. But this is of course no real indication of the importance of women in the actual running of public houses. Most households were small, with generally only the larger

John Lewis Roget's painting of the Yarmouth Packet in 1888. During Amelia Kemp's long tenure as licensee the Beach Street house was particularly favoured by pilots in need of lodgings, and later by French workers at the nearby canning factory.

hotels having live-in servants. Wives, and sometimes daughters, had to play their part in serving customers and generally keeping the house functioning, in addition to their domestic chores within the family.

This was particularly true where their husbands were boatmen and, as the census sometimes put it, had "gone afloat". But other part-time landlords might also be out of the house on business for much of the time. "Are you a married man?" demanded the 1880 election commissioners of Henry Mackie, painter and landlord of the Horse and Farrier after he had denied knowledge of the use made of the committee room in his house: "A: no. Q: who takes care of the house while you are away? A: My sisters"[76]. The absence of the male licensee, leaving the house in the hands of his wife, sister or daughter, was sometimes offered in mitigation of an infringement of the licensing laws. But this did not usually help their cause with the magistrates.

Some wives of landlords had a very unpleasant time of it, and cases of domestic violence were fairly common. Thomas Randall, for example, landlord of the Five Bells in Middle Street, threatened to murder his wife Eliza with a table knife, having ill treated her throughout the two years of their marriage. Mark Funnell of the Noah's Ark received three months' hard labour in 1881 for assaulting his wife, and Thomas Bingham's road to ruin included charges of beating and ill-treating his wife. Amelia Kemp, before finding respect and security running the Yarmouth Packet, experienced brutality when married to Mariner Kemp, landlord of the Crown. To the latter's amazement and fury their daughter Ellen took out a warrant and told the magistrates that "ever since we kept a public house my father has off and on been violent to my mother and all of us".[77] Her mother disclaimed any wish for her husband to be bound over to keep the peace, but the marriage seems to have disintegrated soon afterwards.

Not that women were always the innocent party. Benjamin Ricketts of the Park Tavern, for example, sued his wife in the London divorce courts after less than a year of marriage on the grounds of her "misconduct" with his brother. Some wives could be spectacularly aggressive on their own account. Pride of place must go to Sarah Cooper of the Lord Nelson beerhouse in Short Street. In May 1858 she found herself locked up by the police, at her husband Edward's request, for drunkenness and for threatening to kill him, and was back in custody two months later having struck him on the head with a ginger beer bottle. In October the hapless Edward was claiming to be once again in fear of his life, "his house rendered miserable by the drunkenness of his wife". The magistrates, rather wisely, "suggested that as they live so unhappily together, they had better separate by mutual consent, the husband undertaking to allow his wife 4/- per week and she to take away all her wearing apparel from his premises. Both parties appeared thoroughly satisfied with this arrangement...." [78].

Rivalries between women could also be turbulent. Sarah Cooper moved from fighting her husband to scrapping with Ann Macey of the Bricklayer's Arms, who in turn later got into trouble for hitting a servant. On Beach Street competition between different public houses in close proximity could become disagreeable. In 1878, for example, Robert Wilds of the North Star had to agree to be bound over for the good behaviour of his wife after she had assaulted Mrs Nicholas, landlady of the Lifeboat next door. But women like Mrs Wilds and Mrs Cattermole – the latter, formerly of the Castle, bound over to keep the peace after abusing the wife of the current landlord – did at least have their established places in the life of the town, with networks of friends, acquaintances and indeed enemies. Perhaps more poignant were the experiences of some of those arriving in the town with their husbands to try to make a go of running a public house and put down roots, and very often failing.

Sarah Licence, née Redman, was the first wife of William, landlord of the Saracen's Head. Sarah died in 1889, aged 47, leaving six daughters.

Albert Chambers had been a watchmaker in Sittingbourne but moved to Deal with his wife to take the licence of the Sir John Falstaff, a public house on the High Street, in January 1891. Things went wrong from the start, and he turned to drink. After Albert was charged in February with being drunk and disorderly, his wife Jane told the magistrates:

"a very pitiable tale. They were very short of money, and had very little to eat, while the husband felt too much upset to eat anything, and commenced drinking, which made matters worse. They paid £50 to go into the house, and were not taking, some days, more than twopence. On Saturday they took about 1s 6d, and that was in the evening, when a customer or two came in. Her husband was very much upset, became abusive, and attempted to strike her, but she got away. She did not feel at all safe, having six little children upstairs. They had been very much deceived with the house, and it preyed upon her husband's mind, it being rather weak, and he gave way…".[79]

The magistrates did take pity, and the case was dismissed. But although Albert tried to supplement his income by working as an agricultural labourer, relations with his wife deteriorated further. The brewers (Flint of Canterbury) were by now said to be determined to get rid of the Chambers as soon as possible, and by May 1892 the family had gone. Flint refurbished the house, and installed John Smith, an ex-soldier who had previously kept the Duke of Connaught in Dover. But the magistrates had had enough, and the house was shut. The closure of the Sir John Falstaff, of no great consequence at the time, was in fact a sign of things to come. The high water mark had now passed, in terms of the number of pubs and beerhouses in the town and thus of the opportunities for earning a living as a landlord or landlady. In the following decade, the contraction began in earnest, and has continued ever since.

1. Sidney and Beatrice Webb, *The History of Liquor Licensing in England Principally from 1700 to 1830* (London, 1903) p 111
2. *Municipal Corporations in England and Wales: Report on the Borough of Deal* (1834) para 46
3. S. Pritchard, *The History of Deal* (Deal, 1864) pp 246–7
4. T. R. Gourvish and R. G. Wilson, *The British Brewing Industry 1830 – 1980* (Cambridge, 1994) p 22
5. Quoted in B. Harrison, *Drink and the Victorians: The Temperance Question in England, 1815 – 1872* (London, 1971) p 82
6. S. and B. Webb p 127
7. J. Greenaway, *Drink and British Politics since 1830: A Study in Policy-Making* (Basingstoke, 2003) p 15
8. *Telegram* 30 August 1873
9. *Report by the Committee on Intemperance for the Lower House of Convocation of the Province of Canterbury* (1869) p 23

10. *Telegram* 2 June 1858
11. *Telegram* 15 September 1866
12. *Mercury* 21 September 1867
13. P. Jennings, *The Local: A History of the English Pub* (Stroud, 2007) p 70
14. P. Jennings, *The Public House in Bradford, 1770–1970* (Keele, 1995) p 79
15. J. Bower, "Deal and the Deal Boatmen c 1840 – c 1880", Unpublished PhD thesis, University of Kent, 1990 p 177
16. *Telegram* 16 October 1869
17. *Mercury* 12 August 1876
18. *Telegram* 28 January 1871
19. *Mercury* 22 July 1876
20. *Mercury* 12 Setember 1896
21. *Mercury* 30 September 1899
22. *Telegram* 25 September 1880
23. *Telegram* 22 January 1881
24. *Mercury* 14 February 1903
25. *Telegram* 11 September 1886
26. *Mercury* 26 October 1867
27. Ibid
28. *Mercury* 8 July 1899
29. *Mercury* 6 April 1866
30. *Mercury* 13 November 1875
31. Rules of the Fire Brigade in Kent History and Library Centre De/AF1
32. *Mercury* 11 January 1896
33. *Mercury* 13 October 1877
34. *Telegram* 27 December 1862
35. *Telegram* 23 October 1869
36. Letter to the *Mercury* 5 June 1869
37. S. Glover and M. Rogers, *The Old Pubs of Deal and Walmer (with Kingsdown and Mongeham)* (Whitstable, 2010) p 20
38. *Mercury* 6 March 1909
39. *Mercury* 9 September 1899
40. *Mercury* 11 March 1911
41. *Mercury* 28 September 1872
42. Bower p 178
43. *Telegram* 1 November 1873
44. *Mercury* 9 January 1892
45. M. Winstanley, "The Rural Publican and His Business in East Kent before 1914", in *Oral History* Vol 4 (1976) p 67
46. *Mercury* 30 September 1882
47. *Mercury* 19 October 1901
48. *The Times* 7 May 1860
49. *Telegram* 4 May 1872
50. *Telegram* 9 April 1870
51. Bower pp 131–2
52. *Mercury* 9 May 1903
53. *Mercury* 31 January 1903
54. *Mercury* 21 February 1903
55. *Mercury* 5 September 1903
56. *Mercury* 9 May 1874
57. *Mercury* 5 May 1906
58. *Mercury* 26 September 1891
59. *Mercury* 26 November 1898
60. *Mercury* 23 September 1893
61. *Telegram* 21 May 1870
62. *Telegram* 25 March 1865
63. *Mercury* 14 December 1895
64. *Mercury* 11 April 1891
65. *Mercury* 15 February 1890
66. *Mercury* 3 December 1892
67. *Mercury* 2 March 1907
68. *Telegram* 5 October 1878
69. *Mercury* 21 November 1903
70. *Mercury* 6 March 1909
71. *Mercury* 12 April 1902
72. *Mercury* 18 October 1902
73. *Mercury* 5 November 1898
74. *Mercury* 20 January 1894
75. *Mercury* 30 December 1893
76. *Report of the Commissioners appointed to inquire into the Existence of Corrupt Practices in the Borough of Sandwich* (1881) p 391
77. *Mercury* 21 March 1874
78. *Telegram* 27 October 1858
79. *Mercury* 28 February 1891

Chapter 3

The Users and Uses of Public Houses

Boatmen, marines, lodgers and visitors

In Edwardian Deal, in order to help the magistrates take decisions, the police were asked to summarise the trade of public houses being considered for closure. The Fountain on Beach Street they considered had "an average trade of a fairly superior class". Further up the street the Deal Lugger was "used by labouring classes and boatmen", but round the corner at the Friendly Port in New Street the trade was "rather rough". The Sun was "frequented by working classes both men and women", while the nearby Horse and Farrier was "used a good deal by Royal Marines and for the general class of trade". Others in court sometimes offered their own assessments. The Anchor, according to one magistrate, "was used by carriers, market gardeners and such like, and no in any way objectionable characters frequented it", while the landlord of the White Horse reckoned his trade consisted of "commercial travellers, cyclists, and travellers by train, and tradesmen, and a very large number of country people". But as for the Maxton Arms, according to the magistrates' clerk, "it is a bad class of trade they do".[1]

Arthur Matthews of Thompson & Son, casting around at that point for arguments which might help deter the magistrates from further closures, ventured that "a reasonable number of houses acted as a safety valve, as long as they did no harm. He had a strong feeling that if they mixed people up too closely in these matters, it was not wise".[2] In earlier times Matthews would have had less to worry about on that score. Deal was then overwhelmingly orientated towards the needs of shipping passing through or anchoring in the Downs, and many of the public houses were used almost exclusively by boatmen.

DRINKING IN DEAL

The heyday of the Deal boatmen had been during the Revolutionary and Napoleonic Wars. Deal handled very little foreign trade – in 1791 this was reported to be less than 1,000 tons of shipping a year – but large numbers of boatmen made a living by providing services to crews and passengers of ships in the Downs, and in the activity of hovelling: as Edward Darby, clerk to the brewer Edward Iggulden, succinctly explained, this involved "supplying ships with anchors and cables, and such things as that".[3] Smuggling was rife, sometimes leading to scuffles with the revenue men and the militia. Deal boatmen were admired for their bravery and skill, but had a national reputation for hard-hearted avarice – when in 1794 the British ambassador in Vienna wished to find a parallel for the latest piece of Prussian bad behaviour the comparison that came to mind was "the Deal men [who] avail themselves of the perilous situation of the passengers on the Goodwins to drive a most unconscionable bargain"[4]. In 1838 the writer of a county history conceded that the boatmen were "a bold, active body of men, who perform many important services" but added that they were also said to be "the most egregious plunderers"[5']. It was not until well into the second half of the century that the reputation of the Deal boatmen became largely positive.

With the coming of peace in 1815 the boatmen faced difficult times. In 1833 they petitioned the House of Commons for relief, and the Select Committee then established heard evidence of great hardship. No boatman relying on hovelling alone was said to be paying the poor rate. Of the 21 first-class luggers ("foul weather boat(s), which men go afloat in in the worst of weather"[6]) only 12 were in a sound condition; in 1815 there had been 30. But the total number of boats of all types, even in these hard times, is still very striking. A survey by the local Commissioner of Salvage showed that Deal, Walmer and Kingsdown beaches were also home to 57 30-foot galleys, and 119 smaller 14- to 18-foot punts; with the first- and second-class luggers, 212 craft in total. The commissioner, Edward Boys, reckoned that there were then 437 boatman distributed among the 14 "stations".

Although the fortunes of the boatmen as a whole gradually improved, their numbers fell steadily over the next 80 years as steamships came to dominate the merchant trade. But the decline was not precipitous, and the number of boatmen may even have increased between 1841 and 1851. In August 1869 the *Telegram* estimated that Deal boatmen had recovered some 600 anchors and chains over the previous three years. Large sums could

Beyond the new iron pier, opened in 1864, can be seen the outlines of dozens of ships at anchor. In 1859 the *Telegram* estimated that some 6,000 ships had anchored in or passed through the Downs over the previous year.

sometimes be made from successful salvage operations – most notably the £7,000 shared between 62 Deal boatmen and others following the salvaging in 1866 of the ship *Iron Crown*, stranded on the Goodwins homeward bound from Shanghai. Bower estimates from census returns that in 1851, when almost half of the population of the town lived east of Lower Street, 31% of occupied men living in this tight network of streets worked as boatmen with a further 6% engaged in a related business[7]. There were still an estimated 300 boatmen in the 1880s, and boatmen remained the largest occupational grouping in the town. The striking increase in the number of public houses in Beach Street between 1847 and 1870 has already been noted. The reason cannot have been rising demand by boatmen, except to the extent that individual spending power improved, but it is certainly testimony to the continuing seaward focus of the town.

Furthermore, while not all Beach Street houses depended on the boatmen, most boatmen certainly depended on their public houses. Many of the boatmen's official stations took their names from public houses, past or present, and houses themselves were often the boatmen's unofficial stations. As a witness to the hearings of the 1880 Sandwich election petition noted, "it was the custom in Deal for certain public houses to have their own special clique of watermen"[8]. Another commented that "men on the water all day regarded the public houses as their club, where they spend their evenings. Taverns in Deal had their own special customers.."[9]. (Sixty years before, the irascible William Cobbett claimed to have been glad to hurry through the town "and to leave its inns and public-houses to be occupied by the tarred, the trowsered, and blue-and-buff crew whose very vicinage I always detest"[10].)

As well as being places of relaxation and refreshment, public houses – often run and sometimes owned by boatmen – served as places to meet and to plan, to share news or simply to wait for the chance of work afloat. Boats did not tend to have fixed crews; according to Edward Darby in 1833 "when a boat is launching, as many men as can jump into her do so".[11] The chance might come out of the blue, and if not actually waiting on the beach itself being in a Beach Street public house might serve almost as well. When boatman Richard Orrick heard the night signal in September 1865 he did not hesitate but "jumped out of the window of the Napier Tavern at the risk of breaking his neck" and ran to the boats[12]. One of the houses on the seaward side of Beach Street from which boatmen could step directly down on to the beach, the Napier Tavern was particularly well placed for those hoping for a call. Both the Napier Tavern and the Fountain had verandas from which to watch out for vessels needing help; the latter also had a "look-out"[13] above the veranda and housed the Downs pilot bell. Large sums could turn on the speed with which individual boats could be crewed and launched for, as the *Telegram* noted, "it is usual in [salvage] cases of this kind for those who arrive first on board to have discretionary powers as to whether any that follow shall be employed in conjunction with themselves"[14].

Boatmen might be at sea for several days, particularly if cruising westward for a ship in need of a pilot, and often left or returned home in the early morning. Several of the Beach Street houses, notably the Rose and Crown, held special early morning licences in recognition of the boatmen's particular needs, and closed early in the evening. More contentious, and liable to test the magistrates' sense of fairness to the limit, was the serving of beer or spirits to exhausted boatmen outside of permitted opening hours. Service was often provided by the wife or daughter, the licensee himself being at sea or attending to his boat. The latter might even carry the name of a favoured public house: the Fountain, for example, the Royal Exchange or Yarmouth Packet. Back on land, boatmen would often need a quiet corner or private room in a Beach Street public house to calculate and share out the profits of a voyage. Many examples of this can be found in the local papers, though generally when such meetings ended in a rowdy dispute or a summons to appear before the magistrates for drinking outside of the permitted hours.

Deal was also home to several dozen licensed pilots, many of whom lived in the network of streets built in the 1800s on land to the north of

Beach Street after a storm, probably that of December 1897 when, said the *Mercury*, "wave after wave spent its fury on the parades, moving boats and seats bodily, and driving them towards and into the road". The property of the Royal Exchange (left) included three capstan grounds on the beach.

Hills brewery. They also needed places to wait, and to be found. The Deal pilot William Stanton, when recording his reminiscences of the 1820s, opened one story in the Three Compasses in Lower Street, when "a man came from the beach saying there were several ships adrift, and were making signals of distress", and another when sought out by a stranger while reading a newspaper in the Port Arms.[15] Pilots from other stations around the coast also needed lodgings in Deal, before or after a passage, and favoured public houses on Beach Street did steady business. When Amelia Kemp's Yarmouth Packet on Beach Street was threatened with closure in 1901 a petition signed by most of the Trinity House pilots frequenting the town asked the Mayor to prevent the loss of "what has been our home for many years on landing in Deal, at any hour of the day or night, in summer or in winter".[16] The Railway Tavern, conveniently placed for the train journey home, was also favoured, the landlord explaining to the magistrates in 1911 that he "had some 30 or 40 Gravesend pilots on his list, and set out to come down at all times of the night to receive them".[17]

By this time the numbers of sailing vessels passing through the Downs had fallen sharply. In Victorian times, as photographs show, the sea could be thick with ships at anchor. But Deal had no harbour, and ceased to be classified as a port in 1881. Relatively few merchant seamen set foot in the town, unless shipwrecked or in dispute with the master of their ship and put ashore as "refractory seamen". The master or one of his mates might take a boat ashore – or from 1864 land at the pier – in order to conduct some business and perhaps, like the exhausted captain of the *Zemindar* whose two or three glasses of liquor on an empty stomach had "an effect he had not contemplated"[18], take refreshment at a public house. In December 1878 Sandwich Crown Court heard that Hodges, Deal shipping agents, were in the habit of taking masters of vessels to dine in the Crown (and ruled that they owed the landlord Edward Erridge 3s.10d. for dinners consumed but not paid for).

The guests in question may have been the masters of colliers – until the 1870s colliers from the north east discharged their coal directly on to the beach, and the master and crew might spend a short time in the town. But in most cases those serving on merchant ships in the Downs had no need to come ashore. Before the building of the new pier it was also very expensive to do so – making use of the services of local boatmen might cost several pounds. In 1861 one captain, come ashore to make some essential purchases, told the *Telegram* that he had been "in the habit of passing the Downs about six times a year for the last 12 years, but [had] never been on shore at Deal but once before, which is about eight years since, and then, as on the present occasion, it was a matter of positive necessity"[19]. Another explained that, although sometimes detained in the Downs for long periods, he always tried to avoid taking on provisions until reaching the Isle of Wight.

The new pier greatly facilitated the landing of passengers from ships in the Downs, many no doubt eager for refreshment and accommodation on dry land. Pain records that in January 1873 "nearly 400 ships' boats came to the Pier, landing about 200 passengers, and taking off nearly 80 tons of water and four tons of provisions"[20]. But the pier did little to stimulate the landing of goods and when Deal was downgraded from a port to a creek in 1881 the main business of the custom house transferred to Dover.

Although the great days of the Downs as a naval anchorage came to an end in 1815 it continued to have a role to play, and Deal benefited accordingly. Seamen from naval vessels at anchor might still have the opportunity of a run ashore, like the sailors of the Channel Fleet who in 1860 found landing and departing from the open beach rather a challenge but who created "a din, bustle, and animation which has not been equalled for many years"[21]. But not everyone welcomed the sudden influx of bluejackets, and the consequences were not always happy. In 1860 four "stragglers" from the battleship HMS *Mars* were picked up at the Queen's Arms, only for a police constable to be fined and dismissed for failing to help his inspector to bring them in. Four years later John Outwin, then running the Clarendon Hotel, gave instructions that men from the sloop HMS *Bulldog* should not be admitted in his absence. On returning to find a group of officers being entertained in the hotel kitchen he threw his servant out of the house in a rage, and ended up being fined 30s by the magistrates for assault. Local tradesmen might enjoy a bonanza, or come unstuck. When units of the Channel Fleet anchored in the Downs in July 1862 local bakers worked all night baking bread and biscuit, only for the ships to weigh anchor the following morning "so what was looked forward to by many as a source of profit, turned out, so far as the bakers were concerned, a dead loss, several hundreds of loaves having been prepared for the occasion"[22].

The views of the less welcoming townsfolk prevailed for a good many years. In 1885 the *Mercury* reflected that "time was, when the Downs without a man-of-war would be considered a curiosity, but unfortunately nowadays their presence in our anchorage is considered a much greater one"[23]. The reason seemed to be that at some point in the 1870s, according to Councillor Hayman, there had been "some bother, and complaints were made. They used to come ashore in watches, but it was an old complaint"[24]. As the *Mercury* drolly recalled, "some of our townsmen petitioned the Admiralty to the effect that the men of the fleet should not be allowed to land during their stay in the Downs – a request their Lordships complied with with alacrity, but when a counter proposition was made they were rather slow to see the force of it; and so the thing remains – in our opinion little to the credit of our town".[25]

By now many in the town were eager to welcome the fleet back. Happily for them, in August 1887, for three days running, 200 sailors and marines from warships in the Downs were given 12 hours' shore leave, ending at 7.00am. Most would have lost little time in exploring the town's public houses. Thereafter the anchorage of units of the fleet

Warships at anchor off Deal in July 1908. The *Mercury* rejoiced that the town was "full, full to overflowing with the British public, proud of their fleet, and gratified beyond measure with the splendid spectacle Deal afforded her visitors".

came to be warmly welcomed, not least because, as the *Mercury* observed after large numbers of sailors came ashore in August 1889, "the life and trade of the town have been stimulated to a most appreciable extent"[26]. The presence of warships in the Downs also attracted many visitors from out of town, equally in need of refreshment and perhaps accommodation. The ships' companies might well have included some Deal men, returning to or at least gazing back at their home town, though the common belief that, as the *Telegram* put it, "few of HM ships are without some of their crews belonging to Deal"[27] may have been a little exaggerated.

Shore leave helped keep some public houses afloat. According to the landlady of the Horse and Farrier, striving in 1911 to persuade the magistrates not to recommend closure, her house "did good business in letting in the season, and especially with Marines and sailors from warships in the Downs".[28] Certainly visits by major units of the fleet, sometimes complete with spectacular evening searchlight displays, were a striking feature of the Edwardian period. On 30 June 1914 the 3rd Battle Squadron anchored in the Downs and next day "shortly after daylight provision carts and barrows crowded the entrance to the Pier-gate, all kinds of provisions and market garden produce being ready for the early morning pinnaces...[then at] about 5 o'clock the pinnaces with cutters towing them astern came to the Pier, all heavily laden with men who had been given optional all night leave"[29]. Some 1,800 came ashore, most then staying over night, and a further 1,500 landed the following day. A week later it was the turn of the powerful 1st Battle Squadron. On 7 July, after the exertions of a "black day" filling of the ships' bunkers with 7,000 tons of coal, 1,800 sailors and marines came ashore, most staying until morning. Two days later the number given a run ashore was thought to be 3,000. It is safe to assume the town's public houses did spectacular business. But there would be no repetition. On 29 July the Home Fleet left Weymouth Bay for Scapa Flow and six days later Britain was at war.

Kent had and still has "a larger proportion of its boundaries washed by tidal waters than any English county, with the exception of Cornwall"[30]. Victorian Kent also had a disproportionate number of military installations. In 1911 10% of all adult males in the county were in military service as against only 2% in England and Wales as a whole. At any one time the three Walmer barracks, just south of Deal, were home to 1,500 or more soldiers and then, from 1862, marines. In 1881 the proportion of the male population in military service in the Deal area (the Eastry Registration District including Walmer and Sandwich) was 9.9%; in Kent only Canterbury and Sheerness had higher proportions. Twenty years later the percentage had increased to slightly over 10%.

The presence of marines is remembered fondly today, and from late Victorian times relations between the town and the military were generally cordial. This had not always been the case in earlier days. In 1897 the *Mercury* reminded its readers that "from 1860 to about 1865, the depredations of the Line Regiments stationed at Walmer were really alarming...the memorable raids made by gangs of these fellows on several public-houses in the neighbouring villages will not soon be obliterated from the memories of the victims"[31]. But although such outrages were no longer occurring, and the presence of the marines increasingly valued, there continued to be a steady stream of cases of vandalism, petty theft and drunkenness.

Whereas boatmen and pilots used public houses during the day as well as in the evening, and sometimes in the early morning, marines were usually to be found there in the evening, when given permission to leave the barracks (and sometimes when on the run). PC Chapman, giving evidence to the East Kent Quarter Sessions in 1895, mentioned a second difference: marines were often found in public houses on Wednesday nights, since this was when they received their pay, whilst on Saturdays there was usually more drinking among boatmen and others. Although there are examples of boatmen and marines mixing together in the same public house, in general there was a rough but clear demarcation: boatmen frequented the houses in Beach Street and the streets leading from it, while marines tended to head for houses in Lower Street and on the outskirts of town. But this was not set in stone, and occasionally the clientele of a house could alter quite quickly. The Three Compasses, for example, was one of the many Beach Street houses usually frequented by boatmen, beachmen and fish hawkers, but according to a nearby resident complaining about rowdy behaviour and the presence of women of loose character, "the house became frequented almost entirely by Marines – privates and non-commissioned officers"[32] after a change of landlord in 1893.

The Park Tavern and the Jolly Sailor, both to the west of Lower Street, were popular with marines over a long period. So too was the Maxton Arms, which in 1894 to the chagrin of the new landlord was placed out of bounds for a time. Marines did not have to leave the barracks to take a drink (in 1872 the sale of cheap beer to civilians as well as to marines prompted complaints from the licensed victuallers and the Mayor), and from 1878 they could use a large new canteen; this included a bar for the sale of ales, "one part for non-commissioned officers, another for the men, and the other as a jug department for the married community[33]. But for many marines the chance of an evening out was not to be missed. Not infrequently, particularly in late Victorian and Edwardian times, the landlord of a favoured venue for the military might himself be an ex soldier or marine.

The reports in the local papers of men from the barracks enjoying a night on the town were almost always of those which ended badly. In 1861 a soldier of the 2nd Queens was found frozen to death in a field in Upper Deal after consuming large quantities of rum in the Maxton Arms and the Jolly Sailor. In November 1884 James Smith of the Royal Marines Light Infantry testified to another evening excursion which began in high spirits but which also spiralled down to tragedy. He and two friends "came out of the barracks together at about 8.00pm. We

The Royal Marine band, leading a church parade c.1900, draws level with the Cambridge Arms in Dover Road, Walmer. To the left are the South Barracks.

went from there to the Jolly Sailor, where we had a pint of beer together when we first went in. In about half an hour we had another pint each. After that we had a six pennyworth of whiskey between three of us; a young woman having then joined us and partook of it. After this there was a fight between us and two civilians. We were then taken into custody by the military police..."[34] His intoxicated companion George Holt died the same evening. Two years later, out on a spree, Private Scott became violently drunk in the Noah's Ark, fell down some stairs, struck his head and died later in the barracks hospital. Much more cheerful, though less newsworthy, were the special dinners for non-commissioned officers often held in the town's public houses. The activities of the officers, in contrast – other than notable performances on the cricket pitch or appearances before the magistrates following the misbehaviour of one of their men – rarely appeared in the local press.

Some publicans and their wives looked in turn to the marine barracks for entertainment. In Edwardian times men and women of the town could attend dances and other functions at the barracks, and some did so quite frequently. One such was Hetty Pierce, who accompanied her husband from Sheerness to Deal when he took the Fountain on Beach Street in June 1905, and seems to have lived a rather lonely existence.

She testified, however, at the inquest into her husband's murder the following year that she had – with his blessing – several times attended a Friday evening sergeants' dance at the depot.

Several of the public houses frequented by marines were also lodging houses. The Ship and Castle in Lower Street (which became the Sir John Falstaff in 1872 but closed in 1891) had that function mid-century, among others, as later did the Queen's Arms in what had by then been renamed the High Street. The other public houses doubling and registered as common lodging houses in later years lay further to the west, near the outskirts of town: these were the Jolly Sailor (called the Norfolk Arms between 1866 to 1889) and the Maxton Arms, both in Western Road, and the Noah's Ark in nearby Ark Lane. Although many other houses let rooms to one or two lodgers on an irregular basis, it is a further sign of the rough demarcation that existed between the seaward and landward sides of town that virtually no lodgers are recorded as staying in public houses in Beach Street. The rather touching exception to the rule was Amelia Kemp's Yarmouth Packet. This was not only, over many decades, the temporary home of choice for many Trinity House pilots but also, from the 1880s, of Frenchmen employed at the nearby canning factory. When a French solderer died there in 1907 the *Mercury* noted that Mrs Kemp had often successfully nursed his compatriots through illness and, unsuccessful in this instance, had sent a wreath and opened a subscription list for the bereaved family.

The census returns give only a rough idea of the number of lodgers housed in Deal public houses: perhaps 50–60 or so at any one time in the 1860s and 1870s, with rather fewer in later years. Some were boatmen, usually rather older: men like William Hayward, who died aged 58 in the Queen's Arms, having lodged there for some 12 years and by then unable "to do very hard work. He was able to scrape or varnish a boat, or anything of that kind.."[35]. The largest category of lodgers were the agricultural and "general" labourers. They were for the most part Deal-born, or raised in nearby villages. Some stayed for long periods and made their mark. One such "notable character" was Robert "Cock" Larkins, another lodger at the Queen's Arms, who "in late years gained a portion of his livelihood in assisting the brewers' draymen"[36]. It was in this capacity that Larkins, like so many of those involved in the transport of beer, sustained a serious injury (from which he subsequently died).

Other lodgers were more transitory, willing perhaps to put down some roots if the chance arose but expecting to move on. The 1871 census enumerator could not do better than to list the 16 lodgers in the Maxton Arms, men, women and children, as "travellers or vagrants", and the Shah in the 1880s had a reputation as a lodging house for tramps. But there was often a trade to record: carpenters, sawyers, slaters and shoemakers, for example, and also a fair sprinkling of itinerant musicians. Francesco Randolph, who appeared before the magistrates in 1902, was an organ grinder lodging at the Jolly Sailor. In quieter contrast was Eugene Morgan, who gave evidence at the inquest in May 1870 into the death of Thomas Christy (landlord of the Maxton Arms, who died after a drunken brawl) and described himself as "a collector of ferns... travelling about the country"[37]. In 1906 the lodgers at the Maxton Arms, by then "a very old house, rather low-pitched", were said to be "dealers, fish-hawkers, threshing machine men etc"[38]. Some men lodged together with their wives and families, and there was also a significant minority of single or widowed women. These were almost always listed in the census as dressmakers, needlewomen, seamstresses or laundresses.

Rooms were usually shared, and frequently crammed full. On census day in 1861 the Ship and Castle was temporary home to 12 adult lodgers and five children. The slightly larger Jolly Sailor had 18 adults and six children. In 1887 the Noah's Ark charged 4d a night, as did the Queen's Arms for a dormitory room 20 years later. In 1906 the landlord of the Maxton Arms reckoned to make some 16s a week from up to ten lodgers. Common lodging house rules laid down that beds could not be used between defined hours – lodgers had to be out and about. Food was brought in and cooked on a communal range.

A description exists, recalled by the son and grandson of landlords of the Queen's Arms, of the house in Edwardian times. Lodgers there had their own communal "mess room", with two large elm tables, two wooden forms and a few chairs, a large cupboard and a range for cooking meals. The room was cleaned daily, and the floor covered in sea sand. Down the passage were two dormitories containing 18 beds. Mattresses on iron bedsteads were stuffed with either oat chaff or feathers. Upstairs were four bedrooms, three with double beds at 8d a night and one single at 6d. In the courtyard were the lavatories, a water-butt and sink, a large copper for boiling clothes, and lockers in which the lodgers kept their perishable food.

Transient lodgers at the Queen's Arms included painters, hawkers, tinkers and china riveters. Summer regularly brought pea and fruit pickers, an Italian organ grinder, a German string band and one year "a harpist name Prospero who played in an orchestra having a summer season on the pier". Several Deal boatmen also made the Queen's Arms their home, as did a number of labourers and fish hawkers. Others "made their living from the fields and country in general...in the winter one man used to get the sharp thorns from the blackthorn. In the evenings he would scrape off the black covering and sell the white spikes to the local butchers, who used them for spiking the price tickets to joints. The scrapings of the thorn were used to make a palatable brew which they called Jerusalem tea".[39]

Many public houses also provided accommodation for visitors to the town. These ranged from itinerant tradesmen who might equally have been termed lodgers, to more prosperous businessmen and commercial travellers and, as the century wore on, holiday makers. In the 1870s there were considered to be five hotels, properly so called: the Royal Hotel, Star and Garter and Royal Exchange on Beach Street and the Black Horse and Walmer Castle on Lower Street, though there were many other inns of smaller size which were expected to and did provide accommodation on request. Even the smallest house might offer a room or two to visitors in the summer. Houses often depended for their survival on a mixed economy of residents, regulars and casual drinkers. The balance might change over time or according to the season. By 1911 the Railway Tavern "did not depend so much upon the bar trade, as upon the hotel side of the business"[40], whereas at the Fountain, according to the magistrates' clerk, "the bar keeps the house in the winter time and the hotel in the summer time"[41]. With the magistrates now finding themselves having to decide which houses to close, the significance of the role of individual houses in providing accommodation for visitors became an important element in the mix.

Sea bathing in Deal began in the eighteenth century. In 1754 the *Kentish Post* advertised a "New-Invented Machine for Bathing in the Sea" available on application to the landlord of the East India Arms. Edward Hasted observed in 1800 that "the air of Deal is exceedingly healthy, on which account numbers resort to it in summer, as well for pleasure as for the benefit of bathing"[42] and five years later the compiler of a commercial gazeteer observed that "the result of ... summer visitors [to Margate and Deal] makes for a brisk circulation of money".[43] But the two would not often be spoken of in the same breath in Victorian times, and mid-century Deal was rarely the destination of choice for refined holiday makers: "of Deal it may be said that the general smell is fishy, the general aspect tarry and the general result dreary"[44] wrote a disparaging correspondent of the *Morning Star* in 1865. The site of the old navy yard, sold off in 1864, was slowly redeveloped for residential use (the *Mercury* speculating straight-faced in 1878 that the latest burst of activity "might impress the intelligent foreigner with a conviction, that like other places just now, Deal is fortifying her position against a Russian invasion"[45]) but three years later the Parliamentary Commissioners reporting on corrupt election practices were tersely dismissive of the town: "... a watering place of no great ambition, though provided with a parade and boasting a pier. The resident gentry of these places are very few in number, while of the tradesmen several conduct a respectable business, but none on more than a moderate scale"[46].

But the town certainly did benefit from the late Victorian boom in the popularity of seaside holiday resorts, fuelled by the 1871 Bank Holiday Act and by the rise in middle- and lower middle-class disposable incomes that made such holidays possible for large numbers of people. By 1914 one of 17 seaside resorts in Kent, Deal could not hope to match the remarkable popularity of the Thanet seaside towns notwithstanding the opening in 1898 of a large modern hotel (the South Eastern Hotel)

Boats, boatmen, holiday makers and bathing machines on Deal beach c.1890. In the distance is the Crown, with the landlord's name on the wall. John Fisher, a chess enthusiast, was licensee between 1878 and 1900.

just to the north of Deal Castle. It had previously been a struggle to persuade the railway companies to add Deal to the list of resorts which could be visited by means of cheap day returns, but the council's efforts to promote the town did have some success over time and Edwardian Deal entertained increasing numbers of holiday visitors. The remodelling of the seafront, through the removal of houses on the seaward side and the creation of areas of seafront along which to promenade, had in fact begun as early as the 1830s. Improvements gathered pace later in the century, even though these tended to be detrimental to the interests of the very boatmen – none of whom were councillors – whose activities gave Deal its distinctive character and helped attract visitors to the town. Some of these might even come from across the Channel – "On Parle Francais" advised an advertisement for the Clarendon Hotel in 1889.

By the turn of the century Deal might still be cold and depressing to the visitor and to a good proportion of its inhabitants in winter, but it now had many of the manifestations of a cheerful seaside resort in the summer (albeit that the *Mercury* reckoned the season to be comparatively short, "two months or ten weeks constitute its utmost limits"[47]). It was also increasingly popular as a venue for recreational fishing, with for example the Napier Tavern being reported in 1910 to be used at weekends principally by anglers. But for some in the town the continuing existence of large numbers of public houses was in fact an impediment to the development of Deal as a seaside resort. "We have lately heard the opinion expressed", observed the *Mercury* heavily in 1891, "that to the glaring obtrusiveness of the public-house element must be ascribed our somewhat slow progress as a watering-place"[48].

The meals offered to commercial and holiday visitors might be through a full-or half-board arrangement. Many houses also sought custom from people wanting a single meal of hot food, and advertised accordingly. The Alma, for instance, offered hot joints every Saturday in 1865 and the Fountain chops, steaks and teas in 1885. Nor did the town's landlords have much to learn about the concept of fast food, whether in the form of the "soups constantly kept during the winter months"[49] promised by the Clarendon Hotel in 1860, the "chops and steaks upon the shortest notice"[50] offered in 1883 by the Antwerp or the humble "ha'penny dodger" ("a small loaf that went down well with cheese"[51], explained Thompson's lawyer to the magistrates) that could be purchased at the Sir Sidney Smith in 1910. As today, some landlords, like John Outwin when running the Clarendon Hotel, also provided outside catering for civil and public functions.

To what extent do these patterns of demand help to explain the unusually large numbers of public houses that were able to exist in Deal throughout the period? There is no reason to think that the town was out of the ordinary in terms of the numbers of lodgers or the volume of passing trade it attracted, nor in the extent to which those living in villages and farms within reach of the town spent time in its public houses. On the other hand, although Deal's share of the burgeoning south coast tourist and holiday trade was relatively modest, this did bring welcome new custom during the summer months at a time when activity relating to ships and the sea was in decline, and by the end of the nineteenth century the resident population of the town was also, at last, beginning to increase significantly (in the 1890s by 19%). Certainly the presence of large numbers of marines in barracks close to the town helps to explain the survival of the many public houses around and to the west of Lower Street. On the seafront itself, the modest growth in commercial fishing did something to slow the decline in the overall number of men making a living from the sea, and the continuing interaction between the boatmen of Deal and public houses near and in some cases backing on to their stations and capstan grounds helped prolong into the twentieth century the precarious viability of many of the smaller Beach Street houses.

Conviviality and entertainment

For most of the nineteenth century, until the development of cinemas, clubs and restaurants and the boom in organised leisure activities, Deal's public houses had a virtual monopoly of the entertainment business of the town. The most important exceptions were the lectures and entertainments provided at the Deal and Walmer Institute, based from 1865 in the newly built public rooms in Park Street (in due course named St George's Hall), and those organised by the town's churches and chapels. This section, however, looks exclusively at the kinds of entertainment to be found in the town's public houses, from organised concerts and dinners to the spontaneous conviviality of bar parlours and tap rooms. The following section then considers the wide range of clubs and societies that originated or made their homes in Deal's public houses.

In the first half of the century the Deal Catch Club, a subscription music society, was at the centre of town life during the winter months. This met at the Royal Oak in Middle Street and by 1847 had reached its 21st season. Concerts consisted of overtures, glees, duets and songs (in 1843 vocal and instrumental talent was being engaged "as usual [from] the choir of Canterbury"[52]) and often attracted gentry and visitors from out of town. No "political or party"[53] discussion was allowed, and late comers were refused admission. But by 1859 the club was in trouble, exacerbated by the "defalcations" – financial dishonesty – of the secretary and treasurer. An attempt to revive it in 1865, with concerts at the Park Street public rooms, was abandoned when the number of subscribers fell short of the 150 needed to make the project viable. Ten years later an Apollo Harmony Society, said to have been established on Catch Club principles, met at the Crown on Beach Street, but seems to have been short lived.

As the *Telegram* saw it in 1888, the successors to the old "Catch Clubs, Apollonian and Sicilian Societies" were the smoking concerts: "such good harmonious gatherings come as a pleasure to society in our rather dull town in winter months"[54]. "Smokers" – organised dinners with musical entertainment – were by then very much in vogue. The patrons were often local groups and societies, but the initiative might well come from the landlord himself. The performers could be home-grown, or engaged from out of town. In 1886 Percy Frost at the Rose offered, though not it seems very successfully, a smoker featuring Signor Angelici's Troupe of Mandolinists. Two years later Frederick Wylde engaged Madame Pauline Lorraine of London for a season at the Walmer Castle. When Henry May became licensee of the Saracen's Head in 1896 he immediately set about organising a programme of smokers.

Frost, Wylde and May were new to the town; the holding of an enjoyable smoker was a good way to build a reputation as a genial host. Smokers continued to be popular until the First World War in all but the smallest public houses. By Edwardian times live music was not the only option: a smoker at the North Star in 1907, patronised mainly by boatmen, included songs to the accompaniment of a piano and violin, but also "some very fine gramophone selections for which Mr J Hill was responsible, his instrument, which was an excellent one, giving the selections with remarkably good effect"[55].

Smokers were certainly not the only form of organised evening entertainment. Throughout the period scarcely a week passed without an elaborate celebratory dinner being held in the function room of one of the town's larger public houses, complete with speeches, songs performed by members of the assembled company and dutiful reports in the local papers. Societies and clubs of all kinds, whether or not attached to a particular public house, almost invariably held annual dinners, and bean-feasts arranged by different groups of tradesmen, like the butchers and railwaymen, were also very popular. The brewers were certainly not the only employers to treat their workers to slap up meals on occasion, sometimes to celebrate a special anniversary or event. Well-to-do landlords might also decide to host a special meal at their own expense for their friends and patrons – in Edwardian times the annual dinner hosted by Harry Meakins, boatman and landlord of the Port Arms, to celebrate his wedding anniversary became a well-publicised fixture.

Of all the celebrations in the annual calendar, the mayoral dinner held for many years at the Royal Hotel had the most cachet, but the rival dinners in honour of the unofficial "Mayor of Upper Deal" held during the 1880s at Susannah Marsh's Admiral Keppel were probably a lot more fun. (And perhaps no less elegant: in 1885 the room was "most tastefully decorated with flowers and evergreens. Those who know Mrs Marsh are aware how beautifully she spreads the tables, and it need only be said that this year was no exception to the rule"[56].) The larger public houses were the natural venues for all such gatherings – and, of course, until the development of modern restaurants, there was very little alternative.

When fire broke out at the Queen's Head in June 1892 the flames quickly spread from the inn itself by means of a connecting staircase "covered in by a building of wood"[57] to the club house at the rear. Even relatively small houses like the King's Head often had a room set aside as a club or function room, and brewers modernising their houses might well choose to add one on. In the 1890s, for example, Nalder & Collyer attached a large entertainment hall to the Alma in West Street, and in 1909 the East Kent Brewery Company added a club room to the Harp in Middle Street (its time doubling as a hairdressers long gone).

Some landlords aimed higher still. When James Adams refurbished the Walmer Castle in 1876 he also constructed a skating rink on the opposite corner of South Street ("having secured at great cost the concession of the patent for Deal and Walmer for Plumpton's celebrated skates"[58]). In 1900 Alf and Horace Abrahams, the latter the landlord of the new Walmer Castle, converted part of the old rink into a "much-needed place of entertainment"[59], which they called the Alcazar. This opened in July to considerable fanfare and with twice-daily performances by a large ensemble. But the venture was not a success, and Horace Abrahams moved on less than two years later.

Moorish inspiration had earlier failed in the case of the Alhambra, a house in Robert Street constructed in 1863 by the builder John Friend. This included a large concert room, and Friend attempted to run the place as a music hall. But he seems to have run into difficulties almost immediately. The magistrates granted him a full licence with reluctance, and within a few years the house had been bought or leased by Hills. By 1877, the Alhambra having been closed for more than a year, the magistrates refused to renew the licence and the house closed permanently. After the demise of the Catch Club at the larger Royal Oak an attempt was made in 1861 to run a music hall there but this too seems to have lasted only a short while. The house itself closed in 1873.

The Paragon Music Hall in Middle Street, previously named the Star and before that the Two Brewers, was another Hills house but an altogether more successful musical venue. The landlord James Elson, at that point also a part-time electro-plater and gilder, probably decided to change the name from the Star after some unsavoury goings-on and trouble with the magistrates. By February 1876, claiming the house as "the only place in Deal to enjoy an Evening's Entertainment"[60], Elson was offering a mix of singers, dancers and, during the week in question, a Grand Shadow Pantomime. The price of admission began at 2d, rising to 5s for a private box for eight people. Marines were offered half-price entry, though Elson was also careful to promise "strict adherence to garrison time"[61].

The fortunes of the Paragon fluctuated over the years but it achieved a degree of respectability. When the 1884 season opened, with The Great Van de Velde and his Combination Company of Acrobats, the *Mercury* praised Elson for "doing his best to cater for his patrons by affording them genuine fun free from anything which could possibly be objected to"[62]. In 1899 came a further change of name when the Paragon Music Hall became the Empire Theatre of Varieties (with seating for over 150 people on the ground floor, and for another 69 in the upper circle). But this time re-branding failed to do the trick, and performances were discontinued not long afterwards. In 1903 the owners (Thompson's,

Surprisingly for a house in central Deal, there was space behind the Clifton in Middle Street for a tea garden and a lawn tennis court. The Clifton was owned by the Croydon brewers Nalder & Collyer.

following their purchase of Hills' estate) tried to persuade the magistrates of the value of the licence by claiming that the house could still drum up a large trade as a music hall, and that they held back simply out of responsible consideration for the "great nuisance"[63] this would cause local residents. In the event the house closed down, and the premises were sold at auction for a modest £205 later in the year.

The forms of entertainment offered by or in individual public houses evolved steadily over the period. Cock fighting had made an occasional appearance in Georgian Deal, for example the contest held at the Two Brewers in 1771 between gentlemen of Deal and gentlemen of Bridge for four guineas a battle, but had disappeared by the nineteenth century; it was finally made illegal in 1835. Pigeon shoots persisted for much longer, patrons then dining lavishly in the landlord's public house. One such was organised in 1878 by the landlord of the Swan in a field near the railway station ("birds supplied by Mr S Hammond of London"[64]), another by George Burton of the Liverpool Arms in 1884. Later in the century – in the cause of pest control – came organised sparrow shoots.

Public houses on the outskirts of Deal with reasonably spacious gardens steadily developed less lethal outdoor sporting attractions as the century wore on. In 1864 the former Good Intent, renamed the Castle the previous year at about the time the adjacent Sandown Castle itself was being dismantled, offered Wednesday evening amusements for 4d consisting of "Trap Bat, Rounders, Drop-handkerchief, Dancing on the Green and a Variety of Other Sports"[65] while the Clifton, located in Middle Street but with a large garden, promised al fresco concerts during the summer. Among the games which have since fallen largely out of favour, quoits was probably the most popular. Reckoned by a modern historian of pub games to be "one of the great forgotten sub-cultures of 19th-century British history"[66], quoits was offered in a number of Deal pub gardens, including those of the Anchor and the Bowling Green. Several houses, such as the Deal Hoy, had their own clubs, but by late Victorian times the main venue, and home of the Deal Quoits Club, was the Hare and Hounds on Western Road.

The Hare and Hounds in Western Road was owned by the Dover brewers Leney & Co. This 1887 picture may mark the arrival of Frederick Shelvey as landlord. During his tenure the house became the home of the Deal Quoits Club.

The two outdoor sports offered in nineteenth-century Deal to have retained their popularity to this day, though less often attached to a particular public house, were lawn tennis and bowls. Sixteenth-century legislation which had imposed an enormous licensing fee on bowling greens was finally repealed in 1845, a reform which cleared the way for Richard Verrier to transform his Gun Inn into the Bowling Green. Conveniently located on the road connecting Lower and Upper Deal, this offered tennis and target shooting as well as bowls, and had a large tea garden. Tennis and outdoor refreshment was also to be had at the

Clifton. The Bell, in nearby Robert Street, also boasted a bowling green, as did the Magnet on the London Road, purchased at such great expense by Cobb of Margate in 1896. In Edwardian times both the Magnet (home to the three rinks of "Ye Olde Bowling Club") and the Oak and Ivy had bowling clubs attached to the houses, while the Upper Deal Bowling Club opened a new rink at the Five Ringers in 1910.

Indoor pursuits were a similar mix of the old and the new. Simply gawping at curiosities, such as the Maori chief's head put on show at the Rose at 6d a time, lost its attraction after the 1860s. In the 1880s landlord Robert Redsull's pet monkey was a popular resident at the New Plough until it died through eating cork dust and was interred "with much ceremony"[67]. Skittle alleys, like those to be found at the Deal Hoy, Queen's Head, Lord Warden, Five Ringers and Horse and Farrier, were popular with some, but the noise could provoke the wrath of neighbours: men like "one of the annoyed", who demanded in the *Telegram* to know "what steps to take to rid ourselves of an intolerable nuisance created by a skittle alley situated in a loft converted within the above house [the Sun] …the continued din kept up by the rolling of balls to a late hour is almost unbearable"[68]. The magistrates sympathised, and ordered the landlord to close his alley down. In 1901 the Five Ringers was described as having a dedicated room set aside for bagatelle – a cue game played with nine balls – but traditional public house games, like the two nine-pin frames included in the sale of the Anchor in 1865, were slowly falling out of favour.

Billiards, on the other hand, remained very much to the taste of residents and visitors alike. The 1845 Gaming Act had repealed the ban on billiard tables in public houses, and a good quality table in a dedicated billiards room was a must for many of the town's larger houses: the Royal Oak, until it closed in 1873, the Royal Hotel, the Black Horse, the Clarendon Hotel, and the Walmer Castle (boasting "a Commodious and Light Billiard Room, with a New Table by Thurston and Company"[69] and offering the services of a billiard marker). In 1900 the Rose opened a new billiards saloon, "well lighted and having a separate approach from the Bar"[70] while even the smaller Bell managed to squeeze in a three-quarter-size table. Although billiards ruled the roost, several other forms of cue game, whose hour had not yet come, were also played. In 1859 the Walmer Castle offered pool, as ten years later did the Fountain – "marker always in attendance"[71] – alongside billiards and "pyramids" (an early form of snooker).

DRINKING IN DEAL

A rare, faded image of the interior of a pub, said to be the Five Bells in Middle Street. Four boatmen and a man in a bowler hat pose at a game of cards, clenching (more or less naturally) on clay pipes.

By the Edwardian era newer kinds of indoor games were coming into fashion. A smoking concert at the Crown marked the visit of a party from Ramsgate to play a game of ping pong, and by 1907 – much more the shape of things to come – the Admiral Keppel had an established "dart" club, possibly using a "Kent" board without a treble ring or outer bull. That season the club won 17 of its 21 matches. But there is little evidence from this period of organised sporting competitions or leagues involving teams from different public houses. Nor do one-off contests like the cricket match held in August 1812 on Walmer Sands between eleven gentlemen using the Walmer Castle and eleven using the Black Horse, "won by the former, with ten wickets to go down"[72], or the rowing match in 1868 between the "attendants" of the Royal Hotel and those of the Clarendon Hotel for a silver watch and dinner, seem to have been particularly common.

For many patrons it was enough to take refreshment, alone or with friends and acquaintances, in the form of a pint or more of "Shinny Hilly" or "Roaring Thompson" (local slang as recalled by Frank Simmons many years later). At the White Horse "at 11am or thereabouts on most mornings, there were regular customers for a "schooner" of bitter, in much the same way as coffee is now taken. The regulars were mostly nearby tradesmen"[73]. On Beach Street and the adjoining streets evenings might see a quiet trade of boatmen drinking at rough wooden tables or standing at the bar counter. Or gatherings might develop into something altogether more lively with singing, from the melodious to the raucous, to the accompaniment of a piano, harmonium or banjo.

Paul Jennings, in his recent history of English pubs, maintains that although the majority of customers were men, "women were also in pubs, and in greater numbers than is sometimes believed"[74]. In Deal, to judge from newspaper reports of fracas and disturbances in the late 1850s and 1860s, women were often then to be found in beerhouses and in some public houses. In 1858, for example, they included Eliza Bradley from Folkestone, bound over after hurling a tumbler at her drinking companion in the Dover Castle beerhouse, Mary Banks who complained of the "rough and cowardly treatment" meted out to her in the Bricklayer's Arms, and Jane Wooten who, ejected by the landlord of the Park Tavern, "returned again under the protection of some soldiers and defied him"[75]. The inference that such women were prostitutes, or at least up to no good, was easily drawn.

In contrast there are very few references to women visiting public houses in late Victorian times, other than to buy beer for home consumption. Indeed it is hard to believe that they were quite as absent as the records seem to suggest. But there is no doubt that by now, as Jennings puts it, "many women shunned pubs, either by choice or compulsion"[76]. The granddaughter of George "Cash" Erridge, landlord of the Prince Albert, recalls that in the 1920s a side door "led into a little "snug" for ladies only (they never went into the main bar). This little room had a glass hatch into the bar where the ladies bought their drinks but mostly they passed jugs through to be filled and did their drinking at home"[77]. In rural areas of east Kent, according to Winstanley, "although there is plenty of evidence to suggest that women drank at home, few women would seem to have been regular customers in the pubs themselves unless their husbands took them along on a Saturday evening"[78]. Many houses in late Victorian Deal had in turn become cautious about admitting women. In the blunt words of PC Chapman, giving evidence to the East Kent Quarter Sessions in 1895, "a great many of the houses won't have them"[79].

For the men and women who did visit public houses the price of the beer they drank, from pewter and later glass vessels, remained unchanged between 1870 and 1914 at between 2d and 4d a pint according to the type and strength of the drink. Until 1887, curiously enough, the actual coins used to buy the beer might well have been French made; one estimate was that half of all pennies and halfpennies then in circulation in Deal and other maritime towns in the south east had been minted abroad. In that year the Government banned the import of foreign coinage and inevitably, although the ban did not extend to the private circulation of existing coinage, "persons hitherto unaware of the order [found] that they [were] becoming possessed of a great abundance of foreign coppers....It is stated [in Dover] that certain money changers are giving 8d for 12 of the coins formerly current as pennies. This exchange is very exorbitant when it is remembered that 12 of the coins are worth 11⅓d English, making the rate charged equal to 41½%"[80]. The Government soon afterwards felt obliged to buy up the estimated 8 million French coins in circulation at an exchange of one English shilling for 13 French pennies. In Deal the coins were bagged up by the local post office and dispatched to the Royal Mint, and "foreign bronze money" began to disappear from the town and its public houses. Frank Simmons, who managed the process as a young clerk, recalled much later that "circulation ceased altogether in a matter of six months"[81].

Many drinkers were also smokers. Tobacco could be bought at 3d an ounce, and the clay pipes used to smoke it were for the most part made locally. In Edwardian times the landlord of the White Horse bought these at a shilling a gross from their maker, Francis Harrison of Beach Street, and gave them to customers on request. The free distribution of clay pipes was probably very common practice in the town. Nationally the Tobacco Trade Review estimated in 1896 that publicans gave away on average "eighty to one hundred gross of pipes per annum"[82] – that is, between 11,520 and 14,400 pipes a year. They could sometimes be a hazard, the Deal Hoy for a time being particularly jinxed: smouldering tobacco ash seems to have been the cause of the fire which destroyed the skittle alley in 1866, and four years later the landlord contrived to break his leg by stepping on a piece of tobacco pipe and tumbling down the stairs.

From the 1880s, with the advent of mass production, cigarette smoking became increasingly widespread, and ill-ventilated public houses began to surround customers with the familiar beer-and-cigarette fug they

William Oatridge's restaurant had a prime location opposite the pier. Next door is the Antwerp. In March 1905 Oatridge secured a wine licence despite the opposition of the police.

would retain into the twenty-first century. In 1900 national expenditure on cigarettes stood at £4.8m, roughly a fifth of the total expenditure on tobacco. By 1914, with cigarettes in the middle price range then selling at 10 for 3d, the amount spent in purchasing them had increased almost five-fold and expenditure on cigarettes now constituted well over half of the total amount spent on tobacco.

Boisterous or rowdy behaviour might attract complaints from neighbours and the attentions of the police. The latter were of course also charged with enforcing the licensing hours, as will be discussed in the next chapter, and many of the glimpses of pub life in Deal come from the cases they brought before the magistrates. One of the duties of the police was to prevent unlawful gambling on licensed premises; this was taken to be where the outcomes depended on chance rather than skill. Gambling in moderation on the outcome of games like dominoes and possibly bagatelle might be acceptable. But what about the machine designed and patented by Mr Mancini of Deal – possibly the shopkeeper and ice cream maker John Mancini – incorporating "one fixture winning cup, two sliding winning cups, and two reserve cups"[83] and installed in the Jolly Gardener? According to the police such machines were by 1911 found in 40 or 50 other houses in the town. So here the slot-machine-driven future of twentieth-century in-house entertainment begins to come into view, and the magistrates' conclusion that the use of such machines was probably illegal could not long stem the advance.

Public houses in Deal, with or without slot machines, were now facing increasing competition as the natural venues for dinners and functions. In 1904 the landlords of several nearby public houses vigorously but unsuccessfully opposed the granting of a wine licence to Achille Mangilli's Royal Cafe Restaurant on Beach Street, and the licensing of William Oatridge's restaurant opposite the pier the following year presumably brought to an end the business the Greyhound had sometimes enjoyed in supplying the restaurant with drink. As the licensed victuallers feared, both restaurants steadily drew custom that would previously have been the natural business of the public houses such as the hosting of suppers for boatmen or non-commissioned officers from the barracks. The increasing challenge posed by such competing places of hospitality therefore made it all the more important for public houses to value and sustain their role in providing meeting places for the many clubs, societies, branches and lodges that came to exist in the town.

Clubs and societies

Victorian Deal saw a steady increase in the number and types of associations, clubs and societies active in the town, whether social or recreational, philanthropic or professional, for mutual support or in the pursuit of entertainment. Almost all originated in, or were based in or made use of, public houses. Some in time looked elsewhere or even built their own premises. But – church and temperance organisations apart – it was rare to find an organisation or group that did not depend to a greater or lesser extent on the facilities offered by one or more of the town's licensed premises. Even the regular meetings of the town's clergymen and ministers were, it seems, held for many years in a room in the Star and Garter on Beach Street.

Most numerous, but also the least likely to leave a trace in the record, were the clubs set up for particular and often time-limited purposes, with the landlord usually playing a central part, for the benefit of his patrons and incidentally of the trade of the house in question. These were often variants of small-scale savings schemes, like the Bell's birthday club in the 1860s (where, at one of its fortnightly gatherings in 1865

A charabanc party prepares to leave from outside the Saracen's Head in Alfred Square in 1905. The landlord, Arthur Pain, was a founder and treasurer of the North Deal Bowling Club.

"a party of Ethiopian Serenaders contributed in no small degree to the pleasure of the evening"[84]) or the Christmas Goose and Spirit Club at the Walmer Castle in 1881.

Even a small house, like the Lord Nelson beerhouse, might run its own savings club, while larger houses were often able to sustain for several years well-subscribed clubs offering mutual support and recreation. In the latter case, the highlight of the year was often the annual outing in brakes or later in motorised charabancs. These jaunts were heroic in compass and sometimes celebrated in the local papers, like the summer outing of the Deal Hoy Working Men's Club in 1895:

> forty members started in the brakes of Messrs Spicer and Olds shortly after 8 o'clock. The journey to Sturry was made, via Sandwich (where the East Kent Brewery was visited) and Minster. On arrival a sumptuous dinner was served at the "Red Lion", and a visit was afterwards made to Fordwich. The return was made through Ickham, Wickham, Littlebourne, and Wingham, where tea was provided at the "Dog"[85].

It is interesting to see that even after the rapid growth achieved by the national friendly, life assurance and savings societies in the second half of the nineteenth century there remained a place for small pub-based savings clubs. The Noah's Ark Sick Benefit Club, for example, had income of £34 5s 2d in 1909 (including interest of 9s 4d from the brewers, Ash & Co of Canterbury, with whom the funds were lodged). Expenditure consisted of £3 18s 4d in sickness benefit, £3 14s 11d in doctors' fees, the payment of some secretarial and other expenses, and the distribution of 22s 3d to each of the club's 22 members. The "Slate Club" scheme run by the larger Swan had income of £106 11s 1d in 1913, paid benefits of £6 10s 0d and distributed £1 8s 7d at the year end to each of its 67 members (who also enjoyed a decent dinner). The popularity of these kinds of clubs seems in fact to be have been on the increase in this period, the Bell, for example, having opened a slate club in the same year. Another variant was the Self Help society, like the one run from the Greyhound in Middle Street. In December 1905, at the fifth annual meeting, the 40 members present heard that over £150 had been circulated through investments and loans over the previous year; shareholders then received their £1 stake back, plus 1s 6½d interest.

In earlier times the Bell had played host to the town's main home grown registered friendly society. The Deal United Friendly Association (DUFA) was established in 1817 and in the early days had met in the Royal Oak. In 1848 it divided into separate No 1 and No 2 lodges. By the 1850s both were ensconced in the Bell, which added a "spacious and handsome"[86] new club room in 1860. Business was liberally mixed with entertainment and, inevitably, dinners. ("After a few preliminaries", ran one report, "the usual ... royal and patriotic toasts succeeded, interspersed with a variety of excellent songs of enlivening character"[87].) According to the *Kentish Gazette*, the members of the DUFA were "exclusively of the working classes"[88]. For the *Telegram* a particular point in its favour was that, unlike many friendly societies elsewhere, the Association met the cost of hiring meeting rooms in public houses from lodge funds "rather than requiring every member to spend a certain amount in order that the landlord might clear a profit"[89].

The DUFA flourished in the 1860s and 1870s. By 1872 the No 1 lodge had 129 members, and the No 2 78. Entertainment included trips to Crystal Palace and (for several years in partnership with the Oddfellows and Foresters) huge annual fêtes, complete with processions, banners and bands. But even in 1862 a writer in the *Telegram* was looking back nostalgically to the Association's earlier days. The gala held that year in Morris Thompson's grounds near the Walmer Brewery:

> "reminded me very much of our boyish days, when we looked forward with much joy and glee to the return of Easter Monday, when this society used to meet and celebrate its anniversary by marching with a band, flag and banners to Upper Deal Church, to listen to some appropriate sermon...then returning to the Club House, then at the Royal Oak, which stood A1 in the town of Deal at that time, where a good dinner was provided"[90].

Twenty years later the same paper, marking the death of one of the Association's six founding members, described the DUFA as "a society that has done a vast amount of benefit, but whose funds are now being limited and its usefulness much narrowed by the establishment of younger kindred societies"[91]. The No 1 lodge seems to have been dissolved before 1890 while the No 2 lodge, by that time meeting in the Alma, was finally wound up in 1900.

Friendly societies had existed in the town well before the founding of the DUFA. In the 1760s and 1770s a Deal Friendly Society had met and dined in the Hoop and Griffin on Beach Street, then one of the town's larger hotels, and in 1779 came the founding of a branch of the Order of Enlightened Cottages which survived well into the Victorian period. In the late 1850s and 1860s the brethren of the Order met regularly at the Port Arms and dined lavishly there on the feast day of their patron saint, St John the Evangelist. Their host, the landlord and boatman Thomas Trott, was himself a member of the Order. Later in the 1860s the society could be found meeting and dining at the Pelican and the Eagle. In 1868 the *Telegram* praised "this excellent institution [which] is the only one we are aware of now in existence...several of the present members have been connected with the society upwards of 40 years, and appearances favour the opinion, from the increase in its members, that it will continue to exist for many years longer"[92]. At which point, however, it disappears entirely from the record.

Other small local societies came and went. A Boatmen's Benefit Society ("Happy Britons") was founded in 1851 and its annual meeting at the King's Head in 1860 was attended by most of its 52 members. The

Telegram reported that the society was "in a flourishing condition, from the excellent and economical manner in which it has been conducted"[93]. This was probably the same as the Deal Boatmen's Friendly Society, said to be the last surviving friendly society in the town exclusively for boatmen, which had met for many years in a club room at the Napier Tavern but which called it a day in 1888. "Vulgarly called" – for some inexplicable reason – "the "Scorched Bean Society" it numbered 51 members, some of whom were getting advanced in years"[94]. The remaining funds were then divided, each member receiving £4.14s.6d.

A Pilots Mutual Benefit Society also existed for a time, with 32 members and funds of £502 in 1874, but where it met and how long it survived is unclear. The Deal and Walmer Burial Society No 1, founded around 1839, successfully transformed itself into the Deal and Walmer Mutual Provident Life Association in 1855 and in both manifestations met in a variety of public houses over the years. (At its 20th annual meeting, held at the Sir Sidney Smith, members heard that there had been no deaths for almost two years; "after spending a pleasant evening in the philanthropic endeavour of doing good to their fellow man in the hour of need, the meeting separated at a reasonable hour..."[95]). But some local societies are now almost entirely lost to the record, like the Deal and Walmer Tradesmen's Friendly Society. This was formed in 1857 and evidently took the tactful decision to rotate its meetings between different public houses.

The future undoubtedly lay with the big national affiliated friendly societies. The two largest were the Independent Order of Oddfellows (Manchester Unity) and the Ancient Order of Foresters. Both expanded rapidly in the south of England in mid-century. The number of Oddfellows lodges in Kent increased from 22 in 1845 to 78 in 1875, while Foresters lodges ("courts") proliferated even more dramatically, rising from 5 to 170 over the same period. By the turn of the century friendly societies taken as a whole were the largest set of voluntary associations in Britain, with an estimated six million members, the equivalent to one-half of all adult males.

The Foresters were the first to arrive in the Deal area, with the establishment in 1858 of a Walmer-based court (the Walmer Castle) serving both Deal and Walmer. This met initially in the Royal Standard, thanks in part to the support of the brewer Morris Thompson, before moving to the Queen's Head. From 1881 Foresters Hall was in the former billiard

The Lord Palmerston lodge of the Independent Order of Oddfellows, founded in 1862, was based at the Rose until 1893. David Almond, landlord of the Rose for 23 years, helped to found the lodge and served as treasurer.

room of the Lord Warden. By 1873 the court had 234 financial members, more than doubling to 535 by 1897. A "Deal Loyal and Independent Order of Odd Fellows" had existed for a time during the Napoleonic Wars, meeting in the Three Compasses, but the modern (Manchester Unity) Oddfellows did not reach Deal until 1862 when members of the Dover lodge helped to establish the Lord Palmerston lodge in the Rose. This house was centrally placed in the High Street, next to Hills brewery, and would be home to the lodge for the next 30 years. (Three years later the landlord of the Friendly Port in New Street changed the name of his beerhouse to the Oddfellow's Arms, perhaps hoping to benefit from the revival of interest in the movement, but the name did not stick.) The Oddfellows had 195 paying members by 1876, and twice that number twenty years later, notwithstanding the creation of a separate Walmer lodge (the Earl Granville) in 1886. Unlike the ageing membership of the small local friendly societies, the average age of Deal Oddfellows in 1884 was under 31. Both the Foresters and the Oddfellows also established "juvenile" branches in the 1870s (in this case following the lead of the DUFA).

The Foresters and Oddfellows were very respectable societies, with councillors, clergymen and MPs eager to associate themselves and publicly demonstrate their support. Annual anniversary dinners were extensively reported in the local papers. Summer fêtes, usually held in the grounds of Walmer Castle, were large-scale affairs, though as early as 1867 the kill-joy *Telegram* was wondering if their attraction was on the wane, with outings and excursions to London considered by many to be "a much more rational way of spending a holiday"[96]. Banners, floats and marches kept the societies in the public eye, while enormous care was taken to decorate their club rooms for special occasions. For the Oddfellows' 17th anniversary dinner, for example, their club room in the Rose was "most tastefully festooned with evergreens and flowers, the walls being covered with banners of the Order and Bannerettes with appropriate mottos, the whole being arranged in such an artistic manner as reflect the highest credit on the decorative ability of the committee of management"[97].

Other smaller national friendly societies had a presence in public houses for a time. The Harp lodge of an Independent Order of Friends met in the Bell in the 1900s, and a branch of the Ancient Order of Oddfellows (as distinct from the much larger Independent Order of Oddfellows) also existed around this time. In 1901 the main societies in the area formed a co-ordinating body (the Deal and Walmer Amalgamated Friendly Societies) which met and dined regularly, spreading their custom between different houses in the town.

Several national fraternal organisations also put down roots in Deal, and inevitably sought a home in a public house. The Earl of Goodwin lodge of the Ancient Order of Druids, for example, was founded in 1866 in the Cinque Port Arms, which then took the name Druid's Arms in celebration, though the lodge later set up home at the Royal Exchange on Beach Street. A Deal lodge of the Royal Antediluvian Order of Buffaloes opened in 1883 in the Eagle, and took its name from the house. At a ball held in St George's Hall in 1888, rather impressively, "dancing

The Buffaloes' Eagle lodge was founded here in 1883, but moved out after a time. The RAOB (Royal Antediluvian Order of Buffaloes) initials just visible on the lower front windows suggest that, forty years later, the lodge was back in residence.

commenced at 9 o'clock, and continued without relaxation until five o'-clock in the morning"[98]. The lodge then had spells in the Rose and Royal Exchange, and in Edwardian times in the Fountain, before returning full circle to the Eagle.

There was almost no end to the number and variety of friendly and fraternal organisations late Victorian Deal and its public houses could sustain. When Henry Taylor, landlord of the Clarendon Tap, applied in 1893 for an hour's extension in respect of a dinner for the Orange Institution (the Orange Celebration Heroes of Jordan, No 686) he explained that the branch "had been only recently formed of members of other garrison towns...members were not Irish, but it was a society which upheld the Church and State, and the Crown, and was a wonderfully good thing, and very religious in the conduct of its meetings, it being necessary to have a chaplain present". ("The Mayor supposed that to have an annual supper formed part of their creed. Mr Taylor: No, they have several suppers. (Laughter)"[99]). But on the other hand there could be no question of the Basil Wilberforce tent of the Independent Order of Rechabites, established in Deal in 1887, seeking room at an inn for such frivolity: the Rechabites were strict temperance men and women.

Several masonic lodges had met in public houses in Deal during the Napoleonic Wars. A Royal Navy lodge had existed since the 1760s, and over the years met in at least seven different houses until finally "erased" in 1822. The brewer Thomas Oakley was a member for a time. A second lodge, the Fraternal lodge, founded in 1803, also disappeared from the record in 1822. The Union lodge was founded in 1812 at the Deal Castle and included a good many innkeepers among its brethren. It later met in the Royal Oak and in the Crown. In June 1838 the *Kentish Gazette* observed that the lodge now appeared dormant, and it was formally erased later that year. Modern freemasonry arrived in Deal with the consecration of the Wellington lodge, on the anniversary of the battle of Waterloo in 1858. This met initially at the Walmer Castle before transferring to the Black Horse three years later, and a separate Walmer lodge (the Lord Warden) was formed in 1866. By that time the "secular" Deal and Walmer Friendly Association, set up in 1857 to undertake activity "conducive to the benefits of the locality"[100], was meeting regularly at the India Arms, but seems to have faded away fairly soon after that.

Individual landlords were often active members of one or more fraternal or friendly societies, and there were obvious business advantages in hosting a lodge. David Almond, landlord of the Rose between 1862 and 1885, was one of the founders of the Lord Palmerston (Oddfellows) lodge which established its club room in his house, and served as treasurer for many years. Charles Maltby, landlord of the Eagle, was "most energetic in promoting the re-establishment of the [Buffaloes] Lodge"[101] although it did not remain at his house for long. A landlord might also serve as local secretary for a national benefit society, personally collecting and making payments. Stephen Pritchard, for example, one of Maltby's predecessors as landlord of the Eagle, where he remained for over 25 years, was also secretary of the Provident Benefit Society for a time. Here too, as so often, the evidence comes from a dispute which made the public record, in this case the unsuccessful claim by a boatman before the Sandwich County Court that a payment of 4s 6d made by his son one evening, "having called the defendant out of the bar of his house"[102], had not been placed on the books to his credit.

In time, however, the lodges of some of the larger societies began to look elsewhere for accommodation. The Wellington lodge masons left the Black Horse around 1869 for the newly built St George's Hall in Park Street before finally opening their own Masonic Hall in Sondes Road in 1910. Across the country thriving Forester courts and Oddfellows lodges increasingly aspired to own and run their own premises, and although the Foresters remained at the Lord Warden in Walmer, the Deal Oddfellows left the Rose in 1893 to take possession of a very large purpose built hall in King Street. By then the national lodge-based affiliated friendly societies were facing stiff competition from the insurance-only ("ordinary" or "general") societies, such as the fast-expanding Hearts of Oak Benefit Society, which both collected subscriptions and made payments by post. Yet it is noticeable that when in 1905 an association of Hearts of Oak subscribers living in Deal was set up public houses were still the chosen venues for meetings. Members met at the Greyhound, Deal Hoy and Telegraph, among others, and seem to have decided against adopting a permanent base.

For the town's tradesmen, when meeting in that capacity, nothing could beat a slap-up dinner. An annual Haunch of Mutton supper for tradesmen began to be held around 1820 and took place for many years in the India Arms or the Royal Hotel. The Fountain's annual Punch and Cake Festival was a feature of the 1860s. The more prosaically named Deal Commercial Association was founded in 1858, meeting and dining

A rare photograph of the Deal Castle dressed all over for Queen Victoria's Diamond Jubilee in 1897. The Union masonic lodge was founded here in 1812, with the landlord Richard Piper becoming treasurer.

regularly at the Walmer Castle, Royal Exchange and Royal Hotel, and a Deal and Walmer Trade Protection Association (to be "conducted upon the lines of the Ramsgate society"[103]) appeared in 1888. The modern Chamber of Commerce dates from 1905, Willie Matthews of Thompson & Son being elected president in 1910. On the other hand the use made by local trade union branches of public house rooms was seldom recorded. Rare exceptions are the extension granted in 1879 to the landlord of the Five Ringers for a supper for members of the Labourers' Union and the reference noted by Steve Glover and Michael Rogers to meetings of the Carpenters' and Joiners' Union, Bricklayers' Union and Workmen's Union being held in the Fountain around 1909 ("in one of the finest clubrooms in town")[104].

In Deal as across the country the later Victorian period saw a boom in organised sporting and leisure activities and a proliferation of clubs formed to promote and support them. These almost always used public houses for inaugural gatherings, committee meetings and the inevitable annual dinners. Bowls, tennis and quoits have already been mentioned; clubs also appeared in Deal devoted to cricket, football, angling, rowing and sailing, shooting, cycling and motor cycling, while more cerebral pastimes could be enjoyed at the Downs Reading Club (at the Black

Horse), the Deal and Walmer Bridge Club or the Deal Chess Club. Clubs often came and went or duplicated one another. A Deal and Walmer Bicycle Cub was formed in the Crown in 1879. But in 1891 a cycle club said to have been formed the previous year was dining at the Rose, although at least initially their headquarters were in the Beach House Temperance Hotel. In 1897 the Black Horse (its former stable and coach house doing service as a store and cycle room) was the headquarters of the Cycle Touring Club and in 1905 a Deal and District Cycle Club was described as recently formed. Anglers were among those now being attracted to the town, particularly at weekends, and the Napier Tavern on Beach Street served for a while as the headquarters of the British Sea Anglers' Association.

Some public houses might be the home of several different clubs. The Liverpool Arms, for example, hosted the Upper Deal Gardeners Mutual Improvement Society, the Mongeham and District Sparrow Club and, for many years, the Upper Deal Bell Ringers. In many cases the personal enthusiasm of the landlord for the pastime in question will have determined the choice of public house, and possibly the very existence of the club itself. Selecting the Crown in 1881 as the home for the new Deal and Walmer Chess Club almost certainly reflected the enthusiasm of the new landlord John Fisher, described in 1898 by the *Mercury* as "an excellent and well known player"[105]. Much of the credit for the establishment in 1857 of the Deal Horticultural Society was given to Henry Shipley, founder member, honorary secretary and landlord of the recently opened Alma in West Street. The society met, dined and held its shows in a spacious room at the Alma until Shipley gave up the licence in 1865. Twenty years later, in contrast, the premises were home to the Alma Gun Club ("to be skilled in the use of firearms means more than mere success in bringing down a bird"[106]).

All in all, the town's licensed premises – from the larger inns with spacious club rooms and good dining facilities to the small intimate beerhouses – continued to play an important part in the lives of probably the majority of the male inhabitants of Deal throughout this period. But the surge in new clubs and societies originating in public houses or making use of them as venues was not a pointer to the future. In practice the rapid growth of organised participative and spectator sports and of new forms of mass entertainment offered increasingly attractive alternatives to spending time in public houses, whether drinking or attending meetings or both. In particular, in Deal as elsewhere, the years before the First World War saw the opening of a large number of cinemas: the first, Marina Hall in 1910 (in the old Assembly Rooms in Duke Street), the same year that the marines' Globe Theatre and the Oddfellows Hall in King Street began showing films. Two years later the Queen's Hall cinema opened on the High Street – on land which had once formed part of the Hills brewery estate.

Many people in Deal still spent a lot of time in public houses. In 1904 the town had only a single working men's club – nationally the numbers had risen to 6,371, with significant repercussions for the pub trade in some areas – and those drinking in public houses still consumed, by today's standards, a lot of beer. But per capita consumption in the United Kingdom had peaked in 1875–6, and total beer consumption actually fell after 1900 despite the continuing increase in population. In the late 1870s beer was being consumed at the rate of six pints per head of population per week. By 1914 this had fallen to four and a half pints, though admittedly it was not until after the First World War that consumption fell to the level that had prevailed in the 1840s. Although the price of beer – and of other alcoholic drinks – remained stable between 1870 and 1914, in the context of the rapid fall in the price of a widening range of alternative consumer goods in the 1880s and 1890s drink was now becoming proportionately more expensive. The rising disposable incomes and greater leisure time being enjoyed by large sections of the population during this period tended increasingly to be channelled into forms of recreation in which public houses played little or no part. As Peter Clark has observed, "it is ironic that the licensed house, long a pioneer in exploiting new consumer tastes and promoting the commercialisation of popular leisure, should have been outflanked by the latest developments". As a result, "the golden age of the late Victorian pub was a short-lived affair at best"[107].

Civic and public functions

Despite the rapid evolution since Edwardian times in patterns of recreation, mutual support and voluntary association, and the huge reduction across the country in the number of public houses, many of the activities discussed in the previous sections continue to take place in some shape or form in modern public houses. This section, on the other hand, looks at civic and public functions undertaken in public houses in Deal in the nineteenth and early twentieth centuries which have almost entirely moved out or disappeared.

A key difference, of course, is that unlike today the provision of beer, whether for consumption on or off the premises, was not simply a right, but also a duty. Licences were granted on the basis of public need. Landlords were expected to provide beer to those who needed or legitimately requested it, including importantly those who had travelled significant distances, and the larger houses to offer food and accommodation. Public houses were generally held to provide an essential public service – though teetotallers strongly disagreed – rather than simply being venues offering particular kinds of refreshment and entertainment. The next chapter will look at what this meant in practice in terms of licensing, regulation and control.

In Georgian Deal the relationship between the town's governing structures and its public houses was eminently pragmatic. When commissioners sent to enquire into the state of municipal corporations in England reported in 1834 on the borough of Deal they found "the grand jury to be composed chiefly of the higher class of tradespeople, and the petty jury of the smaller shopkeepers", but that in each case a publican was invariably included. The practical explanation was that "the members of each jury dine together on the day of holding the sessions, and it is customary to have the dinners at the houses of the publicans on the respective juries. Most of the publicans are taken, and nearly in rotation, who, it is thought, can furnish a comfortable dinner"[108]. The practice probably did not survive the reform of municipal corporations in 1835. Nor in the Victorian period is there any sign that the borough magistrates met anywhere other than in the town hall, though the reforming legislation of the 1840s did not preclude this, and the holding of judicial proceedings in public houses continued for many years in some rural areas.

In the early days the business of the town council might sometimes be conducted in a public house, particularly if the landlord were also a councillor. As late as 1860 George Verrier, landlord of the Bowling Green, could see no reason why he should not call a meeting of the town's Finance Committee, which he chaired, in his tavern. But others did, and the practice was discontinued. Another long-standing practice, in this case intensely disliked by landlords, also faded away around this time, namely the billeting of troops in public houses. This had caused huge ructions in the eighteenth century, with Deal landlords taking down their signs in an attempt temporarily to "de-register" as public houses and escape the imposition. An unwelcome reminder that the responsibility still existed came in January 1860 with a shambolic visit by some 60 men of the Royal Artillery to mount Armstrong artillery pieces at Sandown Castle. Notwithstanding the extensive barrack accommodation in Walmer, a short distance away, the men were billeted "at the various hotels and public houses, a step by no means agreeable to the landlords"[109] as the *Telegram* put it. But this may well have been the last such instance in Victorian times.

Another significant function undertaken by the larger public houses during much of this period was that of providing rooms for public meetings at election time, though in due course the town hall or the large new Oddfellows Hall became the preferred venues. Local Liberal and Conservative associations, which also generally met in public houses until late in the century, came and went over the years. These included the Deal and Walmer Working Men's and Boatmen's Liberal Association, and the (Conservative) Deal and Walmer Working Men's Constitutional Association, founded by Benjamin Eastes, the editor of the *Mercury*, which appeared in the wake of the extension of the franchise under the 1867 Reform Act. A related function very willingly undertaken by many houses in Deal came to an abrupt end in 1883, however, when legislation made the practice illegal. This was the habit of providing – sometimes for very generous recompense – committee rooms for the main political parties during election campaigns. As will be seen in the next chapter, the people of Deal played their part in bringing the practice into final disrepute.

An important public function discharged in public houses in Deal throughout the period was that of providing accommodation for the holding of inquests. These were held in cases of accidental, suspicious, violent or otherwise "unnatural" death – nationally, some 5%–7% of all deaths during this period. In 1834 the commissioners reported that there were an average of three inquests a year in Deal, and the number does not seem to have risen significantly in later years despite the increase in population. Throughout the nineteenth century a large proportion of inquests across the country were held in public houses, and for all that the commissioners reported that inquests in Deal were generally held in the "court hall", the town does not in fact seem to have been an exception to the national pattern. It is also likely that informal adjudications, trials and even unofficial inquests took place, below the radar, in boatmen's public houses on Beach Street. Certainly in rural east Kent, according to Winstanley, "even where members of the legal profession had ceased to use licensed premises it was not unknown for members of the community to set up mock trials or inquests in pubs to deal with peculiar, personal or local problems which were outside the scope of the law"[110].

By the end of the century there was a growing feeling in Parliament and beyond that public houses were impractical and unseemly locations for inquests. In Deal some were certainly being held in the town hall. Yet the passing of the 1902 Licensing Act, which forbade the holding of inquests in public houses if any reasonable alternative existed, seems to have had little impact in this regard, and significant numbers of inquests continued to be held in Deal public houses in the years that followed. These were not simply confined to houses situated some distance from the town hall, like the Admiral Keppel in Upper Deal. The Deal Hoy, for instance, was the venue for two inquests in 1903, and was used again in 1905 and 1906. On two occasions the deceased had lived on the same street, but it is not obvious why the house should have been chosen for the inquest of a 55-year-old commercial traveller found drowned at sea, or of a 61-year-old journeyman house-painter who had collapsed and died on the beach having helped turn a capstan heaving a galley punt ashore.

Bodies were sometimes taken immediately to a public house, like the dead seaman placed in the Fountain's outhouse in 1867, for convenience and perhaps on the assumption that an inquest would then be undertaken there. But coroners, and of course the landlords' national representatives, were keen to dispel the misunderstanding that some dead bodies should be taken to a public house as a matter of course. The *Telegram* reported in 1879 that the coroner of West Kent "had told licensed victuallers over and over again not to receive them [i.e. corpses] into their houses. A licensed house was for the living not the dead. In the event of a stranger falling dead in the street, if there were no mortuary the body should be taken to the parish authorities..." Rather disconcertingly, one might have thought, "if there was no other place it should be carried into the churchwarden's drawing-room and left there, but it should never be taken to a public house"[111]. Eventually the town council established a mortuary under the offices of Lloyds on Beach

The New Inn in 1904. In Victorian times the building housed the local excise office. The gentleman standing at the door is probably the landlord Thomas Laird.

Street. In 1890 the *Mercury* reckoned it to be "suitable for both sections of the town and...upon the whole, as completely isolated as is consistent with convenience".[112]

The part played by Beach Street public houses in providing emergency accommodation for merchant seamen injured or shipwrecked in the Downs could also lead to friction. Landlords were usually willing to do this, and often went the extra mile in providing care, but were understandably enraged when captains and owners disclaimed any responsibility for the costs incurred. In 1859 George Mote of the King's Head complained unavailingly to the magistrates that the captain of a Sunderland collier bound for Brest had reneged on a promise to pay for the treatment given to a seaman left in the landlord's care. The *Telegram* sympathised and – perhaps rather over-egging it – felt that after this and other similar instances it should "excite no surprise should innkeepers refuse to submit to their dwellings being converted into hospitals for a season...it is scarcely necessary for us to say that landlords will exercise more discretion in circumstances of this nature, in future...."[113]. But there is certainly no sign that landlords, often boatmen themselves, closed their doors in the face of a genuine emergency. When, for instance, the steamship *Strathclyde* sank in 1876 after a collision in the Downs the survivors were found beds in four Beach Street public houses, and at the Ship in Middle Street. Boatmen taken sick or injured at sea might also be given emergency care, like the sprat boatman "taken to the Rose and Crown Inn, the nearest house open at that time in the morning. Artificial respiration was immediately applied, the landlord (Mr Roberts) paying the poor fellow every attention..."[114].

During much of the nineteenth century a wide range of public representatives found it convenient to organise or undertake their functions in public houses. The Deal Fire Brigade, founded in 1874, made use from the outset of houses in the town for meetings and suppers. So too, in the 1860s and 1870s in particular, did the Cinque Ports Artillery Volunteers. The Lord Warden's Commissioners of Salvage sometimes met in the Royal Oak, and according to Glover and Rogers the New Inn doubled as the local excise office between 1840 and 1884[115]. Public houses were also convenient places at which to pay military pensions; when Major Morrah arrived in Deal in 1878 for that purpose he based himself at the White Horse and 8 October was declared to be Pension Day in the town. And houses themselves might choose to offer the public a wide range of extra services: from the provision of accurate Greenwich Mean Time (Fountain) or acting as a collecting point for milk supplied by a local farm (Rose and Crown, making use of the long-standing permission it enjoyed of opening early in the morning) to the sale of anything from boats, gear and tackle to sacks of potatoes (Prince Alfred) and malt vinegar and mushroom ketchup (Old Victory).

An important set piece event held in the rooms of some of the town's larger houses was the public auction. Between 1800 and 1849 the *Kentish Gazette* carried advertisements for auctions in at least a dozen different Deal houses, with the Black Horse on Lower Street apparently the most popular choice. In Victorian times the Walmer Castle seems to have had the edge. It was convenient that brewers' agents, like Morris Langley who acted for Hills, were often themselves local auctioneers, and it was not uncommon for individual public houses to come under the hammer at such events. In Georgian times several larger houses might also hold copies of the catalogues of important auctions to be held elsewhere in east Kent, with availability announced in the regional and sometimes national press; the Royal Oak continued to play this role in Deal until it closed in the 1870s. By this time the tendency to hold auctions in unattached public rooms – in Deal those in Park Street – rather than in public houses had gathered pace.

The last public function to mention was in fact the original raison d'être of thousands of inns up and down the land, namely acting as staging posts or what might now be termed "transport hubs" for those travelling by coach or carriage, and providing them with food and accommodation. In Deal this included passengers choosing to disembark from their ships in the Downs and to complete the journey to London by coach. Pilots were also frequent coach passengers "since it often happened that the men who had brought ships up the Thames had none to take down and vice versa"[116]. The Royal Oak and subsequently the Walmer Castle were main termini for coaches to London and also to other towns in east Kent, with the landlord of the latter, William Jewitt, advertising in 1867 coaches to and from Dover three times a day. The Swan on Queen Street was another important coaching inn, in 1838 boasting stabling for 20 horses and six coaches, while most of the larger houses in the town would be expected to provide stabling for visitors from out of town. In Great Britain as a whole an estimated 700 mail coaches and 3,000 stage coaches were then in regular service.

Where food was concerned the town was still heavily dependent as late as 1867 on supply by sea. In January bad weather forced the suspension for a month of the round trips of the hoy bringing supplies from London "and the grocers and provision dealers were under the necessity of obtaining supplies at great cost from Canterbury"[117]. But long distance

A group outside the Swan, probably about to set out on a charabanc outing. The sign on the wall points to stabling in West Street. In 1901 this included "a Three-Stall and Two-Stall Stable with Harness Room and double Coach-house, having a large loft over". More stabling was available in the hotel yard.

The Deal, Walmer and Dover coach "Clarence" in South Street. To the right is the old Walmer Castle, destroyed by fire in 1867 and rebuilt.

inland transport, for both people and foodstuffs, was now being transformed. The railways arrived in Deal in June 1847 with the grand opening of the line to Minster, the event which occasioned Charles Dickens' stay at the Swan. "A minor branch line built reluctantly by the South East Railway"[118], it nonetheless opened up a direct route to London. Across the country the expansion of the national railway network would mean the end of the traditional coaching inn. Even the Duke of Wellington, no lover of the railways, had found himself forced to make use of them. Writing from Walmer Castle in September 1847 to Angela Burdett-Coutts, who had enquired if he knew the landlord of the Fountain in Canterbury, the Duke explained that "before the steam invention I was in the habit of stopping at his house six or eight times every summer and I continued to use the road as long as there was any certainty of finding in it horses able to do their work. Since I have used the rails I have not seen him"[119].

Although Robert Allen of the Royal Hotel was reported in 1869 to be promoting a new omnibus route to Ramsgate, this was swimming against the tide. In June 1881 a line between Deal and Dover was finally completed, precipitating two months later the sale by Samuel Olds of four coaches and fifteen horses, previously the stock in trade of his

Deal-Dover coach service. On the other hand the steady influx of visitors arriving by train did bring new custom to the town's hotels and inns, which now included new houses named the Railway Tavern and the Locomotive. It also generated a demand for transport to and from the station for both people and goods. It is no coincidence that the landlord of the Eagle, Stephen Pritchard, was also a carrier (employing five men in 1872) and that both John Hills at the Railway Tavern and William Goodchild at the Anchor were fly proprietors for a time – all three houses were conveniently close to the town's railway station. As late as 1899 the Black Horse was said by a Kent guide to send an omnibus to meet every train even though the station was only some 400 yards away.

Visitors arriving by train might make use of local transport facilities. Or they might need urgent alcoholic refreshment. As bona fide travellers the law entitled them to purchase and consume this in a public house outside of the prescribed opening hours. But how were bona fides to be established? The approach taken in 1872 by Oswald Puckeridge, one of John Hills' successors at the Railway Tavern, was to ask those seeking a drink at his house on Sunday morning, claiming to have disembarked at the railway station after a long journey, to show him their railway ticket. So far so commendable, the magistrates considered. What he should not have done, however, was to appear to solicit trade by standing at the open door of his house rather than leaving it closed and responding to any traveller who knocked upon it. It must have felt at times as if there were simply no end to the mistakes a publican might make, and of the cases the magistrates might have to hear. For Oswald Puckeridge and his colleagues could not of course do as they pleased in providing beer, wines and spirits, but had to manage their houses within a unique and increasingly intrusive framework of scrutiny and regulation. How in practice the police and magistrates went about their task of regulating the public houses and beerhouses in Deal, and what this meant for the people running and using them, is the subject of the next chapter.

1. *Mercury* 3 March 1906; 9 March 1907; 6 March 1909; 5 March 1910; 11 March 1911
2. *Mercury* 6 March 1909
3. *Report of a Select Committee on the Cinque-Ports Pilots* (1833) p 12
4. J. Whaley, *Germany and the Holy Roman Empire*, Vol 2 (Oxford 2012) p 576
5. C. Greenwood, *An Epitomy of County History*, Vol 1, *County of Kent* (London, 1838) p 426
6. *Report of a Select Committee...* (1833) p 12
7. J. Bower, "Deal and the Deal Boatmen c 1840 – c 1880", Unpublished PhD thesis, University of Kent, 1990 p 332
8. *Mercury* 14 August 1880
9. Ibid
10. W. Cobbett, *Rural Rides* Volume 1 (London, 1885) p 319
11. *Report of a Select Committee...* (1833) p 12
12. *Telegram* 23 September 1865
13. *Particulars and Conditions of Sale, Valuable Freehold Estate* (1901) p 4
14. *Telegram* 10 February 1866
15. W. H. Stanton, *The Journal of William Stanton, Pilot of Deal* (Portsmouth, 1929) pp 44, 49
16. *Mercury* 28 September 1901
17. *Mercury* 11 March 1911
18. *Telegram* 27 August 1874
19. *Telegram* 30 March 1861
20. E. C. Pain, *The Last of Our Luggers and the Men Who Sailed Them* (Deal, 1929) p 163
21. *Telegram* 11 July 1860
22. *Telegram* 19 July 1862
23. *Mercury* 31 October 1885
24. *Mercury* 31 August 1887
25. *Mercury* 31 October 1885
26. *Mercury* 17 August 1889
27. *Telegram* 7 May 1881
28. *Mercury* 11 March 1911
29. *Mercury* 4 July 1914
30. A. Armstrong (ed), *The Economy of Kent, 1640–1914* (Woodborough, 1995) p 161
31. *Mercury* 27 March 1897
32. *Mercury* 19 October 1895
33. *Mercury* 2 March 1878
34. *Mercury* 22 November 1884
35. *Mercury* 20 August 1910
36. *Mercury* 28 October 1893
37. *Mercury* 21 May 1870
38. *Mercury* 6 October 1906
39. Taken from P. E. Robinson, "The Queen's Arms Inn, High Street, Deal" (Unpublished article in Deal Library) p 6
40. *Mercury* 11 March 1911
41. *Mercury* 9 March 1907
42. E. Hasted, *The History and Topographical Survey of the County of Kent*, Vol X (Canterbury, 1800) p 12
43. J. Whyman, *The Early Kentish Seaside (1736–1840)* (Gloucester, 1985) p 365
44. Quoted in *Telegram* 14 October 1865
45. *Mercury* 6 April 1878
46. *Report of the Commissioners appointed to inquire into the Existence of Corrupt Practices in the Borough of Sandwich* (1881) p v
47. *Mercury* 4 October 1902
48. *Mercury* 26 September 1891
49. *Telegram* 4 January 1860
50. *Telegram* 4 August 1883
51. *Mercury* 5 March 1910
52. *Kentish Gazette* 3 October 1843
53. *Articles of the Catch Club....to*

Commence on Monday, 29 of October 1827, Article 13. Copy in Deal Maritime and Local History Museum (DMLHM)
54. *Telegram* 27 October 1888
55. *Mercury* 13 March 1907
56. *Telegram* 14 November 1885
57. *Mercury* 11 June 1892
58. *Telegram* 18 March 1876
59. *Mercury* 7 July 1900
60. *Mercury* 26 February 1876
61. Ibid
62. *Mercury* 15 March 1884
63. *Mercury* 30 May 1903
64. *Mercury* 23 March 1878
65. *Telegram* 25 June 1864
66. A. Taylor, *Played at the Pub: The Pub Games of Britain* (Swindon, 2009) p 70
67. *Mercury* 20 January 1883
68. Letter in *Telegram* 9 June 1866
69. *Telegram* 28 January 1871
70. *Particulars and Conditions of Sale...* (1901) p 2
71. *Mercury* 5 June 1869
72. *Kentish Gazette* 14 August 1812
73. Robinson p 6
74. P. Jennings, *The Local: A History of the English Pub* (Stroud, 2007) p 112
75. *Telegram* 22 December 1858
76. Jennings p 117
77. Letter from Kathleen Long to the then landlord of the Prince Albert
78. M. Winstanley, "The Rural Publican and His Business in East Kent before 1914", in *Oral History* Vol 4, No 2, p 73
79. *Mercury* 19 October 1895
80. *Mercury* 9 April 1887
81. Frank Simmonds notes dated 28 November 1852 in DMLHM
82. Quoted in M. Hilton, *Smoking in British Popular Culture 1800–2000: Perfect Pleasures* (Manchester, 2000) p 49
83. *Mercury* 11 November 1865
84. *Mercury* 13 May 1911
85. *Mercury* 20 July 1895
86. *Kentish Chronicle* 14 April 1860
87. Ibid
88. *Kentish Gazette* 15 July 1862
89. *Telegram* 18 January 1860
90. *Telegram* 12 July 1862
91. *Telegram* 16 December 1882
92. *Telegram* 1 February 1868
93. *Telegram* 11 January 1860
94. *Telegram* 24 March 1888
95. *Telegram* 27 April 1859
96. *Telegram* 27 July 1867
97. *Telegram* 2 November 1879
98. *Mercury* 18 February 1888
99. *Mercury* 15 July 1893
100. *Telegram* 12 March 1864
101. *Mercury* 5 May 1888
102. *Mercury* 26 January 1878
103. *Mercury* 24 November 1888
104. S. Glover and M. Rogers, *The Old Pubs of Deal and Walmer (and Kingsdown and Mongeham)* (Whitstable, 2010) p 74
105. *Mercury* 30 July 1898
106. *Telegram* 10 March 1888
107. P. Clark, *The English Alehouse: A Social History, 1200–1830* (Harlow, 1983) p 338.
108. *Municipal Corporations in England and Wales: Report on the Borough of Deal* ...(1834) para 32
109. *Telegram* 18 January 1860
110. Winstanley p 71
111. *Telegram* 4 January 1879
112. *Mercury* 4 October 1890
113. *Telegram* 18 May 1859
114. *Mercury* 14 December 1889

115. Glover and Rogers p 122
116. *Telegram* 23 April 1881
117. *Telegram* 19 January 1867
118. A. L. Minter, *Deal Railway Station A History 1847 – 1995* (Sandwich, 1995) p 5
119. C. B Patterson, *Angela Burdett-Coutts and the Victorians* (London, 1953) p 116

Chapter 4

Disorder, Regulation and Bad Behaviour

Magistrates and police
Shortly after 11pm on Saturday 7 May 1890 PC Chapman, while on his evening rounds, saw lights burning in the bar of the Clarendon Hotel on Beach Street. After a few minutes he decided to seek assistance, and found his colleague PC Mercer in nearby Short Street. The two then returned to the hotel:

> "They listened about twenty minutes to half an hour, and could still hear talking and laughing. PC Mercer stood on the window-sill, and looked through the window blind, which did not fit the window frame within two inches, into the bar. He (PC Chapman) also got upon the sill himself, and looked in. He could see the defendants West and Mackie both in the bar. He then got down, and PC Mercer afterwards got up a second time, and stood there. As they could not both stand there he told PC Mercer to watch there, while he waited at the hotel entrance at the front. He watched there till half-past eleven. The barmaid then came to the door, and unlocked it. Witness was in a stooped position, so that she could not see him through the clear glass of the door. As soon as the lock was turned witness pushed the door open. She shouted "Oh, you are not coming in" two or three times. Witness replied "I am already inside", and walked towards the bar..."[1].

This rather farcical episode, laboriously described to the magistrates and recounted at length in the *Mercury*, is testimony to the countless hours police in Deal spent observing and reporting on the conduct of public houses in the town. Licensed premises were entitled and indeed required to provide beer for consumption off and (in most cases) on the premises, but had to operate within an increasingly detailed regulatory framework. This was interpreted and implemented locally by the borough magistrates and police. In Deal, as across the land, the prevention and punishment of drunkenness and bad behaviour was a central pre-occupation. This is discussed in the next section and is followed by some reflections on the houses which caused the authorities particular problems. There was then the complicated issue of who, in what circumstances and at what hour of the day might be served beer in the first place; the fourth section considers this. The final section recounts the most striking example of collective bad behaviour in Victorian Deal. The part played by public houses and landlords in Deal was at the heart of the election scandal that broke in 1880, though bad – not to say shameful – behaviour had in fact been exhibited by a large proportion of the male population of the town. The chapter begins however by considering the actual mechanisms for maintaining order and policing public houses in Victorian and Edwardian Deal.

Until 1699 Deal had been a "limb" of the ancient port of Sandwich, one of the original Cinque Ports. In that year a determined campaign for autonomy achieved its goal when Deal obtained its own royal charter. Those masterminding the campaign had argued that incorporating the town as a separate borough, with its own magistrates, would mean that justice could be handed out more swiftly and efficiently. They were also determined to take control of the town's public houses and end the situation where "Sandwich puts on us fines for Licences of Public Houses and does whatever it pleases, and keeps the money and returns none of it to us, which would assist our rates if we were separated from that place"[2]. Independence, furthermore, would mean that "ships would then be furnished at most reasonable rates, and all frauds in selling of beer and bread prevented"[3]. Argument and lobbying were eventually decisive, and the new charter was brought back to Deal in triumph on 13 October. Nearby Walmer, however, remained within the jurisdiction of Sandwich, with justice dispensed and licensing decisions taken by Cinque Ports magistrates.

When the commissioners appointed by Parliament in 1833 to report on the functioning of municipal corporations came to investigate the situation in Deal, they found that there was by then "great difficulty in getting persons to come into the corporation...the office of mayor or jurat [i.e. alderman] is one merely of trouble, the corporation having little or no emolument or patronage of any kind". Five of the 12 jurat posts had been vacant not long before, the commissioners noting dryly that they were "all filled up in one day in April of that year. The appointment of the Committee by the House of Commons, for inquiring into the state of corporations, was no doubt the cause of these elections"[4].

After more than a century of government by a self-perpetuating oligarchy, one of the "enclaves of exclusivity and speciality within the normal framework of county administration"[5], the town found itself pushed into a new era as one of 178 boroughs reformed under the 1835 Municipal Corporations Act. Councillors would now be elected for three-year terms of office, with one third retiring each year. They in turn would select one third of their number to serve as aldermen for six years. The reformed corporation of Deal consisted of 18 councillors and six aldermen, with the town being divided into just two wards, North and South. All male rate-paying occupants of premises were eligible to vote, though the franchise in the reformed boroughs was in practice narrower than the parliamentary franchise. Local elections in Deal were often uncontested.

The reformed boroughs gained important new powers to raise a rate to fund deficits. In the eighteenth century the limited powers and capacity of borough corporations had led to a proliferation of local improvement commissions, created under individual private acts to undertake a variety of local sanitation, highway and infrastructure activities. This might even include the appointment, as in Dover, of constables answerable to the Pavement Commissioners, quite separate from those under the control of the magistrates. Deal had secured its own Act in 1791, and although the Pavement Commission then established came in time to be overshadowed by the town council it lingered on until 1873.

Members of the old corporation viewed the reforms with mixed feelings, proud that – in their own estimation – "no interested motive has ever influenced our conduct; we have given up our time to the public service most freely and cheerfully", and hedging their bets about the future:

> "... the time has at length arrived when the Municipal Reform Act is about to come into operation and we trust it is not a dangerous innovation upon those venerable institutions of which Englishmen have been so justly proud, but that it is a measure based upon the principle of sound regenerating wisdom, and as such we must anxiously and sincerely wish it success".[6]

The 1835 Act separated the judicial role of the former boroughs from the administrative functions of the new councils. For Josef Redlich, the Edwardian historian of local government in England, the "peculiar seat of judicial corruption" prevalent in English towns in the eighteenth century had been removed "by two cuts of the healing knife of reform. First, magisterial was severed from corporate office. Secondly, administrative work was withdrawn from borough magistrates and handed over to Town Councils"[7]. On the other hand the campaign by radicals for elected magistrates to dispense justice on relatively minor matters had failed, and borough magistrates would instead be appointed by the Crown. The Mayor did however serve as ex-officio chair of the bench while in office (as Redlich saw it, "the only relic of the old system"[8]). A minimum of two borough justices sitting together now had criminal jurisdiction over "police offences" such as minor theft and larceny, assault and drunkenness, and small scale breaches of the peace. They dispensed prompt, summary justice and could impose terms of imprisonment of up to six months.

In the unreformed borough five justices of the peace had been elected from among the 12 jurats by the jurats themselves and the Mayor; the commissioners had observed tersely that there was "usually no wish to have the office..."[9]. Under the new arrangements, although by convention the Lord Chancellor "sought advice on candidates from a number of quarters, sometimes from Members of Parliament"[10] before making appointments to borough benches, Deal councillors were irritated at times that the process was anything but transparent. The 1835 Act ruled out anyone living more than seven miles from the borough in question, but the leading citizens of Deal clearly expected the Lord Chancellor to do better than this and ensure that he appointed men of their own kind. In 1875 the council petitioned him, indignantly but unsuccessfully, to ask that he take their advice before making appointments, and regretting his recent appointment of "a comparative stranger" when there were "many persons in the town as well qualified for the office [and] who had a greater claim...on account of their being old townsmen"[11].

In practice, although judicial and administrative functions had been separated and the magistrates made independent of the borough council, many justices were past or present members of the council. Furthermore most of those chosen as Mayors seem to have been assiduous in undertaking their responsibilities as magistrates, and took advantage of their entitlement to serve on the bench for another year after their term of office. Their position was reinforced in 1882 when legislation underlined the central role expected of Mayors as members of borough benches by giving them precedence over other justices and confirming their right to chair all sessions.

A drunken marine placed in the cells after an evening on the town, say, or a vagrant locked up after being found begging in the street, might find themselves appearing before two magistrates the following morning. But most business was handled at the regular Thursday petty sessional meetings. These were held in public – according to Pritchard, writing in 1864, the number of people crowding into the magistrates' room in the town hall led to "a deficiency of vital air, as to be really oppressive"[12] – and proceedings were extensively reported in the local papers. In the 1870s the magistrates handled around a dozen cases of indictable offences each year, committing the majority of alleged offenders to trial by jury at the borough quarter sessions. But most of their time was spent hearing and immediately deciding on cases of relatively minor wrongdoing brought either by the police or by an aggrieved party. Reforms in the 1840s had made justices responsible for the trial of many offences which had previously been committed for trial before a jury, and by the 1870s the Deal bench were hearing approximately 150 summary cases a year (though the number could vary markedly from one year to the next). These could involve anything from common assault and breaches of the peace to cruelty to animals, trespass, malicious damage and selling "unsound" food.

A later picture of Deal Town Hall, built in 1803. The police station was in the building on the left. To the right is the Black Bull public house.

In Deal, as elsewhere, many of these summary cases concerned drunken and disorderly behaviour, and in common with their colleagues in other garrison and naval towns in Kent the magistrates found their workload substantially increased by the anti-social and occasionally violent activities of off-duty soldiers, sailors and marines. But the Deal bench had also to hear a uniquely large number of cases involving "refractory seamen" put ashore from ships at anchor in the Downs for refusing their duty. In the 12 months to September 1875 27% of all summary cases (50 out of 186 cases) involved alleged offences under the Merchant Navy Act. In Ramsgate the percentage was 14% (43 cases), and in Dover and Gravesend only some 5% (18 and 29 cases respectively).

According to Pain[13], seamen convicted by the Deal bench would then spend anything from two to ten or even twelve weeks in Sandwich Gaol, at a cost to the borough of 1s 6d per head per day. Fortunately for all concerned the number of cases fell as the century wore on. The *Mercury* observed in 1897 that it was "a most uncommon occurrence for a refractory crew to be brought ashore and tried now, while a few years back delinquents of this calibre were always well represented at Sandwich Gaol"[14]. With the sharp reduction in cases involving either "insubordinate mariners and malicious soldiers …it may not be considered altogether irrelevant to observe that our magistrates are not now nearly so hard worked as were their predecessors"[15].

The importance of the borough magistrates for brewers and landlords was not simply that they dispensed justice in the event of drunkenness and rowdy behaviour. In 1835 the Government had planned to transfer responsibility for the licensing of public houses to the councils of the reformed boroughs, but had thrown in the towel in the face of stiff opposition in the House of Lords. So the function remained with the Deal borough magistrates, subject only to the right of appeal to the East Kent Quarter Sessions should they refuse to renew or transfer a licence. Rather astonishingly, despite periodic attempts at reform, this function would remain with magistrates until 2003. As John Greenaway has observed, the position of English magistrates "…was indeed a complex one. As servants of the Crown, it was their duty to administer the licensing statutes; as representatives of the locality, it was their duty to interpret those statutes in accordance with the needs and requirements of the community; as a quasi-judicial body, they had to assess each case before them strictly according to the rules of law and equity"[16].

In practice the arrangements worked well enough in nineteenth-century Deal. When taking decisions at annual licensing ("brewster") sessions the magistrates drew on their experience in hearing cases of drunkenness and disorderly conduct. They knew well enough which houses tended to cause the police difficulty or provoke complaints from neighbours, and were clearly confident in their ability to discharge the functions of "a body interposed between the licensee and the public for the protection of the public"[17] (as a Law Lord defined it in 1897). Some friction between councillors and the bench did arise during the Three Compasses affair, as will be seen in Chapter 5. But in general there seems to have been a broad consensus about the oversight to be exercised where the town's public houses and beerhouses were concerned, and the conduct to be expected of those running and frequenting them.

Public order in eighteenth-century Deal had been maintained by the town sergeant and 12 parish constables, assisted by a number of watchmen. By 1834 the town had 23 unpaid constables, selected by the magistrates from different parts of the parish of Deal and "usually substantial householders"[18]. There was evidently no disinclination to serve, though the motivation was not zeal for the public good but rather that service as a constable brought with it an exemption from more onerous parochial duties. The 1835 Act marked a watershed here too. It required all incorporated boroughs to appoint watch committees, who were in turn expected to appoint a sufficient number of paid constables to police their town. Deal obediently became one of nine boroughs in Kent to establish a force between 1835 and 1839. Sandwich, in contrast, reckoned a permanent police force and police station an unnecessary expense, and did not change its views until forced to do so in 1856. Kent magistrates were equally resistant, and having failed in 1839 to adopt the new permissive County Police Act held out against a county force until legislation made this compulsory.

Deal's watch committee was constituted in January 1836, and in March reported to the Secretary of State that five night constables had been appointed and that George Hoile, a local butcher, had been chosen as their inspector. Day police were added soon afterwards. Two years later the watch committee decided to reduce the overall strength from seven to four to save money (across the country, observed a later historian, "the new police tended to cost more than the old – at any rate it was easier to say what they cost"[19]) but the visit of Queen Victoria to Walmer the following year prompted second thoughts, and two of the policemen previously dismissed were re-engaged for a time. The work was hard and sometimes dangerous. In 1842 the watch committee awarded Constable Browning 30 shillings in compensation for injuries inflicted by a soldier in the Swan. A few years later Inspector Hoile, though nearly 60, "stood a desperate encounter single-handed against three strangers"[20]. When Constable Cox suffered a fractured arm in arresting a "very strong turbulent man"[21] on regatta day in 1864 there was some indignation that he was awarded only 5s a week and expected by the watch committee to apply to his benefit club for further help and to pay his doctor's bills.

In 1847 the watch committee divided the town into five beats, and bought five whistles. The following year Sergeant Boyd of the City of London Police was appointed to succeed Hoile, but was not a success. In 1850 Henry Redsull, a local man, was promoted from within the force to take his place. Among the constables, "during the whole existence of the force only one man was appointed who was not either from the town itself or from the neighbouring villages"[22]. Their previous occupations included working as seamen, gardeners, cordwainers and general labourers. New recruits were expected to be under 30 years old, and to be at least five foot eight inches tall. The watch committee also seems to have had a policy of only employing married men which, as the historian Roy Ingleton suggests, may have contributed to the stability of employment among members of the force.[23] (Other borough watch committees took the opposite approach and insisted on single men.) In 1866 the Inspector of Constabulary, appointed under the 1856 Act to report annually on every force, noted that only one change had taken place in the force during the year "so that the service seems not to be unpopular"[24] The following year he reported that one member of the Deal force had served for 27 years, and two others 19 and 17 years respectively.

The reassuring figure of James Shelvey Cox, full-time constable with the Deal borough police between 1856, when promoted from the night to the day police, until his retirement in 1877 aged 58. Cox lived in Middle Street and had previously been a shoemaker.

But it was a long time before the Inspectorate pronounced the Deal force efficient, with the borough then able to claim from the Treasury a quarter, rising in 1874 to a half, of the cost of police pay and clothing. Captain Willis, Inspector of Police for the southern region between 1856 and 1880, warned in his first report that there was no effective supervision of constables on night duty – two of whom, part-time, followed their own trade by day – and in subsequent years he repeatedly judged the force to be poorly organised and too small.

The council did not take at all kindly to the 1856 legislation under which Captain Willis had been appointed ("calculated to undermine and supersede the present powers of the Watch Committees and also involve them in principles of concentration which is alike unconstitutional in its tendency, derogatory to the liberties of the People, and hostile to Municipal rights"[25]) and it was not until 1864 that the watch committee and the council finally acted on his recommendations. Having looked at practice in other east Kent boroughs it decided to increase the size of the Deal force to eight full-time officers: a superintendent, a sergeant and six constables. This brought the ratio of policemen per head of population to 1:941. Although this still fell short of the average for borough forces in Victorian England of roughly 1:700, Willis nonetheless now reckoned the force efficient, though warning in 1876 it was "not in any way as regards numbers in excess of the number required for the due performance of the duties, and the protection of the district under charge"[26].

The Deal police force was now a little larger, and was certainly better organised, but it also had more to do. Legislation in 1856 had empowered magistrates to require police forces to undertake a range of other duties in addition to keeping the peace. In Deal the superintendent became inspector of weights and measures and of "low lodgings", and for a time was superintendent of the fire department. The force as a whole acted as inspectors of nuisances, receiving an extra allowance for their pains, and in the 1860s had the task of providing shelter for casual vagrants. Further unrelated tasks continued to be added. These included the inspection of workshops, and of cattle for contagious diseases, and from 1875 the licensing of chimney sweeps. In 1881 the superintendent was appointed inspector under the Adulteration Acts, a post under which he "would have the privilege of tasting the beer"[27]. A few years later, as the town continued to grow, a second sergeant was added to the strength, with the result that the ratio of police to population, which had fallen to 1:1,000, returned to the level achieved 20 years earlier.

The police were based in the town hall until a building next door was bought to serve as the police station and lock-up. The latter consisted of three large cells with beds and fire-places. Two cells were usually earmarked for men and the third for women. In September 1850 the Inspector of Prisons was fiercely critical of the state of the lock-up, reporting in a letter to the Home Secretary that he had found the cells to be "in a most disorderly and dirty condition, reflecting great discredit upon the superintendent of police who acts as keeper"[28]. This brought Boyd's short tenure as superintendent to an abrupt end. The following April Louise Redsull, the wife of his successor, was appointed "matron" of the lock-up, and conditions improved thereafter; Captain Willis regularly found the cells clean and "not unsuitable" for the temporary detention of prisoners. Some incarcerations were more temporary than intended. The escape of Thomas Gimber in 1848 was probably a factor in Boyd's departure, and in 1872 the Mayor reprimanded Superintendent Parker and Constable Cox after "prisoner Chapman" had absconded from custody. The attempt by a marine arrested for drunkenness five years later to escape by "kneeing" his way up and out of the chimney, on the other hand, failed ignominiously. The lock-up was modernised in 1882, following further criticism from the Inspector of Police, with the construction of a charge office and three modern cells to replace the old.

The Inspector's scathing criticisms in 1850 had not been confined to the condition of the cells. Although convicted prisoners were sent to Sandwich Gaol those awaiting trial, unless they became seriously ill, were held in the lock-up. In effect this functioned as a borough gaol, yet "there are no airing-yards [and] neither clothing nor the means of cleanliness are provided for the prisoners". In short, "not one of the legislative provisions in respect to gaols is complied with"[29]. To drive the point home the Inspector reported in some detail on the abject condition of a heavily pregnant woman when finally transferred by the magistrates from the Deal lock-up to Sandwich Gaol. The Inspector's letter had the intended effect of stinging the magistrates and council into action and he was able in publishing it in his annual report to express "much satisfaction...that the evils complained of have been remedied, and the necessary precautions taken to prevent their recurrence"[30]. Henceforth all prisoners, whether convicted or awaiting trial, were sent up the coast

Sandwich Gaol, built in 1829, received prisoners sentenced by the Deal magistrates. It was closed in 1878 and demolished the following year. The gentleman in the top hat is thought to have been the prison governor.

to Sandwich, along with those sentenced by the magistrates to a term of imprisonment or unable or unwilling to take up the option, if offered, of paying a fine. In 1872 41 prisoners were committed there from Deal. This compared with 102 from Ramsgate, 18 from Walmer and 12 from Sandwich itself.

Prisoners from Deal occupied on average five or six cells at any one time. Men were put to work picking oakum, making shoes, clothes or mats or turning the treadmill. Women washed or mended clothes. But in 1878 Sandwich Gaol was closed down by the Secretary of State and sold the following year for £820. Prisoners from Deal were now sent to the new government-supervised county gaols in Canterbury or Maidstone. The borough certainly had no objection. It reckoned that the transfer of responsibility for prisons to central government by the Disraeli Government the previous year, the first transfer of an important service from local to central government and a sign of things to come, would save it around £300 a year.

Many of those given custodial sentences by the magistrates went to gaol for drink-related offences. But actual or potential drunkenness among policemen themselves was a major concern to magistrates across the country. In the words of one historian of the Victorian police "most policemen were assumed to have a drinking problem"[31]. Even as late as the 1880s the majority of dismissals from borough police forces were

DRINKING IN DEAL

drink-related. The 1791 Deal Improvement Act included the provision that if any landlord "shall, knowingly and willingly, harbour or entertain any Watchman...or permit or suffer any such Watchman to remain in such his or her Public House, during any Part of the Time appointed for their being on Duty" he could be fined up to 20 pounds[32], and the rules promulgated in 1836 for the new force required officers to "pay a particular attention to all public houses on the beat, responding to all irregularities" but "on no pretence...enter a Public House or Beer Shop, except in the immediate execution of [their] Duty"[33].

Inevitably some officers did yield to temptation. The new force got off to a shaky start when the night watch were caught in July 1839 accepting beer from a prisoner, and were fined a week's wages. Three then resigned. Drunkenness seems to have played a part in the dismissal of James Beale in 1860, and in May 1868 George Pain was suspended after having been found intoxicated on duty – which may have been the trigger for the introduction the following month of thrice-weekly drill sessions under the charge of Sergeant Burns of the Depot Battalion. In 1877 Superintendent Capps discovered two of his constables being served in the Victoria, "they being at the time in uniform and on duty"[34]. The men were fined by the watch committee, and the landlord by the magistrates (legislation in 1872 having empowered them to fine any landlord serving a policeman on duty). A few years later a mysterious public notice in the *Telegram* inviting anyone who had seen a Deal policeman drinking in a public house to send particulars to an address in London, prompted an anonymous wag the following week to invite anyone who had never had such an experience to make contact[35].

Drink and the conduct of police officers in relation to public houses lay at the heart of the crisis that broke in the 1870s. Both Henry Redsull and his successor Thomas Parker, who died in service in 1874 after 16 years as superintendent, were conscientious and well respected. The watch committee and council then made the mistake of appointing as Parker's successor, in December 1874, his 28-year-old son William. Problems began almost immediately. The following month a late night tussle involving Parker and a commercial traveller staying at the Walmer Castle provoked allegations from the landlord and his wife, supported by the billiard marker and the boots, that the superintendent had been drunk. The magistrates did not believe the story ("Mr Parker had been introduced to the Watch Committee with testimonials of the highest character; his father had held the same position for many years and it was well known his family had been properly trained"[36]) but there was increasing concern in the town. Later that year the watch committee decided unanimously to caution Parker following complaints that members of the force frequented public houses, tended to look the other way when houses opened outside of the permitted hours and failed to maintain due order in the streets.

Parker's deputy, Sergeant Joshua Philpott, had led the force during the short interregnum following Thomas Parker's death but had not been short-listed to succeed him. Although Philpott corroborated his new superintendent's version of events during the Walmer Castle affair, there was clearly bad blood between the two. Discipline began to disintegrate. In May Philpott had to refute suggestions that he had visited the Maxton Arms to see a girl for immoral purposes and later that year the watch committee suspended him for a time for leaving the town without Parker's permission. In February 1876 a constable had to resign after failing to help a woman in distress, Councillor Outwin reckoning he "had never met with a more uncivil person in his long experience of PCs"[37].

There was more trouble in November when Philpott complained to the watch committee that Parker had failed to arrest a marine for drunkenness and "exposure of person". The man in question had been refused beer at the Roxburgh Castle and, as Constable Ramsey put it, "went around the corner and pumped ship"[38]. A fierce row then developed between Philpott and Parker, the latter reckoning (as he later explained to the watch committee) that it was "very hard for a man to be locked up all night...for making water in the street" rather than simply being handed over to the military police. The exasperated committee censured Parker both for his handling of the case and for his use of bad language towards Philpott. No doubt to their relief, the superintendent resigned the following year.

It took time to return to an even keel. The appointment as superintendent of Helder Ben Capps, previously with the Ashford police, led to the resignation of three constables, though one later successfully re-applied, and to the superannuation of a fourth. Among the new appointments was George Ralph, the son of a retired county policeman now the landlord of the Lifeboat. Capps was clearly determined both to improve the discipline and efficiency of the force and to send a message to landlords that infringements of the licensing laws would be acted upon. The next annual licensing meeting had to be held in the main room of the town hall rather than in the small council chamber, "it having been known that almost a score of summonses had been issued against publicans and others against the licensing laws...the spacious hall was nearly full, and the utmost interest was taken in the proceedings"[39]. When Capps brought about the successful prosecution of the landlord of the Jolly Gardener beerhouse in 1881 for serving outside the permitted Sunday hours the magistrates complimented him for his "assiduity in seeking out these cases"[40].

There is some suggestion that the magistrates sometimes found Capps a little too zealous. Certainly the police had at times a difficult course to steer between risking complaints for turning a blind eye and provoking the irritation of magistrates, and of course of landlords, for bringing charges in cases of minor or marginal infringements. But overall Capps' tenure was a success, the *Mercury* acknowledging on his departure that "since he has been in Deal he has given the greatest satisfaction, both to the Bench of Borough Magistrates and the inhabitants of the town generally...his urbanity and consideration in all matters with which he has had to deal have won him general esteem"[41]. The perils of drink to those policing the town were now more likely to be a matter of dry humour. "He was sure the beer was fresh drawn by the froth", said Sergeant Curtis when giving evidence against the landlord of the Victoria in 1893, "and before they left the house it had settled down. He was not an expert in beer, though he had been. (Dr Hardman: It is assumed that policemen don't know the taste of it – Supt Kewell thought that was too much to assume)"[42].

Legally the watch committee of the borough occupied the position of the Chief Constable of a county force, with Superintendent Capps and his predecessors being merely employees. It was the most important council committee, the only one required under the municipal code, and its work was not subject to review by the council. In 1836 the Deal committee consisted of the Mayor, one alderman and five councillors. For many years it met irregularly as the need arose and at the Mayor's discretion; in due course it moved to scheduled monthly meetings. The committee usually had around half a dozen members, selected annually, but disagreements over membership and a feeling that the importance of the business must warrant it sometimes led to it operating as a committee of the whole council. During the 1850s the council see-sawed between the two approaches. When it voted in 1875 to try the whole council approach yet again, Alderman Denne dryly reminded his colleagues that on previous occasions "it often happened that at their meeting they did not muster a quorum, each member appearing to think there would be enough present without him. When they only had about five members each one would see the necessity of attending".[43]

The watch committee's minute book for 1836–76 has survived, and gives a good idea of its work over that period. In practice much of its time was spent in deciding on the purchase of new clothing and equipment. Only in the event of a complaint were issues relating to how the town should actually be policed discussed, or at any rate minuted. Watch committees met in private and – unlike meetings of the full council and of the magistrates, which were recorded in the local papers in enormous detail – their work was not reported in the local press. The historian of the Deal police concludes from the evidence available that "as might be expected of a body of constantly changing members, no effort was made to follow any consistent policy of police management, and suggestions for improvements were allowed to originate with the Inspector of Constabulary. Apart, however, from its lack of generosity over pay...the Watch Committee was not a bad employer."[44]

Borough policemen appointed and supervised by the watch committee were not the only authorised figures of authority in the town. When the force was constituted in 1836 Thomas Langley had already been Town Sergeant, Gaoler and Head Constable for the town for some 35 years, and had won fame in 1816 for his arrest in the smoking room of the Walmer Castle of two men charged with murder on the high seas. Langley declined to join the new force and instead took the reconstituted post of Mayor's Sergeant and Guildhall Keeper. His responsibilities were a mixture of the practical, for example as superintendent of the market and weighbridge, and the ceremonial. "Mr Langley's rhetoric not being first rate", noted the *Telegram*, "he did not always serve in the capacity of town crier, but had the good sense to employ as his deputy Mr Baker...". He died in 1860, still in post, at the age of 85 and after no fewer than 59 years service: " the connecting link between the past system and the present"[45]. His successor, Jonathan Capon, previously landlord of the Sir Sidney Smith, also died in office at an advanced age. In January 1882 the councillors appointed Sergeant Philpott of the borough police to the post, his part in the debacle of William Parker's tenure as superintendent forgotten or forgiven. Gillespie, writing in 1954, noted that even then he was still vividly remembered by the older townsmen "for he had strict views on the proper behaviour of small boys"[46].

The forces of law and order were also supplemented by the annual appointment by the magistrates of 20 special constables for one-year terms of office. They were equipped with badges, armlets and staves, though not given uniforms, and had the same powers and responsibilities as regular police officers. A refusal to serve if nominated by the magistrates could lead to a fine, but in practice the system worked on a voluntary basis (although compulsion was evidently needed around the coast in Ramsgate during the First World War). Special constables in Deal were almost always shopkeepers and tradesmen. Boatmen seem in practice to have been excluded or excused, presumably given their uncertain availability. But being a publican was no bar, in the 1860s at least: Henry Darby (Providence), for example, served in 1866, Edward Grigg (Albion) in 1867 and William Riley (Prince Albert) in 1869. Special constables might take turns of duty as beach inspectors, for instance, and there is some evidence that they took part at times in the inspection of public houses. Until 1914 the basis of the power to appoint special constables was in fact where the magistrates had reasonable fear of "tumult, riot or felony". Such fears might have been real enough on occasion during the eighteenth century. But it is unlikely that the specials in Deal were ever called upon for any serious keeping of the peace in Victorian times.

Both the office of Town Sergeant and the appointment of special constables long outlived the independent borough police force. In 1854 the Palmerston government introduced legislation which would have abolished separate forces in boroughs with fewer than 20,000 inhabitants. This was withdrawn after strong opposition, and the Deal police survived for another 35 years. Legislation in 1888 finally ended the right of boroughs with populations of fewer than 10,000 to have their own forces, so reducing the number of separate police forces in England and Wales from 231 to 183. Efforts to preserve a local force in the Deal area through an amalgamation with Walmer for policing purposes came to nothing, and on 1 April 1889 the Deal police were absorbed into the Kent County Constabulary. In the words of the recent historian of policing in Kent "the Deal force...had a history of some 60 years during which time it was responsible for no great initiatives; it was not involved in any serious or notorious case and none of its members reached an eminent position. Like many another small town, Deal dealt with its own problems of watch and ward with diligence and success and took a pride in its tiny police force"[47].

Superintendent Capps moved on but many of his old force decided to forgo the chance of promotion within the county constabulary in order to remain stationed in Deal. PC John Annall, who had resigned when Capps was appointed but had been quickly granted reinstatement, did make sergeant in due course and retired in 1898 after 25 years service. He then changed horses to become landlord, first of the Brickmaker's Arms, where his occupancy may have been a factor in finally persuading the magistrates to grant an on-licence, and then from 1902 until 1908 of the Hare and Hounds. PC George Ralph, son of the landlord of the Foresters, ran the lock-up at the police station until his retirement in 1902. The last surviving member of the old borough police, PC Ratcliffe, was also lock-up keeper for many years before retiring in 1912.

Many in the town were no doubt saddened or angered by the abolition of their own force, and would have agreed with Gillespie's lament seventy years later that "the supplanting of this sturdy civic patriotism by the administration of distant officials in county town and metropolis is one of the misfortunes of our age"[48]. But given the continuity in personnel they are unlikely to have noticed many practical

Joshua Philpott in his finery as Town Sergeant. Having joined the borough police in 1873 and been quickly promoted to sergeant, he fell out badly with Superintendent William Parker. Appointed Town Sergeant in 1882, he was apparently nicknamed "Shoes" after his effigy was burned in King Street – for some reason – leaving only his shoes.

differences. The police continued to bring cases of drunken behaviour and licence infringements before the borough magistrates, and to be sensitive to the latter's decisions and opinions. There was also a welcome annual saving to the borough of some £250. But the price was an operational chain of command that ran through to the Chief Constable of Kent, until 1894 the long-serving Captain John Hay Ruxton. He and his successors had strong views on the "drink question", including on the need for a reduction in the number of public houses. As will be seen in the next chapter, the fact that the council and the magistrates broadly shared this view did not make them any more appreciative of attempts by the Chief Constable in Maidstone to force their hand.

Drunkenness and disorder
The police in Deal, whether serving in the borough or later in the county force, spent a large amount of time keeping an eye on public houses, entering them in some circumstances, controlling and if necessary arresting drunks, and tackling drink-fuelled rowdy or aggressive behaviour. Drunks might be locked up overnight in a station cell and then sent home, escorted out of town if a vagrant, or taken before the borough magistrates on a charge of being drunk and disorderly. A more violent disturbance, in a public house or out in the street, might lead to prosecution for assault. If the landlord were considered at fault in encouraging or failing to control drunkenness, disorder or immorality in his house, he might also find himself up before the bench and facing a fine or even the loss of his licence. In the latter case the magistrates might allow someone else, reckoned capable of running a respectable house, to take on the licence. Or they might not, and in effect close the house permanently.

Drunks under arrest usually reached the cells under their own unsteady steam but some had to be trundled there in a wheelbarrow. They might be troublesome and argumentative, like the chimney-sweep fighting drunk outside the Sir John Falstaff in 1877 having smashed a pane of glass. He was with difficulty escorted to the cells, and his equally inebriated wife transported there in the wheelbarrow. Having refused or being unable to pay their £2 fines, their reward was 14 days' hard labour in Sandwich Gaol. Others were remorseful and apologetic, offering imaginative excuses for their intemperate behaviour – men like the old soldier up before the bench in 1901 who "had sunstroke in India and when he had had about four pints of beer he didn't know what he was doing".[49] Some, like Lucy Erridge ("I was not drunk, it was nothing but a high wind") maintained their belligerence when in front of the bench ("Much good may it [the payment of the fine] do you. We ain't all dead yet:)[50]. Offenders were often convinced that the dice were loaded against them ("Burnap said it was no use asking them any questions, as the magistrates always believed what the policemen say"[51]), while for the long-suffering police "it was frequently the case that different versions were given when before the magistrates"[52]. Some lamentations in court had a timeless quality: "it is all through women that I got into trouble ...I won't touch another drop of beer"[53] promised Percy O'Neil in 1907.

In many cases of drunkenness the police simply delivered a quiet word of warning, or just turned a blind eye. As far as boatmen were concerned, a show of contrition and what Bower terms their "usual excuse" – "I had just come on shore and had a drop too much"[54] – will have often done the trick. Violence or threatening behaviour was another matter. In October 1863, for example, the brothers Thomas and Henry Redsull were arrested, drunk and riotous, in Middle Street. They had, they said, "been off in their boat all day and required a little beer before going to bed and had been challenged to a fight by another man"[55].

Trouble might follow disagreements after a cruise or the salvaging of an anchor, or spring from a business arrangement gone sour; in July 1870 Oniferous Sneller, landlord of the Napier Tavern, complained of being repeatedly abused and threatened by Thomas Obree "in consequence of some difference existing between us as regards some boats of which we are part owners"[56]. Violence might also be sparked by rivalry between boatmen from different stations or ends of the town, or with boatmen from elsewhere. A tragic example of the latter was the fight between Deal and Dover boatmen in the Star in 1873 which played a part in the death of Frederick Erridge, a drunken young boatman caught up in the fracas. It was not unusual for defendants, ill-advisedly, to offer in mitigation for their rowdy or violent conduct the fact that they were indeed drunk. John and Henry Denton, appearing before the bench in 1895:

> "seemed most anxious throughout the case to impress upon the Bench that they were drunk, and knew nothing of what occurred...Henry, to prove that he was intoxicated, said that just before he entered the Greyhound, he fell over a wheelbarrow, and they had been refused in every house in Middle Street. Asked how

he remembered that, he replied 'We have been told so'"[57].

Sometimes violence could become personal and nasty. When Thomas Bailey, an 18-year-old boatman, appeared before the bench in 1869 after causing damage at the Star, his decision to bring some friends with him backfired badly. As it was "pretty well known that they were quite ready to club round to pay any fine the magistrates might have inflicted", the bench decided instead to impose three weeks' hard labour. The *Mercury* applauded the tough action taken to tackle drunkenness and disorderly conduct "recently...so common among the class to which Bailey belongs". But Bailey's immediate angry reaction was that, had he known that imprisonment was in prospect, he would have given the landlady "a lift under her ear"[58], and he returned to assault her as soon as he was released from gaol. This time his sentence was two months' hard labour, plus surety of £10 for good behaviour for another three.

A modern picture of what was once the Star in Middle Street. In the 1860 and 1870s there were frequent reports of disturbances and the activities of prostitutes. By 1876 the house had become the Paragon Music Hall.

Prosecutions were sometimes brought by the landlords themselves, and an important function of the Licensed Victuallers Association founded in 1893 was to organise legal representation in such cases. This served not only to encourage and support the landlord concerned but also to show the magistrates that the licensed victuallers were responsible tradesmen, determined to play their full part in tackling disorderly behaviour. Relations between the police and individual landlords were generally much improved by this time, and it is unlikely the magistrates then thought, as one of their predecessors had done, that where drunkenness was concerned "the publicans were as much to blame as the men – the former permitting them to get drunk and then hurrying them into the street"[59]. In the Edwardian period the removal of rear and side access to public houses, so facilitating police surveillance and control, could be an important consideration when the council considered plans to rebuild or renovate houses, and the landlord of the Castle probably did not feel the need to deploy a man with a spy glass to watch for the approach of the police, as his predecessor was alleged to have done in 1874.

Violent or aggressive behaviour fuelled by drink had to be tackled. But then of course there were the many who, without crossing that line, became cheerfully and inoffensively lubricated: men like old James Redsull, "'cherry merry' but no more than usual"[60] in the Saracen's Head, or the men reckoned (at least initially) "not drunk but drinky"[61] by the landlord of the Rose and Crown. At what point did the racket created by men in high spirits, laughing, shouting and singing, constitute an unacceptable disturbance, particularly where neighbours and their lodgers were concerned?

For Mrs Philpott, letting out rooms in a house next door to the Crown in 1871, the noise of soldiers and others singing, shouting and clapping to the accompaniment of a piano and a harmonium was beyond the pale, and driving her lodgers away. (Nonsense, wrote men of the Princess Royal Dragoon Guards to the *Telegram* the following week in support of the landlord William Clayton.) A short distance down Beach Street George Porter of the Fountain, charged with permitting "noisy proceedings", admitted candidly that "he could not control boatmen from singing or talking loud, as was their usual custom"[62]. And surely, argued Mariner Kemp, Clayton's successor at the Crown and up before the bench on the same day, "if a person came to his house to have a pint of beer and smoke his pipe, he could not prevent him from singing a song if he wished?" "Yes you must", explained the magistrates' clerk patiently, "if the singing is a nuisance. Although one man's singing would probably not be a nuisance, thirty or forty joining in chorus would be"[63]. No doubt Deal publicans had to show rather more caution than their colleagues in surrounding rural areas where, according to Winstanley, "most landlords encouraged singing, not only because it attracted customers but also because it increased their drinking capacity by making them dry"[64].

It seems clear that, at any rate from the 1870s, the magistrates felt that they and the police had matters broadly under control, and had a reasonably settled approach in dealing with the cases that came before them. The one obvious exception was what on earth to do about "habitual drunkards", as the terminology of the time had it, on whom neither exhortation nor punishment seemed to have any lasting effect: men like the boatman Richard Dawes, persistently brought before the bench for wandering the streets drunk and incapable. In September 1871 the magistrates, admonishing and discharging him yet again, wearily admitted that "he had been so many times before them that they were at a loss to know how to deal with him"[65].

Then there was Maria Tringrove, a "miserable looking woman"[66], who broke a window of the Park Tavern in 1863 and was transported drunk in the police wheelbarrow from the Admiral Keppel in 1865. She comes back into view in 1870 when given six weeks in gaol for breaking the windows of the Chequers beerhouse and again in 1876 when before the bench for the 17th time. Two years later, again in trouble, she blamed her latest misfortune on consuming a combination of "two antibilious pills, three glasses of fourpenny, a morsel of cheese, three cups of tea, a ha'porth of bread and a pennyworth... of bulls-eyes". This time Maria was discharged to the Eastry workhouse and, the magistrates hoping they might see the last of her, "at her request was furnished gratuitously with paper and postage stamps, that she might write to London and Cornwall, at which latter place...she had claimed a parish"[67].

The most notorious town drunk was Tom Brown. First charged in 1847 when in his late twenties, by 1883 he had appeared before the bench on no fewer than 90 occasions and had been committed 38 times. In 1867, during one of his many stays in Sandwich Gaol, he had been pronounced insane. Plans were therefore made to move him to a lunatic asylum, but he was soon back in Deal. Pursued and provoked by small boys in the street, and indulged, teased and bullied by adults (in search of a drink in April 1873 "he was no sooner inside the house [the Eagle] than he was knocked backward into the street by a bucket of water being thrown at him, and he took his revenge by breaking the glass"[68]) Tom nonetheless managed to live well into old age, and even to stay out of trouble for three years in later life. But in June 1895 he succumbed again to "the old propensity, for which, probably, some evil-disposed person who had put temptation in his way is responsible", and the bench reckoned it would "simply be kindness" to send him to prison for another two weeks, without hard labour, "for there he would receive every attention"[69]. Rowdy, remorseful, confused, quick-witted when sober but repeatedly inebriate and violent over a 50-year period, Tom Brown was nonetheless, as the *Mercury* conceded, "rather popular"[70].

Disorder, Regulation and Bad Behaviour

Tom's personal odyssey took place alongside what appears to have been a steady decline in instances of obnoxious drink-related behaviour by his fellow citizens. There is no way of telling if the 1860s, illuminated by reports in the two recently launched local newspapers, were an improvement over the preceding 30 years, but it is clear that behaviour did improve over the following decades. In 1874 the Home Secretary referred in Parliament to annual returns showing that the number convicted for drunkenness per head of population in Deal was 1 in 186, a higher ratio than in Dover (1 in 226) or Sandwich (1 in 235). On the other hand by 1908, according to the local police inspector, the ratio stood at exactly 1 in 755.11 and "compared favourably with other places"[71]. The ratios were susceptible to significant variation year on year, but the overall trend is undeniable. Certainly the claim made in 1902 by a solicitor appearing before the magistrates that "there is less drunkenness in Deal now than there has been for the last 20 or 30 years"[72] was then the commonly held view. According to one local builder – albeit in the context of arguing against further licensing restrictions – "today, out of the number of men he employed, 30 to 40 per cent were total abstainers. Would they have found 3 per cent 30 years ago? And what was more, would they have found not one case of drunkenness in a twelvemonth among 500 men?"[73].

Statistics relating to proceedings and convictions for drunkenness and drunk and disorderly conduct are however notoriously difficult to interpret, and this is certainly the case for the incomplete data available for Deal. In most years between 1870 and 1910 the magistrates heard from 20 to 40 such cases, with roughly four out of five defendants being men. Nationally the statistics for drunkenness showed a downwards trend over the last quarter of the century, but in Deal the 1890s saw the highest average number of cases (38) – a considerable increase over the 1880s – with the highest annual figure occurring in 1890 (56). This almost certainly reflects the impact of the replacement of the borough by the county police force, and the strong views of the Chief Constable, rather than any actual increase in the incidence of drunkenness. Overall, although there were sometimes considerable differences from one year to another – the number of proceedings fell from 39 in 1893 to only 19 in 1894, for example – there is no clear statistical trend over the period 1870–1914 as a whole.

What does seem to have changed is the proportion of proceedings which led to a conviction. In the 1870s it looks as if only around a third of those appearing before the bench were convicted, as opposed to being cleared or simply given a warning. In contrast the percentage rose to some 90% over the next two decades, and to virtually 100% in the period 1900–9. This must surely reflect a deliberate raising of the bar by the magistrates, rather than the exercise of greater discretion by the police in allowing less serious cases of drunkenness, which might not result in a conviction, to escape prosecution. It may be that the near certainty of being convicted if brought before the bench during this period had some effect in restraining public drunkenness (though the proportion of cases resulting in a conviction seems to have fallen in the years immediately before the First World War). Roughly a third of convictions led to a term of imprisonment rather than a fine and, in the 1890s at any rate, women if convicted seem rather more likely to be imprisoned than men.

With a thousand or more troops in barracks on the outskirts of town it is not surprising that many of the instances of aggressive or drunken behaviour involved soldiers or marines, many of whom were raw recruits. This certainly helps to explain why around a half of those convicted were not Deal residents. In June 1862 the *Telegram* told of a rampaging spree by soldiers from the 23rd Royal Welch Fusiliers, warning that "it has been the practice for several months for soldiers to enter public-houses in the neighbouring villages, just as the inmates were retiring to rest, and assistance could not be readily obtained, demanding to be supplied with beer. Resistance under the circumstances being useless, the landlords have submitted to the robbery, as they, of course, were not paid"[74]. The following month (under the heading of "Another Military Outrage") it reported that eight soldiers, probably having attempted just such a trick, had attacked and injured several drinkers in the Sydenham Green public house and chased the landlord down the road. Two soldiers were captured with the help of a sergeant living nearby, and the *Telegram* hoped that the ensuing military tribunal would "mark its sense of such fiendish brutality by awarding them the most severe punishment in its power"[75]. Across Kent as a whole, Conley calculates that between 1859 and 1860 soldiers were involved in 17% of all cases of arson, 10% of indictable theft, 12% of indictable assaults and 10% of sexual assaults"[76]

Friction, or worse, between the military and the people of east Kent was not new. Local readers of the *United Services Magazine* might have felt a little embarrassed to read in the memoirs of Major Edward

Macready, published in 1852, that when returning with the 30th Foot after Waterloo he found that he and his men:

> "..were barbarously treated at Ramsgate, overcharged by the innkeeper at Margate, misled by our guide, and wrongly directed by a ploughman on our road to Sandwich; drenched to the skin each day, and looked crossly on by everyone but the waiters at the inns. As to the peasantry, a civil word could not be extracted from them"[77].

Theft or vandalism by soldiers or marines sometimes had an ulterior motive. When in 1862 Thomas Adamson, another private in the 23rd, stole three ducks from the landlady of the Plough beerhouse the magistrates handed him over to the military authorities after only 24 hours in the lock-up, "the lightness of the sentence being in order that he might not escape the punishment which would be inflicted at the barracks, and that he might not escape being sent out with a draft for foreign service, as he might probably have desired to do"[78]. In 1877, after a house in Water Street was broken into "a private belonging to the Marines confessed to having committed the burglary, with a view to getting discharged from the service"[79]. This was still an issue 20 years later. After a series of window breakings and thefts from public houses the *Mercury* complained indignantly that "it is a mean thing for a man to sneak away from the Queen's Service by committing an offence against the civil law. The Magistrates should make it worth no man's while to play that little game. There should be some arrangement between military and civil authorities to frustrate the device for getting the "ticket"...The public ought to be protected, and the unworthy sons of Mars repressed"[80].

The marines had arrived in Walmer in the 1860s, taking the place of the line regiments and depot battalions of the army. But there continued to be a steady stream of thefts, burglaries and drunken vandalism, across the town and frequently at public houses. Stolen items ranged from a bag of coppers (from the Saracen's Head), the landlord's coat (King's Head) and, of all things, the landlord's canary (Park Tavern). Less successful were the three marines who in 1882 failed to break into the Antwerp, and were then seen running off "with caps turned inside out"[81] in an attempt to avoid detection. Although behaviour slowly improved, the *Mercury* could nonetheless be found in 1891 demanding

An inspection of new recruits and civilian employees outside a store at the East Barracks. The barracks as a whole served as the training depot for recruits to the Royal Marines Light Infantry, and many of those who caused trouble in the town were young men who had only recently joined the colours.

to know "how long are peaceable tradesmen to be submitted to the intolerable nuisances of having their property destroyed by faint hearted individuals, wearing Her Majesty's uniform, but little worthy of such an honourable distinction...there is a strong feeling of indignation in the town, which has been growing in volume for some time..."[82].

Perhaps this was a turning point. Ten years later serious cases of drunkenness or violent behaviour by marines had become infrequent, and it must have been pleasing when at the Quarter Sessions in November 1902 the Recorder repeated his

> "extreme gratification...[at] the extremely good state of order and good behaviour in this town of Deal. If they came to consider that they had the military element in Walmer – that they had so close by a matter of 2,000 men, not men belonging to Deal, or even Kent, but most of them collected from all parts of London, and the poorer quarters more especially – it was difficult to understand how it should be, but the good governance of the military authorities, and the care exercised by the police in Deal, rendered it an extremely rare occurrence to find Marines committing crimes that had to come before the Court"[83].

Nationally, the number and proportion of soldiers fined for drunkenness declined steadily between 1872 and 1899. Indeed, even during the more difficult times there were few echoes among the soldiers and marines stationed in Deal of the problems experienced in Canterbury, for instance, where in "less savoury areas ...brawls between workingmen and the soldiers stationed at the militia barracks were common" and "running fights between police and soldiers were frequent"[84].

Marines usually made for public houses in the Lower Street area or towards the back of the town; there is rarely any sign of interaction with boatmen in their own favoured houses along and near Beach Street. The military police, in conjunction with the magistrates and borough police, naturally kept a close eye on houses where disturbances were most likely to occur. The Bricklayer's Arms in West Street, for example, was said in 1868 to be "a house that gave the military a great deal of trouble"[85]. The Maxton Arms was a particular favourite with marines, and was sometimes put out of bounds. In contrast, the magistrates reckoned in 1892 that "since the marines left, the house has been conducted in an orderly way"[86].

Relations between publicans and the military police could be tense, particularly in the mid-Victorian period. In 1858 the magistrates ruled that the military police could search a public house without a warrant provided that they were accompanied by a borough policeman. The following year William Spicer of the Maxton Arms nonetheless tried to deny entry on the basis that the military police had no right to clear soldiers from his house before 8.00pm. He pleaded ignorance of the law, and escaped with a caution. When the Star was placed out of bounds in 1867 the landlord ejected the corporal who had entered to check for infringements and found himself charged with assault. John Weston "considered the piquet had no business there and that he had a right to expel him"[87], but the magistrates fined him £1 with costs. On the other hand, when Alexander Harvey of the Jolly Sailor was taken before the magistrates in 1865 for refusing to admit a borough policemen who was helping the provost-sergeant to search for a deserter he rather surprisingly won his case. According to the *Mercury* the magistrates concluded that there was no proof the soldier was in the house (though Harvey should have opened the door in any event). The *Telegram*'s version, in contrast, was that "it did not appear that any clause in the Act made it compulsory to admit the police in the middle of the night"[88]. Sometimes ill-feeling spilled out on to the streets. In 1870, for example, Thomas Cattermole of the Castle – always one for an argument – had a violent dispute with a military policeman attempting to round up absconders, and found himself sentenced to two months' hard labour in consequence.

Soldiers and marines absent without leave or attempting to desert were often picked up in public houses, like the soldier found concealed under the bed of the daughter of the landlord of the Deal Hoy in 1863 or the marine who waded twice across the North Stream when being chased across the Sandhills between Deal and Sandwich and was apprehended the same afternoon while recovering "without tunic or cap"[89] in the Bowling Green. The military police, who probably suspected at times that the sympathies of the landlord lay with the deserter, might bring charges under the Marine Mutiny Act for "unlawfully aiding and assisting" a desertion. The arrival of the military police was not necessarily unwelcome if this helped to clear the house of belligerent marines, but a landlord needing help would turn first to the borough police. In practice however most visits by marines to public houses no doubt passed off peacefully, if sometimes noisily, with nothing untoward occurring to attract the attention of the civil or military police, the magistrates or the local press.

A drunken marine risked being locked in a station cell, if arrested by the constabulary, or taken straight back to the barracks by the military police to face a fine or other punishment. In 1885 the *Telegram* reported that 1,100 minor punishments and fines had been imposed at the barracks over the past year, though it is not clear what proportion were drink-related. What the townspeople certainly found objectionable was the practice of "frog-marching" drunken men back to the barracks. In 1865, after an incident resulting in the death of a marine, the *Telegram* fulminated that "a man full of drink cannot be laid on his face in the road and set upon by four or five athletic fellows to be handcuffed and carried face downwards for nearly half a mile without endangering his life"[90].

But matters only came to a head in November 1884 after the military police arrested three marines following a fracas at the Jolly Sailor. George Smith, in his own estimation, "could have walked with the military police. I was willing to do this, but the picket would not let me. I was not violent until they frog-marched me"[91]. His companion George Holt, who allegedly refused to walk, was also frog-marched but died that evening. The inquest jury decided that "he came to his death probably from

Disorder, Regulation and Bad Behaviour

suffocation, accelerated by excessive drinking, and being frog-marched", and made clear their view that "the system called frog-marching is highly dangerous"[92]. In December the *Telegram* reported that an "ambulance stretcher" had now been placed in the police station, with another kept in readiness at the hospital guardroom, and the following month came the news that, after representations to the Secretary to the Navy, orders had been issued that "the "frog's march" be discontinued, and that men are to be carried to the guardroom in a stretcher with suitable straps for confining the struggling drunkard"[93]. In the event the new conveyance does not seem to have been put to use very often, and certainly by Edwardian times instances of drunken misbehaviour by marines had become much less common.

Houses of ill repute

Some soldiers and marines did not simply visit public houses to drink beer. In August 1868 Private Patrick Macnamara of the 101st Depot Battalion was charged with being "secreted" in a bedroom at the Norfolk Arms for an unlawful purpose. Found by the landlord hiding beneath a mattress, he indignantly denied that he had entered the house through a window "and said he went there to see the girl, as he had done many times before"[94]. Their relationship may have been non-commercial. But the police certainly thought that the house was a venue for prostitutes. For the period 1870–81 we know exactly which houses were known or suspected of this because in 1869 the provisions of the Contagious Diseases

The Jolly Sailor in the 1930s. Having been renamed the Norfolk Arms in 1866 after an outbreak of cholera it was repeatedly identified in the 1870s as a brothel. In 1889, by then one of the town's four registered common lodging houses, it became the Jolly Sailor once again.

179

(CD) Acts were extended to the Deal area and began to operate the following February; annual returns to Parliament included lists of houses used as "brothels or houses of accommodation for immoral purposes" in each of the 18 areas of the country then covered by the legislation.

The Norfolk Arms was identified in seven annual returns, as were the Sun and the Seven Stars. Among the eight other houses named were the Bricklayer's Arms beerhouse (named in five returns), the Maxton Arms (four returns), and the Star (four returns). These were all houses particularly frequented by marines. In contrast no Beach Street house appears on the list. Although houses there occasionally found themselves in trouble, as for instance did the Sir Sidney Smith in 1869, it is not surprising that women engaging in prostitution, often arriving from elsewhere and ready to move on if needs be, tended to look for accommodation away from the seafront, amidst other lodgers and transient visitors, rather than among the close-knit Beach Street community. It was also to be expected, given that the aim of the legislation was to reduce the incidence of venereal diseases among soldiers, sailors and marines, that surveillance would concentrate on the houses away from the seafront which marines were known to frequent.

A house could appear on the list without the landlord having been convicted of an offence by the borough magistrates, and it is perhaps not surprising that some of the comparatively few publicans who did appear before the bench in this context reckoned themselves unfairly singled out. When Ann Macey of the Bricklayer's Arms was convicted in 1871, on the evidence of a young female lodger, of accommodating "notoriously bad characters", she complained that eight other houses in the town were doing the same thing and explained, with more honesty than good sense, that "as trade was very slack at her house she thought she might do likewise"[95].

Mrs Macey's estimate of the number of houses then supplementing their business in this way was remarkably close to the official figure for that year: eight public houses and one beerhouse. Thereafter the number of houses reported to be functioning as brothels fell steadily, and in the last four returns (1878–81) none was named. Much the same occurred in Dover and other "subjected districts" in Kent. But this almost certainly reflects the impact not of the CD Acts but of the 1872 Licensing Act. The latter empowered magistrates to fine a landlord who allowed his house to be used as a habitual resort or place of meeting for reputed

Disorder, Regulation and Bad Behaviour

prostitutes (allowing them "to remain longer than is necessary for the purpose of obtaining reasonable refreshment"[96]) and if convicted of permitting his house to be used as a brothel the landlord would lose his licence. No doubt landlords became, at the very least, a good deal more circumspect, and it may be no coincidence that, in contrast, the number of private houses in the town thought to be used for the purposes of prostitution rose from one to four between 1877 and 1881.

Prostitution itself was not a criminal offence. But under the CD Acts a woman identified as a "common prostitute" by a plain-clothes policeman (seconded from the metropolitan police and responsible to the Home Office) would be registered accordingly and then subjected to a fortnightly medical examination. If found by the examining doctor – in Deal, a naval surgeon – to be suffering from gonorrhoea or syphilis she could be placed in a venereal ward of a "lock hospital" for up to nine months. If the woman refused to co-operate she could be brought before the magistrates, where the burden of proof was on her to show, somehow, that she was not a prostitute. The historian of the operation of the legislation in Kent has concluded that there were in fact relatively high levels of compliance with the mandatory medical examination[97] and indeed it does not appear that any woman in Deal attempted to clear her name in this way rather than simply signing the voluntary submission form. There were certainly no instances of the borough magistrates making an order to attend a medical examination.

Nationally a strong movement for repeal soon developed, and there was some local resistance to the operation of the legislation. But the Acts also had many supporters, not least in the garrison towns and ports themselves. Both Folkestone and Dover councils voted in 1870 to tell their borough members that the impact of the legislation had been very positive. Dissenters among the councillors were in a small minority, though vocal. In Deal, by contrast, the legislation seems to have generated relatively little comment or controversy. A meeting convened by the clergy of the town in 1873 to condemn the "degrading and tyrannical"[98] operation of the Acts failed to attract much support.

When William Pittock, tailor and hatter in the town, contrived to appear before the select committee considering the working of the legislation he argued, on the contrary, that the experience in Deal had been very positive. The plain-clothes metropolitan policemen successively stationed in the town were, in fact, kindly individuals, eager if possible

Two marines are among the men standing outside the Roxburgh Castle in Broad Street. By 1904, when the picture was taken, drunkenness and rowdy behaviour by marines had become relatively infrequent.

to help young women rather than "make prostitutes" by placing them on the register, and the regime at the lock hospital in Shorncliffe to which women were sent had a beneficial impact. In his view there was now much less "open vice" and "clandestine prostituting" in the town in consequence of the Acts; the comparison with Ramsgate was now very striking. According to Pittock, of the two "repeal" meetings held in the town "the first one was fairly attended, but there did not seem any inclination to support the repeal; the second was an utter failure"[99].

In 1870, the first year of the operation of the Acts in Deal, 52 women were placed on the register. The number rose to 62 in 1872 before falling steadily to 20 in 1881. The average number on the register at any one time fell from 22 to 9. Roughly two-thirds of the women were aged between 19 and 25, with the average age rising somewhat over the period, as it did in other subjected districts. Very few young women in their teens were added to the register after 1873, and both the number and proportion of women aged over 26 rose. Between a quarter and a half of the names on the register were removed in any one year and in two-thirds of the cases the reason given was that the woman had left the district. It looks therefore as if the number of women residing in Deal who engaged in prostitution did decline during the period, with some probably relocating to Ramsgate and other towns in Thanet where the legislation did not apply. But as much turned on the approach taken at any one time by the metropolitan policeman deployed in the town to enforce the provisions of the Acts, and by the borough police operating within the local frameworks of criminal justice and public order, it is hard to be certain.

Newspaper reports sometimes identified women by name, and at least in the 1860s did not hesitate to described them as prostitutes. One such was Elizabeth Wilkinson, who received a week in gaol for being drunk and disorderly and using profane and indecent language, while 19-year-old Harriet Thompson, similarly described, was charged in 1865 with stealing a pair of ladies' boots while lodging in a room at the back of the Lord Nelson beerhouse. Three years later Sarah Woodward, who had been lodging at the Seven Stars for two months, was brought before the bench having been found sleeping in a haystack. She offered to return to Ramsgate "if the magistrates would forgive her"[100] and the police duly escorted her out of town. (Altogether less apologetic was Eliza Mackenzie when charged in 1908: "a gentleman from the fleet I knew met me [in the Swan] and asked me to have a glass of beer...He lost himself from the ship, and I took his arm and led him on. I was going to lead him up to the ships. Mr Denne: I have no doubt you were going to lead him on"[101].) Conley estimates that some 20% of women committed to Kentish gaols each year were prostitutes, usually having been charged with vagrancy or with drunk and disorderly behaviour.[102]

A woman engaged in prostitution might double as a singer, as for example did Virginia Bell "who represented herself as a professional, specially engaged as a singer for the amusement of the customers of the Park Tavern"[103]. Or a complicit landlord, like John Weston of the Star, might describe the women simply as servants and risk being roundly disbelieved for his pains. (His "frail sisters"[104] stood no nonsense. When Weston failed to return some of their property, including a pair of canvas trousers, they had him up before the magistrates. Forceful too were the women who set upon Private O'Leary when he attempted to search the Dover Castle beerhouse and "handled him very roughly, took off his cap, and pulled him by the hair of his head.."[105].) When James Elson, another arrival from Ramsgate, applied for the licence of the Star in 1871 Superintendent Parker reported that he had brought four or five prostitutes with him from his previous house. Elson, of course, was having none of this: "two of the four young women he had brought with him were servants and the others went on the stage"[106]. The magistrates made further enquiries and, surprisingly, allowed the transfer to take place. Elson later enjoyed success and some esteem in running the

Paragon Music Hall, as the Star became in the 1870s, and served for a time on the town council.

Compulsory examination under the CD Acts was suspended in 1883 and the legislation itself repealed three years later. Nationally, though largely in consequence of the new licensing rules, "the number of public houses letting out rooms to prostitutes [had] experienced a significant decline...women largely *resorted* to rather than *resided* in these houses"[107]. In Deal prosecutions for harbouring "persons of notoriously bad character" or, as they in time became, "women of bad repute", became infrequent, though landlords of houses like the Norfolk Arms and the Maxton Arms continued to find themselves in trouble at times. In the event both houses survived into the next century, but Ann Macey's Bricklayer's Arms, probably to no one's surprise, did not. The Rector of St George's, leading a delegation to the magistrates in 1875, referred to scenes he had witnessed when visiting the sick which "he would not attempt to describe...it was looked upon as a refuge for loose women and soldiers and as a nuisance to the neighbourhood"[108], and the house closed down that year. The Duke of York, another beerhouse with a reputation for harbouring prostitutes, closed down several years later.

Closures of any kind directly brought about by the actions or censures of the magistrates were however very rare. A formal warning by the bench, following complaints or a particular incident, or at the annual licensing meeting, that the licence might be withdrawn was often sufficient for the landlord to move on or be moved on by the brewers owning the house. On the rare occasions when a licence was withdrawn, the magistrates usually made clear that a fresh application by a new landlord might be successful. A licence to sell beer, wine and spirits at a particular house was a valuable asset in itself and one which brewers were very loath to see forfeited – particularly after 1870, when new licences became very hard to come by. The degree of control and supervision by the brewers increased during the late Victorian period, and we can be sure that behind some of the otherwise unexplained short tenures of tenants noted in Chapter 2 lay quiet warnings from the police or magistrates to the brewers or the landlord (or landlady) that all was not well. In 1895 PC Chapman explained to the county magistrates that complaints were reported to the superintendent or inspector and kept track of by being "put on the slate at the Police Station"[109].

Some houses, like the Maxton Arms and the Lord Nelson (which also survived, rather against the odds, into the twentieth century) gave intermittent trouble over many years under successive landlords. Others led a generally unremarkable existence but plunged into trouble for a time. The Sir Sidney Smith was an old-established house on Beach Street, well-conducted in the 1850s during the tenure of Jonathan Capon, the future Town Sergeant. In 1861 the licence was taken by Joseph Maxted, who had previously run the Sydenham Green on the outskirts of town. Maxted was a boatman and boat owner. He renovated his new house, advertised in the local paper ("made in every way convenient for customers"[110]) and opened at 4.00am to meet the needs of his fellow boatmen. But his troubles began to mount. By 1869 he and his wife were said to be rowing incessantly, and in August he was charged with assault. The following month, at the annual licensing meeting, neighbours complained about "fighting, obscene and filthy language"[111], though the police reckoned that the disturbances tended to be caused by the family of the previous landlord, whose daughter Maria Marsh continued to live in the house ("I don't know in what capacity, although I believe it to be an illegal one"[112] advised Superintendent Parker). Maxted's licence was not renewed.

He then, rather surprisingly, appealed the decision to the East Kent Quarter Sessions at Canterbury. Although Maxted's counsel produced a string of witnesses, including the Chief Officer of the North End Coastguard Station, willing to affirm that the house was well conducted, his client's case was undermined by Maria Marsh who "stated that she had been kept in the Sir Sidney Smith by Maxted and his wife for immoral purposes. Both of them were great drunkards, and they never sat down to a meal without quarrelling"[113]. The keeper of the Royal Adelaide Baths across the road confirmed seeing Marsh entertaining men in a bedroom of the house on many occasions and, for good measure, reported witnessing Maxted lying "heels upwards" in the bar before breakfast. The magistrates had no difficulty in believing counsel for the magistrates that the house was the worst conducted in Deal, and Maxted lost his appeal. The whole episode, according to the *Telegram*, "created a great deal of amusement"[114] in the town, but the Maxteds were in no mood to forgive; four years later Mrs Maxted found herself before the bench for repeatedly abusing a neighbour she considered to be the author of her misfortunes.

The Sir Sidney Smith on Beach Street, taken from an advertisement in 1936 (and now spelt Sydney). When the borough magistrates refused to renew Joseph Maxted's licence in 1869 he took the unusual step of appealing to the county magistrates.

The Deal magistrates were in two minds about granting a licence to a new landlord, and uncertain about the law. Some were content to see the house close. The Mayor, on the other hand, although he "quite approved of withholding the licences of the beer-shops... thought they should not do so with respect to public-houses"[115]. The clerk reckoned it would be unfair to punish the owner (Hills) for the misconduct of their tenant: "they had not taken the licence away from the house but from the tenant...there was no clause in the Act that bore directly upon the question, however, and it was just one of those points where the balance might be either way; but he was inclined to think that the Bench might grant the application"[116]. In the event the magistrates decided not to penalise the brewers. Later in the year the house reopened in the charge of the former boots and ostler of the Black Horse (another Hills house) and it remained open until the Second World War.

The Park Tavern was another example of a house which narrowly escaped closure and in time achieved respectability. In 1858, when still a beerhouse, it survived the efforts of local residents to persuade the magistrates to close it down. Two years later Benjamin Eastes attempted a fresh start, securing a full licence and reopening the house "on strictly respectable principles"[117]. But Eastes soon moved on, and in 1861 came complaints of "fights and rioting, with filthy language [and] indecent scenes constantly occurring....[which] rendered the windows looking into Park Street unfit to be occupied by modest persons"[118]. The magistrates instructed the police to keep a close watch, and Superintendent

Parker soon reported seeing at closing time "14 females in the house, who he knew to be of a disreputable character"[119]. The following year came allegations of half-naked women and soldiers leaving the house on Sunday mornings, and after the Superintendent reported finding "five or six prostitutes and 60 or 70 soldiers in the room where music and dancing was going on"[120] the magistrates refused to renew the licence to the landlord Charles Pryor.

This was the turning point. The magistrates granted a licence to a new landlord two years later ("several of the inhabitants who had previously been instrumental in the licence being suspended, now having supported this application"[121]) and henceforth, particularly during the 55-year tenure of Henry Webb, the house and its neighbours enjoyed an apparently peaceful co-existence.

Enforcing the licensing laws

Public houses were only allowed to sell beer, wine and spirits, for consumption on or off the premises, during times specified in the licence issued by the magistrates. The enforcement of these restrictions took up a huge amount of police time, in Deal as elsewhere. As a historian of the drink trade noted in 1940, "the public-house is the only shop in this country which has to be supervised by the police, and a large part of

Local residents complained repeatedly to the magistrates between 1858 and 1862 about the behaviour of drunken soldiers and "lewd women" at the Park Tavern. The house was lucky to escape closure. But it survived and prospered, not meeting its end until destroyed by a German shell fired from across the Channel in January 1944.

their time has, especially prior to the war, been spent in watching these houses and in dealing with the people who come out of them"[122].

The frequency with which even the most apparently minor transgressions, like the one with which this chapter began, were brought before the magistrates and then punished with a fine seems, at this distance, quite extraordinary. But, in the magistrates' view, being punctilious in refusing to serve beer outside the permitted hours was a mark of a respectable landlord and of a well-run house, as well as a way of preventing drunkenness and bad behaviour. The character and record of the individual landlord or landlady, insofar as these could be ascertained, were therefore important considerations in the granting, renewal or refusal of a licence.

In Georgian Deal a person applying for a licence was expected to be or to become a freeman of the town – paying the required fee for the privilege – but the practice had fallen away by 1830. Until 1828 he was also required, by law, to find a friend or business associate to stand surety. The records for that final year show, unsurprisingly, that many of those entering into a £30 recognizance were boatmen, though bakers, cordwainers, grocers and painters were also well represented. But after 1830 confidence that a landlord would be a fit and proper person depended primarily on the magistrates' judgement in the light of any knowledge they and the police had of the individual in question – it helped of course that most of those wanting to run a public house in the town in the early Victorian period were Deal born and bred. The serving of public notices by those applying for a spirit licence, which included having them fixed to the doors of the parish church courtesy of the sexton, helped improve the chances of the magistrates knowing what they might need to know about particular applicants.

Arrangements were tightened from the 1870s against the backdrop of the doubling in the number of public houses in the town, a steady increase in the proportion of those wishing to become landlords who were not from Deal and the stricter licensing regime put in place by the 1872 Act. Local weekly newspapers now existed to carry public notices, and the magistrates attached increasing importance to written testimonials. Pride of place here must surely go to the coup de théâtre staged in 1896 by the brewers George Beer. Their previous tenant at the Eagle having been convicted of drunkenness, the brewers needed to conjure up an extremely respectable candidate to keep the house open on an interim basis. Enter Alfred Sawford, "for ten years a messenger in the Treasury...He was formerly in the services of the Gladstone family, Mr Gladstone obtaining a post for him in the Treasury, and he produced a very kind personal letter written him by Mrs Gladstone in 1891"[123]. The magistrates saw fit to agree the application. Their task was also relatively straightforward when, as by then was increasingly common, the applicant was a former marine or soldier able to produce their discharge papers and pray-in-aid good conduct badges and, in some cases, campaign medals.

A second important though not infallible safeguard was to take advice from the police. This was relatively straightforward where the individual was a Dealite, possibly wanting to move from another house in the town, or hoping to turn a temporary endorsement of the licence into a full transfer. But the local police were also expected to make enquiries through other forces when, as was increasingly common, the applicant planned to move to Deal from elsewhere in east Kent or beyond. These did not always yield results, of course, and sometimes the applicant had simply to be given the benefit of the doubt. When, for example, the former proprietor of the Gloucester Arms, Bayswater, applied for the licence of the Walmer Castle the magistrates agreed "not knowing anything against Mr Adams"[124].

In the 1860s the magistrates stretched the benefit of the doubt a remarkably long way for some of those wishing to take over the Maxton Arms. It is hard to fathom why in May 1868 they granted a licence to David Simpson, who had failed previously in both Canterbury and Sandwich, and the bench having heard from a superintendent from the county police that Simpson had been convicted on several occasions and was "a constant companion of thieves"[125]. The following year the magistrates initially refused a licence to George Cawthorne, who had previously appeared before them charged with drunkenness "in connection with the female with whom he was living"[126] and with assaulting the police – but then for some reason, relented. Cawthorne left almost immediately, his wife – now identified as such – having attempted to drown herself in a pond in Middle Deal. It is equally hard to understand why the agent for the brewers (the Maxton Brewery in Dover) attempted in 1876 to have James Lines reinstated in the house despite the fact that he had absconded two years before; further police enquiries convinced the magistrates to have none of it. The following week the hapless agent tried again with Charles Hamilton, only for the borough superintendent, consulting his charge book, to remind the magistrates that Hamilton had been up before them several times for various offences. Perhaps the brewers were simply becoming desperate. The licence had been transferred on ten occasions over the previous twenty years, at least three landlords had absconded, and one had died after a drunken fight which led to a visiting horse dealer being tried for manslaughter.

In 1879 the county justices advised magistrates in petty session to be much more vigorous in combating drunkenness through the existing licensing laws: when considering transfers "the terms of the agreement [between the brewer and the tenant] and the character of the transfers [should] be carefully considered...and the Justices should require evidence on oath, whenever it may be deemed necessary"[127]. In late Victorian Deal the local papers began routinely to record details of the previous domicile and employment of applicants for a licence, and police enquires were extended and tightened. When Amos Allen, for example, applied for the licence of the Deal Lugger in 1892 he was nonplussed to learn that the police had made enquiries in Bromley and that the transfer would be refused on the basis of a report from his previous employer.

By Edwardian times it was common for the applicant to be represented by a solicitor if difficulties were expected. When George Skinner sought the licence of the Noah's Ark in 1908 he could see that he had a fight on his hands given his conviction for serving a drunken scissors-grinder lodging at his previous house in Ashford, though he himself had called in the police. His solicitor did him proud, emphasising Skinner's otherwise excellent record, stressing the respectability of his family

The Old Victory, formerly the Clarendon Tap, was a small house in Middle Street. Unlike the nearby Lord Nelson, it seems to have kept in the magistrates' good books and was rarely in the news.

– his father a licensed victualler before him and seven brothers also in the trade – and wearing the magistrates into submission with the help of testimonials from the Superintendent of Police at Ashford, the Ashford Brewery, a local justice of the peace and, for good measure, the surveyor of the Ashford Urban District Council.

Licences had to be renewed every year at the magistrates' general licensing meeting – the "brewster" session. This took place in September (changed in 1903 to February) and publicans were expected to attend. Notwithstanding the urging of county magistrates and others that renewals should not be agreed simply as a matter of form, and that the police should be told to oppose any application from a landlord convicted of an offence the previous year, the Deal bench were usually content just to issue stern words of warning to the previous year's offenders. Until the managed reduction in the number of public houses set in train by legislation in 1904 it was rare for a licence actually to be refused or withheld, either on the grounds of the landlord's inability to run a respectable establishment or because the house was thought to have insufficient trade to justify its continued existence. Sessions were occasionally complicated by a clutch of objections or cases brought by the police, as happened in 1878 following Superintendent Capps' arrival in town, or more frequently by petitions and objections from temperance representatives (to be discussed in the next chapter). But for most landlords in most years the annual licensing meeting posed no threat.

For the town council a useful benefit of the licensing system was the leverage the magistrates could exert to keep landlords up to date in paying their rates. Individual transfers during the year might be refused if the applicant owed rates on their existing house, and the annual licensing meeting gave purchase across the board. In 1867, for example, an otherwise uneventful session was enlivened by the refusal of the magistrates to renew the licence of any house where rates were outstanding "in consequence of which several of them [ie the landlords] were very eager to obtain an interview with Mr John Brown, the rates collector, in an adjoining room"[128]. Brewers, to their considerable irritation, sometimes found themselves expected to pick up the tab for rates left unpaid: "it came very heavy on him [Daniel Hills] when his tenants got into arrears before leaving"[129] complained Hills' agent in 1887 after the rates collector opposed the transfer of one of his houses on the grounds of rate arrears.

But the main cause of friction among magistrates, police and landlords was inevitably the regulation of the hours during which houses could be open to sell beer (and spirits if so licensed). Until 1872 the statutory framework was confusing but relatively permissive. In essence public houses – though not beerhouses – could open from 4.00am until late at night. But they could not do business on a Sunday morning, and from 1854 had to close for several hours during Sunday afternoon (reduced the following year to two hours). The 1872 Licensing Act regularised the position across the country, but still left magistrates some flexibility at the margins. The Deal magistrates took pains that September to ask each landlord in private what hours they would prefer before fixing the evening closing time at 11.30pm on weekdays and 10.00pm on Sundays; beerhouses would have to close 30 minutes earlier in each case. Other than on a Sunday all houses could open at 5.00am. A few weeks later, however, having learnt about the decisions taken in other areas, the publicans petitioned the magistrates to extend Sunday closing until 11.00pm, as had been agreed in Folkestone, arguing that it was "very hard that they should have to close at ten on Sunday evenings, before the arrival of the last train"[130].

The magistrates deferred a decision until the following year, by which time both sides had marshalled their forces. John Outwin led a delegation from the Licensed Victuallers' Protection Society to argue for extended opening until midnight from Monday to Saturday, and to 11.00pm on Sundays, during the four summer months. He was opposed by a delegation led by the former Baptist minister who presented a memorial signed by 99 inhabitants and most of the clergymen of the town. Outwin's claim that reports from across the country "showed that where the restrictions were the severest, there the greatest amount of drunkenness prevailed. It encouraged private tippling..."[131] was rather undermined by the evidence of Superintendent Parker of the borough police – subsequently noted in the Inspector of Constabulary's annual report – that since the new legislation had come into force in Deal "the streets were much quieter, and there were seldom any brawls or rows after twelve o'clock"[132].

In the event the magistrates hedged their bets, agreeing the extended Sunday opening between June and September but leaving the weekday closing time unchanged throughout the year. The town council, for its part, claimed in reporting to the Home Office that "the present hours are quite to the satisfaction of the inhabitants"[133]. They did not think that the restriction on opening hours had led to a significant increase in drinking in unlicensed premises. The council did have a concern, but this was nothing to do with the sale of beer. It was rather that the consumption of spirits in the town had increased in consequence of the number of "grocers' licences" (not at that stage under the control of the magistrates) which permitted the sale of spirits in bottles. In particular, warned the council – giving credence to or simply repeating a common allegation – "women have been known to obtain spirits at the grocers, and have it placed in account as grocery to deceive their husband"[134].

In the event the care the bench took in exercising its discretion under the 1872 Act proved rather a waste of effort; legislation introduced in 1874 by the new Conservative Government put an end to local flexibility. For the *Mercury* it was all to the good that it would no longer be in the power of magistrates "urged on by noisy fanatics" to decide such matters. "The evils of the present system may be illustrated by the case of a borough within our own knowledge wherein the majority of magistrates being Good Templars insist on the closing of public houses an hour earlier than in a contiguous borough where the magistrates are less fanatical"[135]. Legislation fixed the hours for towns and "populous places" at 6am to 11pm from Monday to Saturday and 12.30pm to 2.30pm and 6pm to 10pm on Sundays, Christmas Day and Good Friday. These took effect in Deal in October 1874, and remained unchanged until the First World War.

The county police, for their part, initially attempted to enforce a Saturday 10.00pm closure on Walmer public houses, on the apparently reasonable grounds that the place was neither a town nor populous. For the *Telegram*, enjoying the chance to deplore the practical consequences of a piece of Conservative legislation, this amounted to "treating the public like a parcel of schoolboys, to be hurried neck and heels out of a respectable house at so early an hour as ten, in fact we consider it a downright infringement on our social liberties"[136]. Amid general relief, Walmer was discovered to be a town after all, for this purpose at any rate, by virtue of becoming an Urban Sanitary District under the 1872 Public Health Act.

Most claims in the local press of a widespread disregard of the rules pre-date the 1872 and 1874 Acts. Typical was a letter from "An Unwilling Member of the Night Patrol" who referred to, though did not name, many offending public houses including "the –, which recently drew 300 pints of beer one Sunday morning...I do not know of but one publican in Deal, that pays regard to closing at the proper time, which is Mr -"[137]. A visitor to Deal in 1865 claimed to be able to walk through the town on a Sunday morning and see:

> "the doors of most of them [i.e. public houses] wide open with not even a shutter put up...Let me ask whether a man could get beer between 9 and 10 o'clock on Sunday morning in Ramsgate or even in Walmer, and whether a policeman seeing a man drinking in a public house between 11 and 12 on a Sunday night in any other town than Deal would not summons the landlord for having his house open after the proper hour"[138].

The magistrates agreed that the problem was real enough, and also believed that the tighter supervision exercised by the county force had the effect of encouraging many labourers from nearby villages to visit Deal on Sunday mornings, confident of being able to drink without being disturbed by the borough police. Superintendent Parker observed in his defence that "if spoken to on the subject the landlords shielded themselves from blame on the grounds that the hours for closing were not specified in their licences"[139]. The magistrates, no doubt rather irritated, ordered that all publicans and beerhouse keepers should be warned that serving customers on a Sunday morning would henceforth result in prosecution, and instructed the police to report every instance of non-compliance.

This was not the last time that the magistrates pressed the police to exercise stricter control, but certainly after 1872 – with permitted opening hours now written into each individual licence – landlords could no longer plausibly claim ignorance of the rules. Miscreants still offered a wide range of excuses, however, from an inaccurate clock to the "usual excuse"[140] that the drinkers simply would not leave. (Some publicans, complained Superintendent Parker, "seem to have an idea that it was the duty of the police to clear their houses for them, but such was not the case"[141]). A frequent explanation was that an innocent mistake had been made in ignorance by the wife or daughter of the landlord, the publican himself being at sea or otherwise engaged. But this rarely cut much ice with the bench. Superintendent Capps, who led the borough police from 1877, came down particularly hard on houses serving outside the permitted hours, as both landlords and drinkers found to their cost. As the wife of one of those caught drinking in the Jolly Gardener one Sunday morning sadly commented, as she paid her husband's fine of 10s with costs, "it was a very dear glass of beer for a poor man"[142].

The magistrates did however often show sympathy when cases involved boatmen weary from a night at sea or who had helped launch or heave up a boat in the early morning. When George Norris, landlord of the Deal Lugger, put to sea at 5.00am one Sunday in 1870 he told two boatmen, cold and wet having helped with the launch, to ask his son to serve them "some warm beer with sugar in it"[143]. The bench let this pass with a warning. As they observed after dismissing a similar case two years later, "Deal was an exceptional town and some little allowance was required to be made for its peculiar position and the calling of the boatmen"[144].

The magistrates might also be sympathetic when spirits were sold out of hours for medicinal purposes. The law made no such allowance but, at least according to the magistrates' clerk in 1901, it was "generally winked at in times of illness"[145]. (But not in this case. The Chief Constable had personally ordered the prosecution of the landlord of the Fountain for selling gin on a Sunday morning to a man who claimed it was for his sick wife, and the bench fined him 5s with costs.) The medicinal value of spirits, and the role of public houses in providing it in case of need, was certainly not in question. When, for example, the brewers George Beer applied that year for a spirit licence for the Oak and Ivy beerhouse, one of their arguments was that as matters stood local residents had to go "pretty well a quarter of a mile in case of an emergency, which they knew would occasionally occur"[146].

Cases of out-of-hours drinking often turned on whether the drinkers were lodgers, and thus entitled to take alcoholic refreshment at any time, or were alternatively personal friends of the landlord rather than paying customers. Particularly tricky were cases involving travellers – that is, those who claimed to have travelled a long way and to be in need of refreshment. Public houses had traditionally both the right and the duty to meet such needs, and the 1872 Act was clear that restrictions on opening hours did not apply to bona fide travellers. The 1874 Licensing Act defined this as someone who was at least three miles from their previous lodging. But were soldiers who had walked round from their barracks in Dover entitled to beer on a Sunday morning (probably not,

DRINKING IN DEAL

The Railway Tavern c.1922. Purchased in 1881 by the Deal and Dover Railway Joint Committee, the house drew a lot of trade from those arriving at the station. But the definition of "bona fide travellers" who might reasonably be served out-of-hours was anything but straightforward.

thought the magistrates), or mariners arriving on foot from Sandwich (possibly). A court judgement in 1893 ruled that someone who had travelled primarily to obtain a drink was not "bona fide" for this purpose, but another that the three-mile restriction did not apply to railway travellers.

Come to that, what about boatmen who had been at sea all night, perhaps several miles out – were they automatically bona fide travellers entitled to refreshment? The landlords of the North Star and the Fox, two Beach Street houses, were quick to test this in 1872. The magistrates were equally quick to refuse to give any general sanction, and to fall back instead on the mantra that every case would have to stand on its merits. Nor did they ever seem to have gone as far as the clerk to the Cinque Ports bench, who had no doubt that the landlord of the Stag was not only entitled to serve two returning Walmer boatmen but "from the fact of their exhaustion was bound to supply them"[147]. It was all very confusing.

In practice many suspected infringements of the licensing laws coming to the notice of the police passed off with an informal warning, the proportion depending on the individual officer and the pressure being exerted at the time by his superiors and the magistrates for tight control. The number of actual prosecutions was relatively small – at most 3 or 4 a year – and naturally some landlords brought before the bench considered themselves the victims of extremely bad luck, or worse, in being prosecuted for behaviour that they felt sure went unchecked in other houses. Some infringements were spotted by policemen on their rounds. In other cases, often as a result of complaints and information received, particular houses were surreptitiously watched around closing time or on a Sunday morning. The police sometimes had to judge their moment carefully. When challenged as to why he had waited two minutes having seen two marines enter the Victoria after closing time, PC Chapman patiently explained "you don't want to be in too great a hurry in entering a public-house or you may make a mistake". He clearly thought it was equally obvious why he did not detain some soldiers who left the house shortly before: "it would be of no use to me to catch them outside. I want them in the house"[148].

Police surveillance of public houses might be undertaken in plain clothes – the deployment of police out of uniform had begun in the town in the 1850s and was used regularly after that. With the absorption of Deal within the area policed by the county force came the practice of outright entrapment by plain-clothes officers, sometimes going to what now seems absurdly disproportionate lengths. In 1898, for example, the bench reluctantly convicted Emma Gunner of the Brickmaker's Arms, which at that time had only an off-licence, of serving beer on the premises to PC Simmons who, dressed as a labourer "with a bag on my back"[149], had fabricated an elaborate story of having come down from Margate to look for work laying water pipes. A few years later evidence from a plain-clothes constable who took part in Sunday morning drinking at the Fox led to the conviction of the landlord Henry Wells and to his immediate removal by the brewers (George Beer). Perhaps in this instance there was rather better cause – certainly the police inspector considered it "very unfair to other licensed houses in the vicinity. They are all struggling to get a living, and here is a man doing more on a Sunday morning than plenty take all day during an ordinary week". On the other hand the boatmen caught drinking and fined 5s with costs could see the funny side, and left the court laughing at having been taken in by "this 'ere sham boatman"[150].

Landlords could legitimately open their houses outside of the statutory hours in one of two ways. One was by persuading the magistrates to grant a special early morning licence under the 1872 Act. The first to apply to open at 5.00am was James Redman of the Rose and Crown, on the basis that "his had always been an early house, being used by pilots and boatmen, who landed at all hours of the night"[151]. Redman was successful, and the house retained the right through repeated applications well into the next century in the face of a certain amount of opposition from the police and others. This was a privilege to be jealously defended. In 1884 Charles Redman, the landlord's son, took to the pages of the *Mercury* to deny the allegation made by George Startup of the nearby Pier Hotel, when applying for his own licence, that "men complain that I do not get up for them"[152]. Several other Beach Street houses, in particular the Deal Lugger, the Napier Tavern and the Globe further to the north, also held early morning licences at times. But only the Rose and Crown, which also tended to close early in the evening, was able to sustain permanent legitimate early morning trade.

Several houses away from the seafront were also eager at times for the privilege of opening at 5.00am, variously citing the needs of fish dealers (Providence), gas workers (Hare and Hounds), men unloading coal trucks (Park Tavern, Eagle), brickmakers (Oak and Ivy), agricultural labourers at harvest time (Admiral Keppel) and market gardeners ("who come in very early... and like to take something with them for their luncheon"[153] according to the landlord of the Magnet, adding two years later – though to no avail – that "beer bottled overnight would not be up to much in the morning"[154]). New early morning licences were hard to come by, and agreement to the renewal of an existing licence was certainly not automatic. When John Skinner of the Jolly Gardener was refused a licence for harvest time he was very aggrieved, though chose a rather odd line of attack: "he considered that he had an equal right to the same privilege as the other applicants, his being the only house of the four owned by a local brewer"[155]. By the 1890s early

The Rose and Crown in the 1920s, "Flint" Roberts at the window. For a hundred years or more landlords had opened the house early in the morning to serve boatmen and pilots.

morning licences had to be renewed every quarter, and only four houses seem to have possessed them for an extended period.

Nor did the magistrates, under pressure from temperance spokesmen, care to grant evening extensions other than for genuinely special events – a celebratory dinner, say, or to meet the needs of visitors on regatta day. Giving Edward Erridge of the Crown blanket permission to remain open an extra hour every Wednesday –"for the convenience of a Club soon to be established at his house"[156] – was considered in 1875 to be against the spirit of the new legislation. The bench became irritated in due course at the sheer number of individual applications, which, they grumbled in 1888, "would soon do away with the hour of closing"[157]. By the 1890s their reluctance to agree reasonable applications – as the publicans saw it – became a matter of concern to the town's Licensed Victuallers Association, and applications for two days' late opening to mark the 1902 coronation saw further friction between the publicans and the temperance lobby. By 1906 there was said to be an "unwritten rule"[158] that the bench did not grant extensions beyond 11.30pm on Saturdays. But there was sometimes scope for a certain amount of creativity in applying for special dispensation. When Charles Slawson of the Rose, applying for an "occasional licence" to cater for a Conservative smoking concert at the Oddfellows Hall, was told that such licences could only be granted on the occasion of a ball or dinner, he rather wearily supposed that "they could have a few sandwiches and make it a sort of luncheon"[159]. (But this still did not wash with the magistrates' clerk.)

By this time many brewers were coming down hard on tenants who came to grief with the magistrates, like the tenant of the Eagle quickly removed by George Beer after being convicted of drunkenness in 1896. Indeed as early as 1879 the principal brewers in Kent were warning their tenants that should they be convicted under the Licensing Acts, "and thus endanger the licence of the house"[160], they would have to leave immediately. Both Hills and Thompson seem to have cut their tenants in Deal rather more slack than this, perhaps having some sympathy with their tenants for the sheer number of different ways in which, by Edwardian times, a landlord might fall foul of the law.

The sale of beer to children under 13 was prohibited in 1886, and the age raised to 14 in 1901. In 1907, the landlord of the Brickmaker's Arms came to grief for selling "twopennyworth of ale to one Edward Shelvey, under 14, for consumption off the premises, unsealed and in quantity less than one pint"[161], the bench considering it high time that the police properly tackled the issue in the town as a whole. The following year children under 14 were banned altogether from the bars of licensed premises. In 1907 the magistrates in Deal, Dover and Sandwich had also to wrestle with the complexities of the local practice of "Two of Ale", a variant of the inducement of the "long pull" – giving customers an over-full measure – which so vexed legislators and temperance reformers at the time.

In 1902 magistrates acquired new powers to require structural alterations to licensed premises, and these too were deployed in the town: the following year, for example, the licence of the Rose and Crown was renewed subject to the closing of a side entrance while the Jolly Gardener was required to erect a seven-foot fence around the premises and to keep a side gate locked during prohibited hours "to compel bona fide travellers to go to the front door"[162]. Personal inspections by magistrates of public houses before granting or renewing a licence were nothing new however. In earlier days these were not necessarily pleasant experiences. In 1870, after the magistrates decided to visit the Maxton Arms following the abrupt departure of the landlord, the brewer's agent helpfully advised them "not to inspect the interior unless they wished to be devoured by fleas"[163].

Laws relating to the adulteration of spirits had a long history. Legislation in 1872 included a fearsome list of substances which, if added to an intoxicating liquor (and which by implication sometimes were) would lead to a fine of £20 for a first offence; these included cocculus indicus, chloride of sodium, copperas, opium, Indian Hemp, strychnine, tobacco, darnel seed, extract of logwood, alum and salts of zinc or lead. Most prosecutions in Deal, increasingly common later in the century, seem however to have involved the sale of spirits that were simply below strength. Caught out in 1883, David Almond, landlord of the Rose, pleaded guilty and "said he supposed he had lowered the spirit a little below what he ought to have done"[164]. But the usual excuse was that the stopper had been left off – most probably, according to the landlord, by his wife or daughter – with the liquor losing strength as a result.

The consequences for the licensee could be serious; Mary Baker, for example, lost her tenancy of the Prince Albert in 1903 after adulterating brandy, albeit having performed the same disservice to her whisky some

Disorder, Regulation and Bad Behaviour

years earlier. The very respectable Elizabeth Denne at the Star and Garter, however, escaped with a very light penalty when she was caught by Superintendent Chaney's agent selling woefully under strength brandy in 1899. Her solicitor explained to the bench that although she was "experienced in mixing and breaking down spirits, and always did it herself, and test[ed] them with a hydrometer and proper appliances"[165], she had unfortunately been called away at a crucial point in the process. (Not that spirits were the only substance capable of being mistreated: in 1876 the landlord of the Forester was fined the large sum of £5 for possessing tobacco adulterated with licorice.)

Elizabeth Denne's embarrassment before of the magistrates must however have been as nothing compared to her husband Charles' excruciating experience some 20 years before in front of a panel of Parliamentary Commissioners. He had been summoned to explain, in detail, the basis on which he had charged the Liberal by-election candidate the very handsome sum of £84 for the hire of rooms over a period of 11 days, and an equally impressive £80.11s. for the supply of refreshments. Denne had a very difficult time of it, stumbled over his answers, and found himself summoned back for a second grilling the following week. But, as will be seen, he at least had the consolation of knowing that he was only one among an astonishingly large number of Deal publicans suspected of blatant wrong-doing.

Bad behaviour at election time

At this distance the framework of supervision and control within which public houses in late Victorian and Edwardian Deal had to operate can seem absurdly intrusive and hair-splitting, and excessively time-

The magistrates punished Elizabeth Denne's slip in 1899 in serving under-strength brandy with the lightest possible sentence. She had run the house for 35 years, at first alongside her husband and from 1881 as licensee, without previous complaint. The Star and Garter was by now almost the only house in Deal not brewery-owned.

consuming for both the police and magistrates. In sharp contrast, the extent to which the flagrant bad behaviour of the town's publicans at election time was tolerated by almost everyone as part and parcel of a hugely enjoyable and, for many, blissfully profitable election contest, seems quite extraordinary. Matters finally came to a head in 1880, when the behaviour of the people of Deal made national news and helped change public policy. Both Deal and Walmer were then included within the parliamentary borough of Sandwich and it may have been a small crumb of comfort – though in fact very few in Deal seemed to have felt the least bit ashamed or apologetic – that the name most often associated with the unfolding scandal was not that of the town itself but of the constituency.

In October 1880 Richard Emmerson, clerk to the Sandwich magistrates, recalled to the election commissioners (almost fondly, it would seem) that:

> "years ago it was customary, before the Reform Bill, that every freeman when he went to the booth should receive a pound. That was the old system, and to a certain extent, of course, that has never been eradicated from their [i.e. the electors'] minds. Elections have become so pure now... There used to be a dinner, which was given by the members after the result had been announced, and you either had your dinner or you had your pound, if you chose to demand it, in the hall, when you went to tender your vote. That was the old system"[166].

Emmerson was certainly right that the expectations of electors in the borough were more or less unchanged. But notwithstanding legislation in 1857 to prevent corrupt practices and the introduction of the secret ballot in 1872, he was wildly off the mark in reckoning that elections in the constituency had become "pure". There was no doubt that electoral corruption had in fact "long and extensively prevailed"[167], and certainly Sandwich was known to be a very expensive constituency to fight and to "nurse". During the 1874 general election, for example (according to the *Telegram*) two men had been seen visiting houses "of poorer classes of voters and handing them in some instances a sovereign, half sovereign, and occasionally more if asked for" to vote for the Conservative candidate[168].

Henry Brassey, Liberal MP from 1866, had been notably lavish in his disbursements, both at and between elections. In 1877 he had given £489 to various institutions and causes in Sandwich, Deal and Walmer, followed by £551 in 1878, £573 in 1879 and £315 in the early months of 1880. He seems to have done so in part to support his fellow Liberal, Edward Knatchbull-Hugessen – Sandwich being a double-member constituency created under the 1832 Reform Act – and at the general election of 1874 both had been returned with handsome majorities. By 1880 their position was considered unassailable. The Conservatives did not run a candidate at the March general election, leaving Sandwich one of the country's 43 uncontested constituencies. But even without what would no doubt have been prodigious expenditure in the borough, the election as a whole was reckoned to have been the most costly ever to have been held in Britain.

The absence of a contest in Deal was a grave disappointment to many. In the words of the biographer of Alderman Edmund Brown, the Liberal agent, the townspeople "looked back on a long series of contests, animating, exciting and entirely profitable... When after six dull years, this crowded hour of glorious life, this festival, should have come again, and there came instead the lenten fare of an unopposed return, the popular resentment was not loud (it could not judiciously be called that) but deep. But Fate had still one golden day for Deal"[169]. It dawned in March when Knatchbull-Hugessen was elevated to the peerage – where, rather ungratefully one might have thought, he took the Conservative whip – and a by-election was called for 18 May. This time a contest was assured.

The Conservative candidate, Crompton Roberts, was quick to arrive in the town, followed soon after by his agent Edwin Hughes. The Liberals were slower off the mark but after some hesitation Sir Julian Goldsmid, previously MP for Rochester, threw his hat in the ring. Soon the town was festooned with flags – blue for the Liberals, red for the Conservatives – flying from an enormous number of poles, and with banners hung across the main streets. Public houses were plastered inside and out with posters and bills. It was clear that large amounts of money were being spent in every possible way. The *Telegram* marvelled at "how remarkably friendly the Conservative upper crust have become with the working men and boatmen, when other than at election times they would pass by without even a sign of recognition"[170], while the *Mercury* in turn rejoiced that "not only was the Conservative feeling apparent in the nautical element, but the public houses, with comparatively few exceptions, gave expression to it"[171]. When the votes were counted 1,445 were found to have been cast for Crompton Roberts, and 705 for Sir Julian Goldsmid. In Deal itself Roberts was only slightly less successful, having triumphed by 700 votes to 419.

After the party came what proved to be an extended hangover. The following month the town learned that Goldsmid had lodged a petition to have the result of the election overturned. Such petitions were no longer decided by the House of Commons but were entrusted to the High Court, with trials taking place in the constituency concerned. Justices Lush and Manisty duly held court in Sandwich Town Hall that August, took evidence, and reached the striking conclusion that "the election forming the subject of this inquiry was distinguished from all others with which they had had to deal in that the more important provisions of the Corrupt Practices Prevention Act seemed to have been totally disregarded from first to last"[172]. The election was therefore declared void.

The *Mercury* greeted the decision with disgust, considering that Crompton Roberts had been unseated entirely thanks to the actions of his agent in distributing bribes and taking pleasure in the fact that Sir Julian Goldsmid was also criticised and would have to meet his share of the costs. According to the paper the indignation of the town was overwhelmingly aimed at Goldsmid for bringing the petition in the first place – particularly from those who had not in consequence received the second instalment of their bribe. As Edwin Hughes, Crompton's agent, later observed, "a petitioner becomes so unpopular, and is always looked upon as a tale-bearer"[173].

The next step was the appointment, following an address by both Houses of Parliament under reforms introduced in 1852, of a commission "to inquire into the existence of corrupt practices" in the parliamentary borough. The hearings began in Deal Town Hall on 5 October, the borough police being reinforced by a detachment of county police as an (evidently unnecessary) precaution. In all the three commissioners sat for 21 days, took evidence both in London and Deal, examined 1,171 witnesses and asked no fewer than 22,533 questions. The transcript of the hearings, which appeared alongside the commissioners' report in February 1881, exposed in extraordinary detail the networks of bribery that had operated during the election and the very large number of people

An 1887 *Vanity Fair* cartoon of Sir Julian Goldsmid. He claimed after contesting the by-election in 1880 that, having realised how much illegal expenditure would be entailed, he considered withdrawing from the race and "only did not do so because I did not wish to incur the reproach of the Liberal party by giving up the seat".

involved. Most witnesses were candid about their own involvement, and named those from whom they had received money. There was a good reason for this: the commissioners were able to issue certificates granting immunity from prosecution to those it considered had made a full disclosure. As the Attorney General subsequently observed, it was noticeable that "on the trial of the petition all the voters bribed denied their guilt, but before the commissioners many of them admitted it and got their certificates"[174].

The commissioners confirmed that there had indeed been, throughout the borough, "not only indirect bribery of various kinds...but direct bribery, the most extensive and systematic"[175]. A notable example of the former was the paying of money out of all proportion to the services rendered to men who happened to be electors for the manufacture of flags, for the supply of rope, for the hire, purchase and erection of flag poles, and (as a precaution should "the elaborate structures of poles and cordage... be injured by the opponents or perhaps by the friends of their constructors") for guarding the flags once in place. The Conservatives alone spent £796 on flags, poles, rosettes and associated business. The 1852 legislation limiting extravagances was simply ignored, and "the two sides vied with each other in extravagant and still more extravagant display of colours, till fairly tired out in the rivalry"[176].

The Conservatives had set up their central committee room in the Royal Hotel, the Liberals in the nearby Star and Garter. But this was just the start; the renting of committee rooms in as many other public houses and beerhouses as possible, and with it the right to display bills and posters, was central to both parties' campaign strategies from the outset. The Conservatives started earlier, and established a clear lead. Samuel Olds, a town councillor and local coach and fly proprietor, visited a large number of houses on 4 May carrying with him a heavy bag of gold, and within a short time rooms had been taken in 71 of the 105 houses in Deal and Walmer. The going rate was £5, irrespective of the size of the room or the house. John Outwin, landlord of the Clarendon Hotel, did his best to secure rooms for the Liberals, their final tally, at the same rate, being 27 houses. Rare indeed were landlords like William Redman at the White Horse, who declined to let a room to the Conservatives since "his principles were on the other side"[177], or George Hurst at the Victoria who agreed to let the Liberals have use of a room but did not want payment – the petition trial judges, understandably, found his approach rather refreshing.

John Outwin in later life, at the door of his Beach Street newsagent shop. At the start of the 1880 by-election campaign Outwin, then landlord of the Clarendon Hotel, hired committee rooms in a large number of public houses on behalf of the Liberal candidate, but could not match the Conservatives' tally.

It is not all that surprising that most landlords had no hesitation in accepting an offer: £5 was the equivalent of four months' rent, or more, for most houses. The only regrets voiced to the commissioners were that elections were not very much more frequent. Nor were some landlords at all embarrassed about taking money from both sides. John Skinner (Jolly Gardener), Charles Smith (Lord Warden), Patrick Harris (Norfolk Arms) and William Appleton (Three Compasses) let rooms to both parties, while Charles Redman (Rose and Crown) confirmed that he had in effect let the outside of his house to the Conservatives for the posting of bills, and the inside to the Liberals. Small wonder that he cheerfully admitted to the commissioners that "I should like to see another election next week"[178].

The Conservative agents insisted that they did not enquire about voting intentions when hiring rooms, and claimed that – although the majority of landlords clearly favoured the Conservatives – a good many of those they paid for a room had voted Liberal. According to Samuel Olds, the chief importance of the investment lay in the opportunities this gave for secure bill-posting:

> "My object was...to go round fast and secure a great many public-houses.... It is important in many ways. With regard to the bill posting, the literature put upon the walls is pulled down and covered up with other bills, whereas in the windows there is no difficulty in hanging the bills, and you can send the boys and they can replace the bills two or three times a day if you feel inclined. Many of the voters living in outlying districts perhaps do not attend any meetings, but they see the bills at night when they come in to have a quiet pint, and they can read the bills much better than when they are posted in the streets. In the windows they are not subject to being covered up or being torn up and made use of"[179].

But the commissioners, like the petition trial judges before them, simply did not believe that this had been the main motivation. Closer to the mark was Edwin Hughes' acknowledgement that the publicans were a significant body of voters in the constituency (roughly 10% of the electorate) and that "they always have a dozen or so, more or less, in their parlour company, and that is of itself an influence no doubt"[180]. Many of the committee rooms were scarcely used, or not used at all, and the commissioners were quite clear that "the taking of a considerable portion of these public-houses was a colourable means of gaining the votes of their proprietors and of influencing the voters"[181].

Then there were the hundreds of instances of bribes being offered and readily accepted. Here the going rate was £3 with, in many cases, a further £2 to follow if the election went the right way. The list painstakingly compiled by the commissioners showed that 21 Deal landlords accepted bribes to induce them to vote Conservative or to cement them in that intention, and another eight took money from the Liberals. Nine landlords themselves bribed small groups of electors using gold supplied by Samuel Olds, while eight bribed for the Liberals. Prominent among the former were Henry Spears (Antwerp), Edward Rea (Fountain), and Robert Wilds (North Star), while among the latter were Thomas Finnis (Fox) and William Riley (Prince Albert). Stephen Pritchard (Eagle) found himself admonished for neither distributing his full allocation nor returning the residue ("bribery is bad enough, but theft is worse"[182]).

A particular feature of the campaign was the effort both sides made to induce boatmen to return home to vote, or to persuade them not to set out, and to recompense them handsomely for their trouble. George Ralph (Lifeboat), for example, gave £32 of the £90 he received from John Outwin to the crew of the lugger *Albert Victor* (which, as it happens, they did not consider enough). He explained to the commissioners that he "learnt as the lugger ...was down at Portland, and when I heard the election was coming off, I wrote and telegraphed to several places to get them home. They were people who used my house, and four out of the six had got votes, and I know they had been in the Liberal interest..."[183].

The commissioners' tone throughout was one of sustained if sometimes ironic disbelief. They found that there had been relatively little treating, "the superior attraction of direct bribery [having] rendered the seductions of treating superfluous"[184]. Many thousands of pounds had been spent by both sides. In practice "the actual distribution of money was effected without difficulty. We could find only one or two instances in which a bribe was refused"[185]. They concluded that there had been, rather, "a general expectation that money would be distributed in bribery, [and an] almost universal willingness and even avidity to accept bribes"[186]. The commissioners found that 128 people were guilty of acts of bribery and 1,005 – that is, half the electorate – of accepting bribes; and 27 of those bribed had been paid by both sides. (The tally in

Canterbury during the 1880 general election, in contrast, had been a paltry 61 bribers and 180 bribees.) The secret ballot had made no difference: "on the contrary, while it enabled many voters to take bribes on both sides, it did not, as far as we could ascertain, render a single person unwilling to bribe for fear of bribing in vain"[187]. As for the licensed premises, the engagement of committee rooms, while not in itself illegal, "afforded a method by which the keeper of the public-houses and his clientèle were very easily bribed"[188].

The question then became what punishment would be meted out to the eight witnesses from Deal and Walmer to whom the commissioners had refused to grant certificates of immunity. In July they were brought to trial at the Maidstone Assizes. Among their number were Samuel Olds, the Deal landlords Edward Rea and Henry Spears and the coxswain of Walmer lifeboat and landlord of the Stag, John Mackins. According to the *Mercury* no fewer than 450 witnesses from Deal, Walmer and Sandwich received subpoenas to appear; "the exodus of so many witnesses, chiefly working men, will be attended with no little inconvenience to employers of labour... especially...the brewery firms of Walmer and Deal, many of whose workmen are among the witnesses required"[189]. All eight were found guilty. Olds, and the Liberal James Barber Edwards, were sentenced in December to six months imprisonment. The remaining six received two or three months each. When sent down from Holloway to serve their terms in Canterbury Gaol they arrived handcuffed and in prison dress as though, as the *Mercury* put it, "they were felons of the deepest dye"[190].

Virtually none of those appearing before the commissioners had shown remorse. Thomas Theobald, storekeeper at Hills brewery, probably came as close as any ("I could not resist the temptation; it was offered to me, and I took it"[191]). It is also unclear what the clergy, councillors and other leading figures in the town made of the commissioners' tart observation as to "the total absence of a voice to warn, condemn, or denounce"[192] while the election was in progress. Nor had the police or magistrates been at all in evidence. But any inclination there might have been to repent was now buried beneath a torrent of sympathy for the "crushing sentences" the court had imposed, and for the treatment the prisoners then received. On 4 December the morning service at St George's "was conducted throughout without music or singing of any kind"[193]. For Reverend Bruce Payne, writing as a lifelong Liberal to the liberal *Daily News*, the sentences inflicted were "purely vindictive" and offended against "the first principle of a Liberal creed...to do justly and to love mercy"[194]. His colleague the Rector of Mongeham could not understand why "men of high moral and social standing should be degraded to the level of ordinary prison punishment, while offenders such as Charles Stewart Parnell were privileged as first-class misdemeanants"[195]. According to the *Kentish Observer* "never perhaps has more universal sympathy been expressed for any victims of the law than now finds utterance on all sides for the sufferers by the unjustly harsh bribery sentences...the columns of the London press have teemed with indignant letters"[196].

Sympathy for the prisoners was certainly widespread, and a committee was quickly formed in London to petition the Home Secretary for their early release. On 17 December the *Mercury* reported that "the memorial is being very extensively signed by all classes. On the Stock Exchange, and Lloyd's, in Mincing Lane, and the Corn and Hop Exchanges, the petition is being very generally subscribed to, and the solicitors throughout the kingdom are getting up a special petition of their own..."[197]. In all, petitions to the Home Secretary for the remission of sentences were signed by no fewer that 43,841 people, including 32 peers, 75 MPs, 313 bankers, 1,113 clergymen and 3,587 solicitors. But Sir William Harcourt, responding on Christmas Eve, flatly refused to intervene and, with the exception of one early release on the grounds of serious ill-health, the sentences ran their course. In March Spears, Rea and Benjamin Wood arrived back in Deal to be greeted by cheering crowds, flags and gunfire. When Mackins arrived home the same day "flags flew from the masts of all the boats at Walmer, and cannon gave [him] a thundering salute as he reached the portals of his house, the Stag Inn"[198]. Olds returned, more quietly, three months later.

Less cheering for the people of Deal was the fact that the commission's costs, which came to £2,139, were chargeable to the parliamentary borough, and that the town was obliged to levy a special rate of ten pence in the pound to meet its share. Furthermore, as expected, the constituency was disenfranchised. But here the town was more fortunate than it probably deserved. Legislation in 1884 abolished two-member constituencies and in 1885 established the principle that constituencies should have roughly the same number of electors. As a result Deal found itself part of the new constituency of St Augustine's, which took in a large part of rural east Kent and had an electorate of more than

The coxswains of the Deal, Walmer and Kingsdown lifeboats. John Mackins (right), coxswain of the Walmer lifeboat and landlord of the Stag, spent three months in gaol for his part in bribing electors in the Conservative interest during the 1880 by-election.

12,000. It was the massive extension of the franchise that took place across the country which, as much as anything else, helped bring about a rapid decline in electoral corruption. But the 1883 Corrupt Practices Act, which limited expenditure and sharply increased the penalties that could be imposed on candidates and their agents, also played an important part. Its provisions included banning committee rooms on licensed premises, a ban extended the following year to cover municipal elections. The 1880 by-election proved to be a last hurrah of blatant electoral corruption in Deal and the last joyous windfall of gold sovereigns to be showered down upon the publicans, their customers and their friends.

1. *Mercury* 10 May 1890
2. J. Laker, *History of Deal* (2nd ed, Deal 1921) p 239
3. B. Collins, *Discovering Deal (Historic Guide)* (Deal, 1969) p 56
4. *Municipal Corporations in England and Wales: Report on the Borough of Deal* (1834) para 10
5. F. Lansberry (ed), *Government and Politics in Kent, 1640–1914* (Woodbridge, 2001) p 64
6. *Message to the Inhabitants of the Town and Borough of Deal*, 11 December 1835 in Kent History and Library Centre (KHLC), De/AC3
7. J. Redlich and F. Hirst, *Local Govern-*

ment in England (London, 1903) Vol 1 p 410
8. ibid
9 *Municipal Corporations ...* (1834) para 25
10. T. Skyrme, *History of the Justice of the Peace:* Vol 1 *England to 1689* p 276
11. *Mercury* 13 November 1875
12. S. Pritchard, *The History of Deal* (Deal, 1864) p 298
13. E. C. Pain, *The Last of Our Luggers and the Men Who Sailed Them* (Deal, 1929) p 145
14. *Mercury* 27 March 1897
15. Ibid
16. J. Greenaway, *Drink and British Politics since 1830: A Study in Policy-Making* (Basingstoke, 2003) p 77
17. Quoted in G. B. Wilson, *Alcohol and the Nation* (London 1940) p 112
18. *Municipal Corporations...* (1834) para 36
19. J. Hart "Reform of the Borough Police 1835–1856", *English Historical Review* Vol LXX (1955) p 422
20. Obituary in *Mercury* 28 November 1868
21. Letter to the *Telegram* 10 September 1864
22. W. H. Gillespie, "An Old Force", *The Police Journal,* Vol 27 (1954) p 307
23. R. Ingleton, *Policing Kent: Guarding the Garden of England, 1800–2000* (Chichester, 2002) p 43
24. *Report of the Inspector of Constabulary,* 1866
25. *Vote and petition against Sir George Grey Police Bill,* Assembly Minutes 20 February 1856 in KHLC, De/AC4
26. *Report of the Inspector of Constabulary,* 1876
27. Gillespie p 313
28. *Fifteenth Report of the Inspectors of Prisons I – Home District,* 1850 p 96
29. Ibid
30. Ibid
31. C. Steedman, *Policing the Victorian Community: the Formation of English Provincial Police Forces, 1856–80* (London, 1984) p 151
32. *Act for...Paving, Cleansing, Lighting and Watching the Highways etc of the Town and Borough of Deal* (1791) para 29
33. *Rules and Regulations for the Deal Municipal Police* (Deal, 1836)
34. *Mercury* 8 December 1877
35. *Telegram* 18, 25 June 1881
36. *Telegram* 6 February 1875
37. *Mercury* 19 February 1876
38. Watch committee minutes 2 November 1876 in KHLC, De/ACC1
39. *Mercury* 1 June 1878
40. *Telegram* 26 November 1881
41. *Mercury* 6 April 1889
42. *Mercury* 11 March 1893
43. *Mercury* 13 November 1875
44. Gillespie p 315
45. *Telegram* 14 March 1860
46. Gillespie p 313
47. Ingleton p 44
48. Gillespie p 317
49. *Mercury* 13 April 1901
50. *Telegram* 9 April 1881
51. *Mercury* 10 April 1886
52. *Mercury* 13 September 1890
53. *Mercury* 6 April 1907
54. J. Bower, "Deal and the Deal Boatmen c 1840 – c 1880", Unpublished PhD thesis, University of Kent, 1990 p 303
55. *Telegram* 10 October 1863
56. *Telegram* 9 July 1870
57. *Mercury* 7 December 1895

58. *Mercury* 20 March 1869
59. *Telegram* 26 September 1863
60. *Telegram* 15 January 1887
61. *Telegram* 10 April 1886
62. *Telegram* 5 July 1873
63. *Mercury* 5 July 1873
64. M. Winstanley, "The Rural Publican and His Business in East Kent before 1914", in *Oral History* Vol 4 (1976) p 71
65. *Telegram* 16 September 1871
66. *Mercury* 22 September 1865
67. *Mercury* 22 June 1878
68. *Telegram* 5 April 1873
69. *Mercury* 29 June 1895
70. *Mercury* 8 July 1876
71. *Mercury* 8 February 1908
72. *Mercury* 21 June 1902
73. *Mercury* 18 April 1908
74. *Telegram* 14 June 1862
75. *Telegram* 19 July 1862
76. C. A. Conley, *The Unwritten Law: Criminal Justice in Victorian Kent* (Oxford, 2003) p 154
77. Quoted E. M. Spiers, *The Army and Society, 1815–1914* (London, 1980) p 73
78. *Telegram* 20 September 1862
79. *Mercury* 8 September 1877
80. *Mercury* 19 January 1895
81. *Telegram* 22 July 1882
82. *Mercury* 29 August 1891
83. *Mercury* 8 November 1902
84. Conley, p 10; Lansberry p 238
85. *Telegram* 7 March 1868
86. *Mercury* 15 October 1892
87. *Telegram* 5 January 1867
88. *Telegram* 16 September 1865
89. *Telegram* 16 June 1888
90. *Telegram* 24 June 1865
91. *Mercury* 22 November 1884
92. Ibid
93. *Telegram* 24 January 1885
94. *Mercury* 1 August 1868
95. *Mercury* 5 August 1871
96. *An Act for Regulating the Sale of Intoxicating Liquors* (1872) s14
97. C. Lee, *Policing Prostitution 1856 – 1886: Deviance, Surveillance and Morality* (London, 2013) p 146
98. *Telegram* 27 September 1873
99. Parliamentary Papers 1881 (351) VIII pp 271–2
100. *Mercury* 29 February 1868
101. *Mercury* 30 May 1908
102. Conley p 166
103. *Telegram* 9 November 1861
104. *Mercury* 23 June 1866
105. *Telegram* 22 December 1858
106. *Mercury* 14 January 1871
107. J. Walkowitz, *Prostitution and Victorian Society: Women, Class and the State* (Cambridge, 1980) p 24
108. *Telegram* 18 September 1875
109. *Mercury* 19 October 1895
110. *Telegram* 21 December 1861
111. *Telegram* 18 September 1869
112. *Mercury* 18 September 1869
113. *Telegram* 23 October 1869
114. Ibid
115. *Mercury* 5 March 1870
116. Ibid
117. *Telegram* 18 January 1860
118. *Telegram* 17 August 1861
119. *Telegram* 31 August 1861
120. *Telegram* 13 September 1862
121. *Telegram* 10 September 1864
122. Wilson p 183
123. *Mercury* 12 September 1896
124. *Mercury* 1 January 1876
125. *Mercury* 16 May 1868
126. *Telegram* 6 March 1869
127. *Mercury* 5 July 1879
128. *Mercury* 14 September 1867
129. *Mercury* 21 May 1887
130. *Mercury* 2 November 1872

131. *Mercury* 13 September 1873
132. Ibid
133. *Reports from the Borough Authorities in England and Wales Relating to the Licensing Act* 1872
134. Ibid
135. *Mercury* 2 May 1874
136. *Telegram* 17 October 1874
137. *Telegram* 8 February 1860
138. *Telegram* 30 September 1865
139. *Telegram* 25 September 1869
140. *Telegram* 30 March 1871
141. *Mercury* 14 October 1871
142. *Telegram* 26 November 1881
143. *Mercury* 15 January 1870
144. *Telegram* 13 January 1872
145. *Mercury* 6 July 1901
146. *Mercury* 28 September 1901
147. *Mercury* 19 February 1887
148. *Mercury* 11 March 1893
149. *Mercury* 5 November 1898
150. *Mercury* 23 May 1903
151. *Telegram* 7 September 1872
152. *Mercury* 6 December 1884
153. *Mercury* 24 April 1897
154. *Mercury* 4 March 1899
155. *Telegram* 17 July 1880
156. *Telegram* 27 February 1875
157. *Mercury* 28 January 1888
158. *Mercury* 24 October 1906
159. *Mercury* 20 May 1905
160. *Telegram* 27 September 1879
161. *Mercury* 1 June 1907
162. *Mercury* 14 March 1903
163. *Telegram* 2 July 1870
164. *Mercury* 31 March 1883
165. *Mercury* 25 February 1899
166. *Report of the Commissioners into the Existence of Corrupt Practices in the Borough of Sandwich* (1861) p 25
167. *Report...* p xv
168. *Telegram* 4 April 1874
169. E.B.V. Christian, *Edmund Brown: A Deal Worthy* (Canterbury, 1931) p 79
170. *Telegram* 15 May 1880
171. *Mercury* 22 May 1880
172. *The Times* 11 August 1880
173. *Report...* p 339
174. *The Times* 14 July 1881
175. *Report...* p viii
176. *Report...* p viii
177. *Mercury* 7 August 1880
178. *Report...* p 134
179. *Report...* pp 43–4
180. *Report...* p 340
181. *Report...* p vii
182. *Report...* p 135
183. *Report...* p 136
184. *Report...* p x
185. *Report...* p ix
186. *Report...* p xv
187. Ibid
188. Ibid
189. *Mercury* 16 July 1881
190. *Mercury* 10 December 1881
191. *Report...* p 134
192. *Report...* p xv
193. *Telegram* 10 December 1881
194. *Mercury* 24 December 1881
195. *Telegram* 10 December 1881
196. Quoted in *Mercury* 17 December 1881
197. *Mercury* 17 December 1881
198. *Mercury* 4 March 1882

Chapter 5

Controversies and Closures

The temperance movement in Deal
The Deal borough magistrates, in their capacity as the licensing authority for the town, had to operate against the backdrop of an increasingly active and vocal temperance movement. A large number of Deal men, and some women, made very regular use of the public houses and beerhouses that filled the town. But others strongly disapproved of anything beyond the very moderate consumption of alcoholic drink, and some of any such consumption at all. They did not enter drinking places, unless perhaps to attend a respectable function at one of the larger inns, and they wanted to see far fewer of them. Deal was a very long way from the nineteenth-century temperance heartlands in the north of England, and in Brian Harrison's assessment "the temperance movement never prospered in the Home Counties, centres of malt and hop production"[1]. So it is all the more striking, and testimony to the strength of one of the largest popular movements the country has ever known, that virtually every significant manifestation of the temperance movement in Victorian and Edwardian England can be found to have existed or made an impact in the town.

The first temperance society in England was formed in 1830. For many years the focus of the movement was on proselytising and on "moral suasion" – reforming the drunkard through exhortation, example and help – rather than on seeking changes in the licensing laws, though this took place alongside a lively debate about the relationship between a more (or less) free market in the sale of beer and the drinking habits of the nation. In 1832 came the start of what would become a national teetotal movement, and for the rest of the century and beyond the distinction between those advocating total abstinence and those prepared to accept and sometimes partake in moderate drinking marked the central divide within the wider temperance movement. This was compounded by acute disagreements over both strategy and tactics. Was banning the sale of alcoholic drink, as the prohibitionist United Kingdom Alliance strenuously argued, the only sure path to the radical transformation reformers hoped to achieve? Were less fundamental reforms to the licensing system worth pursuing in themselves, or were they compromising and possibly harmful distractions? The temperance movement as a whole was energetic and highly visible, but it was also fragmented and fractious.

There was certainly temperance work in Deal well before 1858, but it is only with the launch that year of the *Telegram* that the activities of temperance men and women in the town can be followed. It is clear that, as in many other parts of the country, levels of activity and commitment ebbed and flowed a great deal during this period. A summer programme of talks and lectures, usually delivered by peripatetic speakers from national organisations, could spark a good deal of interest. But it was hard for local organisers to sustain enthusiasm and activity thereafter.

In 1860 a programme of outdoor temperance lectures attracted large crowds. "Mr Black", reported the *Telegram* approvingly, "does not talk the elegancies that some folk do – so elegant and beautiful that you wonder what is meant – but plain, good, hard, common sense; facts logically applied..."[2]. The existing Deal Temperance Society was reorganised, and in September sponsored three set piece events at the town hall featuring a speaker from the United Kingdom Alliance. Next month saw the opening of a reading room and a small temperance hotel in Lower Street, and over the next few years the *Telegram* carried regular reports of speeches, meetings and tea parties, not to mention the formation of a marching band of boys aged 8 to 14 to parade the town before lectures. Public meetings usually concluded with an invitation to sign the temperance pledge. In February 1865 the secretary reported that 176 pledges had been signed over the previous fifteen months (though "would that we could say, they had all stood firm to their pledge"[3]). Yet by 1869 an anonymous writer to the *Telegram* was complaining that "when [he] left Deal some years ago there was an active Temperance Society...but now there seems to be nothing of the sort in the place, and so far as I can judge, little or no interest in Temperance Causes"[4]. The following year the *Mercury*, reporting on a meeting at the Wesleyan school rooms, referred to the Deal Temperance Society as having been "dormant for a long time"[5].

From the 1870s onwards the efforts of national temperance campaigners focused increasingly on Parliament. Legislation to introduce a "local veto" (enabling ratepayers to vote on whether to ban the sale of alcoholic drinks in an area) and, from 1879, resolutions in favour of a "local option" (broader local control) were regularly put forward by prohibitionists, and just as regularly defeated. Local temperance commitment became more institutionalised and tended to find expression in membership of one or more branches of national temperance organisations and networks, many of them church based. At the same time as men and women in Deal were joining friendly, fraternal and recreational societies in increasing numbers, and usually holding their meetings in public houses, a significant minority of their fellow citizens were banding together in temperance organisations which viewed the impact and even the very existence of public houses with strong disapproval.

An early example of the impact of national and indeed international temperance organisations came in 1872 with the founding of a local lodge of the Independent Order of Good Templars. This was christened Goodwin Light. The Good Templars were a quasi-masonic teetotal fraternal organisation, uncompromisingly zealous for the cause, which had been founded in America in the 1850s. It reached England in 1868 and six years later could claim over 200,000 adult and juvenile members, though this had fallen to about half that number twenty years later. The organisation was unusual in admitting women on a equal basis with men and allowing them to stand for all elected offices. The founding of the Deal lodge, which began life in the Primitive Methodist chapel in Park Street, was part of the initial surge of interest in the new movement. Although it drew much of its support from non-conformists in the town, notwithstanding the dislike of some co-religionists elsewhere for the Order's "ritual, regalia, titles and degrees"[6], it also received strong backing from the town's Church of England clergy. Reverend Bruce Payne, Vicar of St George's, took the chair at many early meetings. Indeed it is noticeable that across the spectrum of temperance activity clergymen of all dominations had little hesitation in sharing temperance platforms and addressing meetings organised by other churches and societies.

The lodge quickly got into its stride. It soon boasted a Good Templar choir, and a junior lodge (the Hope of Deal). The adult lodge met in a variety of church premises over the years, including the Wesleyan mission rooms in Duke Street, with larger gatherings and entertainments often taking place in the Anglican Blackburn Hall in Middle Street. In 1909, still going strong, it was reckoned by the *Mercury* to be the oldest temperance society in Deal. The nearby Walmer Castle lodge, founded in 1874 and meeting in the Foresters Hall in Walmer (even though this adjoined the Lord Warden public house), had similar staying power. In Deal itself a second lodge, the True Unity, also existed for many years, apparently based around members of St Andrew's church. Good Templar numbers fluctuated a good deal, partly because subscriptions were relatively expensive but also because membership of the various lodges included many marines quartered in the Walmer barracks for limited periods of time. In 1882 the Goodwin Light lodge was said to have gained 132 members over the previous year but to have lost 141 in "removals", in most cases marines posted elsewhere.

The second American-inspired temperance initiative to have a powerful impact in Deal was the "Blue Ribbon" Gospel Temperance movement. This reached England in 1877. Between 1880 and 1885, in the words of a modern historian of temperance, "England was gripped by a temperance fever that rose and fell continuously like the temperature of a sick man"[7]. The fever took hold in Deal in 1882. In June 250 people were said to have adopted the Blue Ribbon at a crowded meeting at St George's Hall. The following month Edward Chitty, helping to organise the campaign in Deal, estimated that between 600 and 700 people had now done so. This meant, he calculated rather optimistically, that with the inclusion of Band of Hope children one in eight of the people of Deal were now committed to total abstinence. In November came a week-long gospel temperance mission. The momentum was sustained the following year, with a further round of public meetings, missions, pledge taking and ribbon wearing, enlivened by temperance choirs, bands and amateur theatricals. In July the "Blue Ribbon Army" helped inspire and organise a temperance demonstration in the grounds of Walmer Castle which attracted an estimated 5,000 people.

Inevitably this rush of activity made existing temperance activities seem rather old hat. In May a report in the *Mercury* contrasted a rather uninspiring Good Templar meeting ("less pregnant with the quality that seizes the attention of the people"[8]) with the enthusiasm generated at a recent Blue Ribbon gathering. It also considered that being able to don the Blue Ribbon for a fixed period of time was a much more attractive and realistic proposition than signing the Good Templar teetotal pledge, since the latter was expected to last a lifetime. Although by the end of the decade a million men and women in England had donned the ribbon, the wind behind the Blue Ribbon's sails dropped almost as quickly as it had risen. The habit of ribbon wearing, be it blue, white or, in the case of Roman Catholic teetotallers, green, would be a feature of the temperance movement for many years to come, but many individuals inevitably slipped away from their good intentions. On the other hand, many of those inspired by the gospel temperance message continued within the temperance movement by making a home within one of the church-based temperance societies which were now coming increasingly to the fore.

Reverend Bruce Payne served for 18 years as a curate in Walmer and for 45 years as Vicar of St George's, Deal. A lifelong Liberal and temperance advocate, he established a branch of the Church of England Temperance Society in his parish in 1879.

By the end of the century the Church of England Temperance Society (CETS) was the largest temperance society in England. It welcomed not only teetotallers but also, in a separate "general section", non-teetotal supporters of temperance – "all those who were interested in the suppression of intemperance", as the *Mercury* put it[9]. Teetotallers provided much of the local drive but nationally the CETS's moderate and incremental approach to reform put it at odds with the prohibitionists. A parish branch could only be established with the permission of the incumbent, who was then expected to be president of the branch and to control its work. In Deal Reverend Bruce Payne, Vicar of St George's between 1868 and 1913, was an energetic promoter of temperance throughout his long incumbency. In 1879 he established a branch of CETS in his parish, which took the name of Deal Temperance Union in the early years. His colleagues in the two other Deal parishes, St Andrew's and St Leonard's, followed suit in due course, and in 1888 came the formation of the Deal, Walmer and District Branch to coordinate the work of five local parish branches.

In 1880 the St George's branch had 60 members, "mostly teetotal". This had risen to 166 three years later, though 28 teetotal members were said to have violated their pledge and only four had returned. The level of activity dipped later in the decade, but the three Deal parish branches of CETS seem to have sustained their vitality and carried this through into the Edwardian era. In October 1913 Deal hosted the annual festival of the CETS in the Canterbury and Rochester dioceses in the course of which the Archbishop, Randall Davidson, preached in St Leonard's church. By now a practical manifestation of CETS's philosophy had become visible in the town through the work of their Police Court Missions, from whose activities the modern probationary service would emerge. As the *Mercury* saw it "the advice and help that an experienced police court missionary can give is often just what is needed to give a first offender a new start in the right direction"[10]. The men and women the missionaries tried to help were often before the bench for drunkenness, and in Deal as elsewhere the helpers acquired quasi-official status in the eyes of the magistrates. In April 1912 for example, George Friend, a labourer, was bound over under the supervision of the police court missionary "a condition of the recognizance (added at Mr Kilford's suggestion) being that during this period he abstain from all intoxicating liquor"[11]. In 1913 there were nine such "missionaries" in Kent working in 33 different courts, and were reported to have helped in 9,397 cases.

The most notable temperance advocate and recruiter for CETS was Reverend T Stanley Treanor, Chaplain to the Missions to Seamen for Deal and the Downs between 1878 and 1910. Treanor's three books, in particular *Heroes of the Goodwin Sands* published in 1892, did a great deal to burnish the reputation of the Deal, Walmer and Kingsdown boatmen, in particular those who crewed the three lifeboats. When visiting merchant ships at anchor in the Downs – with, on occasion, a publican among those taking an oar – Treanor would arrive well equipped with temperance pledge cards . He appears to have been relatively tolerant about drinking on land but for those at sea, as the *Dover Express* explained in 1887, "he recommends the pledge of total abstinence because many of the men tell him they cannot take the drink without going too far and taking too much"[12]. In memoires published in 1894 he explained that "whatever may be our opinions as to the right of every man to the temperate and legitimate use of God's creations, there can be no doubt that total abstinence is the safest and easiest cause for sailors, and therefore the wisest"[13]. The fact that Reverend Treanor, "a staunch Irish Protestant"[14], was a committed Unionist and Reverend Payne a lifelong Liberal may have been a factor in the existence of a separate CETS Missions to Seamen Branch in the town.

In Deal as elsewhere teetotal non-conformists were at the heart of the temperance movement. Ministers in the town were almost invariably strong advocates. Although there does not seem to have been a specifically Wesleyan adult temperance society (nationally the church was relatively late in throwing its hat in the ring) a branch of the Baptist Total Abstinence Society was founded around 1884 and Wesleyans, Baptists and Congregationalists alike put a great deal of energy into running their respective Bands of Hope, as indeed did the Anglican churches. These taught the temperance way of life to children aged 6 to 12 and required them to sign a teetotal pledge. The first Band of Hope had been

"Enrolling temperance seamen after a service on board the Lunesdale", from Reverend T Stanley Treanor's memoir *Log of a Sky Pilot* (1894). Treanor was the long-serving chaplain to the local branch of the Missions to Seamen.

formed in Leeds in 1847, and a Band existed in Deal from the 1850s. The role that women were permitted to play in organising Bands of Hope varied considerably, and irritation at the limitations imposed on their activities may have been one reason for the founding later in the century of the Deal and Walmer Branch of the (largely non-conformist) British Women's Temperance Association. This too organised meetings, sponsored missions and held events in the grounds of Walmer Castle.

Reverend James Bartram was minister of the Congregational church between 1856 and 1879 and, like very many of his non-conformist colleagues, a teetotal temperance campaigner.

By now, in the words of Lilian Shiman, the temperance movement had created "so many different social and cultural groups that it was possible for many members to lead a well-rounded life with only minimal contact with the drinking world"[15]. For teetotal men and women in Deal this included the option from 1887 of joining a branch ("tent") of the country's largest temperance friendly society, the Independent Order of Rechabites (Salford Unity). This took its name from an Old Testament nomadic tribe forbidden to drink wine, and was formed in 1835 "of none but abstainers and their wives"; part of its mission was "to counteract the baneful influence arising from clubs held at public-houses"[16]. Membership fell to only 6,000 in the mid 1850s but then recovered, and the founding in Deal of the Basil Wilberforce tent 30 years later was part of a national surge in membership which took the Order from 60,000 members in 1885 to 142,000 in 1897. As the secretary of the Deal tent explained, the order "shielded [the working men] in a double sense, from drink and its many temptations, and helping them in sickness"[17]. Strongly supported by the clergy in Deal, by 1899 the tent had 118 adult members with another 114 young members of the juvenile tent. Although smaller than the local Foresters' court and Oddfellows' lodge

– whose members no doubt included some temperance supporters – the Rechabite tent was particularly active in recruiting new members after the passing of the 1911 National Insurance Act. By this time the Order had become the country's third largest friendly society.

Temperance groups in Deal and Walmer were eager to help spread the message among soldiers and marines stationed in the Walmer barracks. In 1865 124 of the 176 new pledges gathered by the Deal Temperance Society came from men at the depot, and in the 1880s the Goodwin Light lodge of the Good Templars initially recruited strongly among the marines. A separate Royal Naval Temperance Society had existed there for a time and men in the barracks increasingly looked to their own temperance groups: these included a branch of the National Temperance League founded in 1872, the "Per Mare, Per Terram" Good Templar lodge from 1886, and a Royal Marine Depot Band of Hope. In 1890 Samuel Jefferson, baptist and manager of the Beach House Temperance Hotel, claimed to have seen a remarkable change over the previous 25 years:

> "at that time he only knew one total abstainer there, now they could be counted by hundreds, and he very much questioned if there was a room in the barracks without one of its inmates being a pledged abstainer"[18].

Five years later the *Mercury*, in commenting on the work at the depot of the Royal Naval Temperance Society, reported that over 1,200 pledges had been taken over the past year. It is wise not to take such exuberant claims at face value, but there is no reason to doubt that the general reduction in drunkenness and rowdy behaviour noticeable among regular soldiers in late Victorian and Edwardian times was also felt among the marines stationed in Walmer. For Reverend Payne, looking back in 1908, the exemplary conduct of the Royal Marines stood in sharp contrast to the behaviour of the line regiments and depot battalions of the army that had once been stationed there: "anybody was thought good enough to be a soldier then...the men were a wild and reckless lot"[19]. The turning point, he considered – speaking with some authority, having served as curate in Walmer between 1850 and 1868 – had been the Crimean War.

Given the plethora of temperance groups and activities in Deal, it is not surprising that efforts were periodically made to re-create a single over-arching temperance body in the town. The *Telegram* had hoped that the foundation of the St George's CETS branch in 1879 might have been the catalyst for such a body, under Reverend Payne's leadership, but it was not until 1892 that a non-denominational Deal and Walmer Temperance Union was formed, on the initiative of the Wesleyan minister. In the event, this proved to be another membership organisation for "bona fide abstainers". By 1897 the DWTU boasted around 200 members paying subscriptions of 1d a month, a programme of monthly meetings, the delivery of free copies of the Temperance Mirror and a choir which took part in mass temperance rallies at Crystal Palace. But it was hard to make further headway. In 1907 a speaker at a Wesleyan temperance festival in Sandwich admitted that "...in Deal membership was stationary, as every church had its own society, and there were in addition Rechabites and Juvenile Templars, there was not much room for great advance"[20].

What was the impact of all this effort? It is clear that committed total abstainers remained a small though not insignificant minority in the town and that, vocal though they were, they did not come close to capturing the centre ground of local opinion. Non-abstaining temperance supporters – a much more fluid category – were more numerous, though this might amount to little more than a disapproval of persistent or excessive drinking. These men and women certainly played a successful part in promoting the view that Deal was very much at fault in having so many public houses, and that something should be done about this. Less tangibly, the temperance movement in Deal also reflected and contributed to the decline in drunkenness and disorder that, difficult though this is to quantify, was such a marked feature of late Victorian society. But although temperance missions and other forms of outreach (to use the modern term) continued in the town throughout this period, the pioneering days of a movement eager to "reclaim the drunkard" had long since passed. Temperance activity in Deal certainly did not buck the trend evident across the country for the movement to become "less concerned with rescuing the intemperate than with providing fellowship for members of the temperance community"[21].

Some temperance campaigners set great store by promoting, as an alternative to the public house, refreshment rooms and other premises at which only tea, coffee and soft drinks were offered. This approach had some impact in Deal, though it is also true that attaching the temperance label could also be useful in attracting a particular class of custom. The area in and around Lower Street, from 1879 the High Street, usually had at least one temperance establishment. Mr Jordan's Temperance Refreshment Room, for example, was the venue in 1873 for an entertainment provided by the Goodwin Light lodge of Good Templars for their visiting colleagues from the Channel Fleet lodge, and 1880 saw the establishment at 37 Middle Street and St George's Passage (connecting Middle and High Street) of the Central Coffee Tavern, Temperance Hotel and Dining Rooms. This seems to have prospered for a good many years. A second coffee house (the Victoria) and temperance hotel operated in the High Street in the 1890s, but the largest establishment, which featured prominently in countless photographs taken from the pier, was the Beach House Temperance Hotel. This opened in 1890, "A Want Supplied" according to the *Mercury*[22]. Sold for £2,000 three years later, the hotel continued as a temperance establishment and was enlarged in 1895. Later in the decade came an attempt by the Temperance Union to bring about the building of a dedicated Temperance Hall, but this came to nothing.

There was also a growing market for aerated and other soft drinks. In 1858 a manufactory near the Swan was said to be able to produce "250 dozens of Soda water, etc, per day"[23], but the most successful enterprises were those of Stephen Parker in Upper Deal and J W Court & Son of Walmer. In 1890 the latter's products included "soda water, seltzer, potash, lithia, lemonade, ginger beer, ginger ale, zolakone, and the old-fashioned home-brewed ginger beer, for which latter, especially, an enormous demand exists"[24]. Of less enduring popularity, it seems, was the Blue Ribbon Army Brain Restorative, advertised in the *Telegram* in 1883, by which "the craving for stimulants is abated"[25]. The market for non-alcoholic drinks was not of course exclusively a temperance one. "Here are gallons of lemonade – is lemonade a very favourite drink in your house?" asked the barrister scrutinising Charles Denne's accounts during the 1880 by-election inquiry. Denne agreed that it was. But there was also the matter of "two bottles of lemonade and brandy, one bottle of lemonade, one bottle of lemonade and brandy, three bottles of lemonade and whisky, two bottles of lemonade and brandy, and so on – that is all upon 8th May. Who had this great mass of lemonade? – I could not say"[26].

For most temperance activists in Deal the promotion of "dry" venues and non-alcoholic drinks was much less important than throwing their weight behind national campaigns for legal restrictions on the sale of alcoholic drink. This activity usually took the form of large public meetings featuring a speaker from one of the main national organisations, and the passing of resolutions. Speakers from the Central Association for Stopping the Sale of Intoxicating Liquors on Sunday were regular visitors, and campaigning on the "Sunday Closing question" continued over many years. Typical was a gathering at the Wesleyan Hall in October 1901, "the whole of the Free Church ministers in the town being on the platform"[27]. The visiting speaker had arrived in Deal on a Thursday early-closing afternoon "and found there was no business doing. Shops were closed everywhere, but the public houses were open, and raking in the money. This was again repeated every Sunday"[28]. The arrival in Deal of the Salvation Army gave local campaigning on this issue extra impetus, while the founding of groups of the charmingly named Pleasant Sunday Afternoon (PSA) Brotherhood in 1905 and, separately it seems, of the Sisterhood, extended the opportunities available for wholesome Sunday activities. But most of those taking part were no doubt passing the time between morning and evening worship rather than choosing a sober afternoon of good fellowship as an alternative to Sunday lunchtime or evening conviviality in a public house.

The second national campaign supported locally over many years was the repeated efforts, driven primarily by the prohibitionist United Kingdom Alliance, to secure the passage of "local veto" or "local option" legislation. Liberal Governments repeatedly failed to fulfil teetotallers' hopes but the defeat in the 1895 election of the Liberal Party as a whole and of temperance candidates in particular was a huge disappointment. Legislation introduced by the Conservative Government in 1904 to manage a phased reduction in the numbers of public houses with compensation to the brewers was not at all what the teetotallers wanted to see, and the possibility of radical temperance reform did not come again until 1908 with the introduction of licensing legislation by the Liberal Government. This held out the prospect of reducing the number of houses by a third or more over a 14-year period with only modest and diminishing levels of compensation, and sparked some of the largest public demonstrations the country had ever witnessed. As will be seen, Deal temperance organisations pitched in with a will, as did their opponents.

Taking a lead from Brian Harrison, historians have tended to see the 1870s as a significant turning point in the history of the British temperance movement, with the focus increasingly on licensing issues both national and local. Local campaigners increasingly targeted their elected representatives and, in particular, the licensing magistrates. Successes were eagerly seized upon, and trumpeted in the temperance press as examples of what might be achieved. In September 1878 the editor of the *Church Temperance Chronicle*, writing to the *Mercury*, ascribed the decision of the Dover bench to refuse a new licence and withhold four existing ones to pressure from the local branches of the Church of England Temperance Society, and in July 1882 rumours circulated that at least 19 public houses had been closed in Folkestone as a result of the pressure exerted on the magistrates by the Blue Ribbon movement.

As will be discussed, temperance spokesmen in Deal also made frequent attempts, through petitions and delegations, to influence the decisions taken by the magistrates on the licensing of public houses in the town. But they did not have the field to themselves. The publicans, feeling under increasing pressure from a number of directions, made repeated and eventually successful efforts to combine more effectively to shore up their defences and to build support among the opinion formers and decision makers in the town.

The Beach House Temperance Hotel enjoyed a commanding position facing the South Esplanade (and largely concealing the Port Arms immediately behind). "The entire arrangement of the place eminently fits it for the purposes of a first-class private hotel", enthused a town guide in 1890.

The licensed victuallers mobilise

The most notable attempt by Deal publicans in the eighteenth century to take a united stand occurred in 1776 when 30 houses took down their signs in an attempt to avoid the billeting of troops. Legal advice to the corporation had previously been that although licensees could not be required to open their houses, a refusal to do so might reasonably be taken into account when licences came up for renewal by the magistrates, and the revolt seems to have been fairly short lived. In Victorian times the first coordinated action visible through the local press came in response to national rather than local developments. In 1860 13 publicans assembled in the Walmer Castle, at a meeting convened by the London-based Licensed Victuallers Protection Society, to condemn the intention of Gladstone, then Chancellor of the Exchequer, to throw open the sale of wine by retail and to enable spirits merchants to sell liquor in single bottles. The chairman of the meeting, Alexander Bird, himself a wholesale wine and spirits merchant, admitted that "the trade in Deal was already nearly thrown open [but nonetheless] there could be no doubt but if the measure now before the country were passed into law the interests of licensed victuallers would be materially affected"[29]. In the event, although Gladstone had his way, the publicans seem to have gone about their business much as before.

Indeed it is noticeable that, in contrast to many other parts of the country, the debate about the sale and consumption of beer, wine and spirits did not generate much heat in Deal in the 1860s. Temperance activity in the town had reached a low ebb by the end of the decade, and although Deal, Walmer and Sandwich had a combined population of some 12,000 it was thought to be one of the few districts in England without a permanent licensed victuallers' association. A meeting in the Black Horse in September 1868 tried to put this right, but was poorly attended despite the draw of an address by the secretary of the Manchester-based Provincial Licensed Victuallers Defence League. At a meeting in Sandwich the following week local publicans resolved to work with others to "resist the threats from Teetotallers and Sabatarians"[30], and urged their colleagues to probe candidates' views on local veto legislation before casting their votes in the forthcoming general election. But although groups of publicans combined to make their views known to the magistrates and others over the next few years this continued to be on an ad hoc basis.

Controversies and Closures

The catalyst for the first really determined attempt to set up a permanent trade protection body was the 1872 Licensing Act, and in particular the element of discretion this gave to the magistrates – short lived though it turned out to be – in deciding when public houses might open. In June 1873 a meeting of publicans at the Crown (supported this time by the Licensed Victuallers Protection Society of London) agreed to constitute a Deal, Walmer and Sandwich Licensed Victuallers' Protection Society. Captain Gillow, a Sandwich brewer, became chairman, and the indefatigable John Outwin was appointed secretary. The new society quickly recruited 50 members and in September, as recounted in Chapter 4, had some success in persuading the magistrates to sanction extended opening hours. The *Telegram* reckoned that the new body would become "one of the most prosperous trade organisations in the County...we wish [it] the most hearty and unqualified success"[31].

This prediction proved rather wide of the mark. Although the society remained active until at least 1879 it seems to have faded away not long afterwards. The absence of a functioning trade association in the 1880s is a puzzle. Although the next attempt by central government at major licensing reform did not come until 1888, temperance reformers were making palpable headway in persuading legislators that action was needed. It may be that the shenanigans that took place during and after the 1880 by-election campaign, which led to Outwin becoming persona non grata among some of his erstwhile colleagues, badly affected the willingness of publicans in Deal to band together, and that the efforts of the temperance movement to influence the magistrates, though persistent, were not sufficiently alarming to trigger an organised response. An attempt in 1888 to set up a body "upon the lines of the Ramsgate society[32]" came to nothing, and it was not until April 1893 that 16 publicans meeting at the Rose successfully re-constituted a trade protection society for the district: the Deal, Walmer and Sandwich Licensed Victuallers Protection Association (hereafter LVA).

The publicans now had every reason to stand up and be counted. The Liberals, successful in the 1892 general election, had included prohibition in their "Newcastle programme" the previous year, and the founding of the non-denominational Deal and Walmer Temperance Union (DWTU) showed the determination of the local temperance movement to speak with a stronger voice. Two months before the publicans gathered at the Rose the new Government had sponsored a bill to give local ratepayers in a parish, ward or borough, if they could secure a two-thirds majority in a referendum, the right to prohibit most liquor licences after three years. The bill was withdrawn later in the year, but it was clear that further attempts would be made. In February 1894 the DWTU convened a large public meeting at the Oddfellows Hall in King Street addressed by a speaker from the United Kingdom Alliance. The publicans came out in force, and after a representative of the National Trade Defence Fund secured a hearing and was loudly cheered the evening descended into pandemonium. The chairman closed the meeting and brought down the curtain on the stage, whereupon Councillor Soloman mounted a chair and a "volley of hands" supported a resolution "that in the opinion of this meeting, the Liquor Traffic Control Bill is contrary to temperance, justice, and democracy"[33].

In 1895, after a further unsuccessful attempt to introduce licensing legislation, the Liberal Party suffered a heavy election defeat. But the LVA could certainly not assume that all danger had now passed, and the following year – though rather late in the day in comparison to many other Kent associations – it decided to federate to the National Trade Defence Fund. This had been created by the brewers in 1888 to defend "the general interests of the whole trade in and out of Parliament"[34] and, in David Gutzke's assessment "[its] subsequent power derived primarily from one change, the handful of full-time, salaried agents appointed in 1891"[35]. It was one of these agents, John Dunne from the Eastern Counties District, who followed up a barnstorming speech at the LVA's annual dinner in March 1896 by securing a unanimous vote in favour of federation at a special meeting in June.

Within two years the LVA had some 90 members of all kinds, rising in 1901 to 86 trade members – roughly half of all licence holders in the district – and 25 honorary members. In 1873 beerhouse keepers had been refused membership of the Licensed Victuallers' Protection Society, but times had changed. Now the priority was for the whole trade, widely defined, to try to pull together. Beerhouse keepers, wine and spirits merchants and soda water manufacturers were all welcomed as full or honorary members, and the public support and sponsorship of local brewers was gratefully received. Membership cost several shillings, though exactly how much is unclear; in 1905 the *Mercury* reported that members had decided not to increase the rates to 7s 6d for full licence holders and 5s for beerhouse keepers. Committee meetings and general meetings open to all members were held every month, the venue rotating between different public houses as decided by ballot.

The LVA was not simply a campaigning body. Three months after its launch a solicitor acting on behalf of the Association successfully prosecuted a general dealer for threatening the landlord of the Clifton; this was one of six prosecutions brought by the LVA in its first year. According to John Outwin, apparently back in the fold though no longer in the trade, "the few prosecutions that had taken place had done much to relieve [publicans] of the trouble in checking, and ridding them of, characters who created disturbances in the various public-houses, which at one time was a perfect nuisance. In every case they had carried their point..."[36]. The prosecution of those threatening or assaulting a publican would remain an important function of the LVA. It was no doubt "a great help to them in the conduct of their houses, especially when these unruly people saw some of their pals sent to prison"[37] but it was also useful, as they squared up to the challenge posed by temperance campaigners, in promoting themselves as responsible traders determined to run orderly houses.

No less important than the prosecution of aggressive troublemakers, and the occasional defence of landlords brought before the bench for licensing infringements, was the continuing dialogue with the regulating and enforcement bodies on a wide range of practical issues, from the basis on which occasional licences should be granted to the way in which new legislation would be interpreted in the borough. How, for instance, would new rules restricting children from entering public houses to buy beer for their parents work when "very few houses...were so situated as to enable them to set aside a bar exclusively for the off trade?"[38]. The protection of members' interests might sometimes entail taking on other groups of tradesmen. In 1912, for example, the LVA threatened to prosecute oilmen and general dealers who used beer and mineral water bottles for "Paraffin, Disinfectants and other obnoxious liquids"[39], thus reducing the flow of returns to the brewers, or rendering the bottles unusable, and in either case leaving publicans out of pocket. The Association also tried to clamp down on what it considered unfair competition between different houses. Members were not allowed to sell beer below an agreed minimum price – some argued that this should be extended to spirits – and the committee did its best to support irate law-abiding publicans by working with the police and the inspector of weights and measures to stamp out the illegal local practice of "Two of Ale" (a means of giving favoured customers an over-full measure).

Members embraced the social benefits of LVA membership with gusto. Annual dinners were lavish and well attended, and one can only admire the professional stamina displayed during the annual summer charabanc outings. In 1902, for example, the publicans set out at 9 o'clock in two brakes and proceeded:

> "via Sandwich (where members residing there joined them), Eastry, Fredville Park, Nonington, Barham, Chillenden, Kingston, and Woolwich, to Bridge, which was reached at 1.30. A sumptuous dinner was provided by Mr Swail, of the White Horse, which was a credit to the host, and gave the utmost satisfaction. The party stayed at Bridge for about two hours, and then proceeded to Littlebourne, Ickham, Wickham, and thence to Wingham, where, at the Dog, a capital meat tea, provided by Mr Smith, awaited them. After a stay of three hours the homeward journey was commenced, the route followed being by way of Staple, Eastry, Sandwich, and the party arrived at Deal at 10.45, having spent a most enjoyable day".[40]

Enjoyment was in shorter supply in the years that followed. Nationally, in David Gutzke's words, "the rank and file became increasingly dissatisfied and apathetic. Deteriorating markets, heavier taxes imposed by both parties, shortages of funds and three consecutive [Conservative] defeats at general elections demoralised many in the trade"[41]. Locally the LVA had its work cut out supporting members as closures under the 1904 Licensing Act began to take effect, in mobilising local opposition to the 1908 Licensing Bill and in coping with a range of legislative and budgetary changes with threatening implications for public houses. In 1910 the retiring chairman admitted that the Association had been going through the most troublesome period in its history, and that at one point the committee had been obliged to convene at his house (the New Plough) every day for a fortnight. Membership had fallen to 71 by 1909 and plunged to 50 a year later. This seems to have reflected not only the closure of 24 houses in the district since the 1904 Act came into force but also some dissatisfaction with the committee's handling of affairs. The LVA's finances were now badly stretched, and annual meetings and summer outings less well attended. But the Association managed to weather the storm. By 1912, although another 12 houses in the district had closed, membership had bounced back to 74 and the budget was in a healthy state once again. The following year the number had risen to 82 with, according to the chairman, "the greater part of licence holders, with few exceptions, members"[42].

Publicans in Victorian and Edwardian Deal could draw comfort from the fact that neither of the two main local papers, although sympathetic to the efforts of temperance societies to encourage sobriety, had any truck with prohibitionist arguments. The *Mercury* was launched in 1865 with the promise of being "Independent in Politics, Impartial in Reports". But when sold in 1875 it was as "the only Conservative organ in the locality" and in 1881 the mast-head said simply "Conservative in Politics". An editorial that year praised the cause of temperance as "at once beneficial and requisite", particularly if promoted by "concurrent agitation for Thrift, Food reform and other preventative measures"[43]. The "weeding out" by the magistrates of superfluous licences was also a worthy cause, but pursuit of prohibition through the local veto was a hopeless one; "to prohibit the sale of liquor because some persons took too much would" – as William Wheelhouse MP, Conservative Member for Leeds, had argued – "be just as reasonable as to stop the sale of Sheffield knives because outrages and murders were committed with them"[44].

The Liberal-supporting *Telegram* had been launched seven years before the *Mercury*, but closed in 1888. It too remained firmly opposed to temperance reform through restrictive legislation. In 1864, commenting on an attempt to introduce a Sunday Beer Bill, it warned that "legislation is but a lazy expedient for the extirpation of a personal and social evil...More advantages and less restraint is the prescription which best suits our views of [the working man's] condition. Offer him something better than public-houses and the excitement of drink, and in the course of time he will follow the example of the middle classes and forsake them"[45]. It had no more sympathy than the *Mercury* for the repeated attempts orchestrated by the United Kingdom Alliance to introduce a Local Veto Bill, which "in some mysterious way always seems to be before the country and before Parliament"[46], and considered the effort involved wasteful and misguided: "persuasion is invariably a more powerful weapon than force"[47]. "Let us", it proclaimed in 1880:

"promote working men's clubs and mechanics institutes, together with well managed music halls and places of public entertainment; let us aid the movement for establishing coffee taverns; let us endeavour to improve the dwellings of the working classes, and thus we shall greatly aid the cause of temperance without any desperate repressive measures"[48].

A cause much closer to the *Telegram*'s heart was the reputation of the town's two Liberal MPs. The double-member constituency of Sandwich, created in 1832, usually returned Whig and then Liberal members, and the 1868 general election saw the victory under Liberal colours of Henry Brassey and Edward Knatchbull-Hugessen. Brassey, the second son of the railway constructor Thomas Brassey and son-in-law of George Stevenson, was careful to keep a low profile on the drink question (or, as the *Mercury* saw it, to manifest "a supreme indifference"[49]). This was not an option for his colleague Knatchbull-Hugessen. Second son of the county grandee Sir Edward Hugessen and married to a niece of Jane Austen, he was for a time a rising star in the party.

First elected in 1857, Knatchbull-Hugessen served as a junior minister under both Palmerston and Russell and became Under Secretary for the Home Department following Gladstone's election victory in 1868. According to Brian Harrison the Home Secretary, Henry Bruce, "had not wanted this jealous and ambitious man in the post, and felt that he had "no personal weight" and very little information"[50]. It was probably a relief to both when Knatchbull-Hugessen was moved sideways in January 1871 to become Under Secretary for the Colonies. It certainly suited Knatchbull-Hugessen to distance himself from the legislation introduced by Bruce in April – though this never came to a vote – which seemed to open the way to the suppression of large numbers of existing on-licences. He was nonetheless a member of a government which the following year secured the passage of legislation which restricted opening hours, gave magistrates more power and increased the penalties for wrong doing. What view would Deal licensed victuallers take of all this?

In 1868 Knatchbull-Hugessen had been warmly praised by George Candalet of the Provincial Licensed Victuallers Defence League. Now, four years later and to the *Telegram*'s great satisfaction, Candelet joined with John Homer of the London licensed victuallers to laud Knatchbull-Hugessen once again as a great friend of trade; during the last session of

Studio portrait of Edward Hugessen Knatchbull-Hugessen in the 1860s. Liberal MP for Sandwich between 1857 and 1880, he joined the Conservatives on becoming Lord Brabourne in 1880. Four years later he edited the first collection of Jane Austen's letters.

Parliament he had "supported our interests and sought to render us no unimportant service...he was in communication throughout with representatives of the Wholesale and Retail trade, and exerted himself to meet their wishes by making the Bill less stringent"[51].

When Homer repeated his gratitude the following year at the launch of the LVA the *Mercury* was beside itself with indignation at what it perceived as political whitewashing. The truth, as it saw things, was that "Mr Hugessen never lifted up his voice against the [1871] legislation in or out of Parliament". As for the LVA, "Liberal policy has unfortunately rendered such an organisation absolutely essential to the safety of the interests of a large and deserving class"[52]. The *Telegram* of course would have none of it: "the Brewers and Licensed Victuallers are too wise not to perceive the folly of identifying their cause with one particular party or the other, and the wisdom of emphatically supporting those Liberals who have supported their interests in Parliament"[53]. The *Mercury* returned to the charge later in the year after Knatchbull-Hugessen had laid the foundation stone of a new Temperance Hall in Ashford, observing caustically that "it is indeed difficult to play at the same time the rôle of the publican and teetotaller – even for the most Procrustean of aspiring statesmen"[54].

But in reality the licensed victuallers had good reason to be satisfied, and teetotallers correspondingly little to hope for. In November 1874, having held his seat at the general election earlier in the year, Knatchbull-Hugessen chaired a banquet of licensed victuallers in London in honour of his friend George Candalet, and was rebuked by the Good Templars for his pains. The following year Sir Wilfrid Lawson, the prohibitionists' leading Parliamentary spokesmen, was reported to have told a meeting organised by the United Kingdom Alliance in Sandwich that Knatchbull-Hugessen had "helped to break up a Government of which he himself was a member, and overthrow the party to which he belonged"[55]. A strained exchange of letters then followed between the two Liberal MPs. Two months later, speaking during the second reading of Lawson's next futile attempt to secure the passage of local option legislation, Knatchbull-Hugessen explained his views in detail. He also recalled, with amusement but clearly also with lingering irritation, how, when Sir Wilfrid visited Sandwich:

> "...some of his [Knatchbull-Hugessen's] constituents were so much astonished at the appearance of his hon friend that they proposed to give him practical proof that there was cold water as well as beer in Sandwich, by subjecting him to summary immersion in the canal...he had fortunately escaped to an adjoining school-room in which he held a quiet meeting, and revenged himself by a hostile criticism of his Parliamentary conduct upon the question now before the House..."[56].

There matters seem to have rested. Both Knatchbull-Hugessen and Brassey were returned unopposed at the 1880 general election – whereupon, as has been seen, the former accepted a peerage and precipitated a by-election. Teetotallers in the town could expect little from the Liberal candidate. In 1875 Sir Julian Goldsmid had urged prohibitionists not to waste the House of Commons' time any further in bringing forward legislation, and the *Mercury* reported with satisfaction that on election day "a strong portion of the temperance party remained unpolled up to a late hour of the afternoon. This was, we believe, owing to the inability of the candidate to satisfy the cause on the local option question"[57]. As we have seen, lavish disbursements of Conservative and Liberal gold did the trick in satisfying large numbers of electors but led to the disenfranchisement of the constituency.

By the time the franchise was restored to the voters of Deal, Sandwich

The Conservative Aretas Akers-Douglas in 1910. Between 1885 and 1911 he represented the St Augustine constituency, which included Deal. As Home Secretary between 1902 and 1905 he took though the 1904 Licensing Act which largely satisfied the brewers and outraged the temperance lobby.

and Walmer their place was now within the new and much larger single-member constituency of St Augustine's. Between 1885 and 1911 the seat was securely held by the Conservative Aretas Akers-Douglas. As Chief Whip between 1885 and 1895, and later as Home Secretary responsible for taking through the 1904 Licensing Act, Akers-Douglas had no wish at all to antagonise the drink trade. In the 1880s a substantial minority of landlords in Deal had favoured the Liberal Party. Twenty years later Liberal supporters were probably few and far between. When members of the LVA met in January 1906 a recommendation that they should give "the most hearty and strenuous support"[58] to Akers-Douglas, and "work with vigour and enthusiasm" to help secure his return at the forthcoming general election, was agreed unanimously.

The support of local MPs was certainly valuable to the LVA but the views of town councillors – particularly since some also served as magistrates – were more important still. Two hundred years before, Thomas Powell, Mayor of Deal in 1703, had achieved fame and notoriety for his determination to bring about a "reformation" in Deal. This included ensuring that public houses remained closed on the Sabbath. Initially Powell found the landlords took no notice of his orders "but kept the doors open as formerly; upon which I made them shut them – not their inner doors only, but as many of them as had portals, their outward doors also"[59]. But none of his successors showed any wish to follow in his footsteps as a temperance crusader. Individual councillors might sometimes express temperance sentiments or even claim to be temperance men when condemning insobriety or disorderly public houses, but there is no sign that anything resembling a temperance "block" ever existed on the council. Only one ardent teetotaller served on the council. Indeed it is noticeable that, although the various temperance societies in Deal were well supported, their spokesmen were almost invariably Anglican clergymen or Nonconformist ministers. Laymen like Edward Chitty and William Ramell tended to play a supportive organisational role, and did not sustain a high profile.

Brewers were a significant presence on many borough councils but not, after mid-century, in the case of Deal. Neither Thomas Hight nor Daniel or Edwin Hills became councillors, though at least two of those who acted as their agents did: the auctioneer Morris Langley was a councillor in the 1860s and 1870s and later in the century the estate agent William Hayman served as councillor, alderman, Mayor and JP. On the other hand, unsurprisingly, a succession of landlords of the larger public houses could be found taking their place among the local tradesmen who ruled the roost as councillors and aldermen in Victorian Deal: men like George Mockett (Royal George), William Kelsey (Alma), Alfred Weston (Walmer Castle) and Robert Allen (Royal Hotel). They were never especially numerous, though, and until late in the century there was no suggestion that such men attracted support or opposition by the simple fact of their involvement in the drink trade. What mattered was an individual's standing and personal reputation, the strength of his social and professional networks and, sometimes, his political views.

These factors helped launch John Outwin's council career, and then brought it abruptly to an end. By the 1870s he had earned respect as an experienced hotelier and wine merchant, and in 1875 successfully stood for election in South Ward. Then came the 1880 Parliamentary by-election. It was one thing for Outwin to act as chief organiser and dispenser of funds for the Liberal candidate but quite another to be associated with the successful election appeal which then ruined the fun. When the *Mercury* referred the following year to "the informer...as black as black can be, secretly stabbing his fellow-townsmen in his own as well as in the opposite camp"[60] it must surely have had Outwin in mind. In November 1880, a month after the commission of enquiry began its hearings at the town hall, Outwin was pitched out of the council having received a paltry 85 votes. When attempting a return the following year he did even worse. This came as no great surprise to the *Mercury*: "that Mr John Thomas Outwin would head the poll upside down was equally certain"[61]. In later life Outwin pursued a new career as a newsagent, and seems to have made his peace with the licensed victuallers, but he did not return to the council.

By the 1890s the national battle lines had solidified, with the Liberal Party now embracing prohibition – at least until the crushing defeat in 1895 made many of its leaders think again – and the drinks trade firmly aligned with the Conservative Party. Knatchbull-Hugesson, now the Conservative Lord Brabourne, claimed that the Liberal Party need (and by implication should) never have offended the drink trade, but the demarcation was increasingly apparent from the 1880s. In Deal the drink question spilled over into local electoral politics for the first time in the 1890s. This was in part thanks to the zeal of William Ramell, house decorator, baptist, passionate Liberal, "one of the first to take up the blue ribbon movement in Deal"[62] and member of the United Kingdom Alliance.

In 1891 Ramell stood as a candidate in North Ward. Narrowly defeated on a platform of opposition to the building of a harbour in Deal – plans which in the event came to nothing – he claimed that "the greatest thing he had to fight against was spelt in a word of four letters". ("Cries of "Beer", amidst much cheering and hooting"[63].) The following year, defeated a second time, he bitterly advised anyone wishing to represent the ward to "proceed with caution...[and] if he wanted to get in there, never to try to do it honestly"[64]. But he persevered, and stood for a third time in 1893 – "an effort", said the *Mercury* rather patronisingly, "which has the merit of courage and persistence. He takes his beatings kindly.."[65]. This time, on a very high turnout, Ramell swept to victory with 432 votes. This was a record for North Ward, and put him a full 150 votes ahead of his nearest rival. The *Mercury*'s prediction the previous week that "those who value pluck and determination are certain to go solid for him[66]" can hardly be a full explanation. Perhaps, although denying that party politics had a place in local affairs, he succeeded in mobilising temperance and Liberal Party supporters to the full whilst also gathering up the votes of those agreeing with his opposition to expensive "visionary schemes". It was in any event a notable triumph.

Although one of those elected alongside William Ramell was the landlord of the Royal Exchange, Ramell's success had come at the expense of an experienced councillor supported by many local landlords. In 1895 – three serving councillors having been returned unopposed for North Ward in 1894 – the LVA decided to support a full slate of candidates in the town's two wards. Their campaign in North Ward was

William Licence, landlord of the Saracen's Head in Alfred Square between 1869 and 1896, took the lead in organising the licensed victuallers in north Deal in the 1890s and in promoting candidates for the council who were either landlords or sympathetic to their interests.

coordinated by William Licence, long time landlord of the Saracen's Head in Alfred Square, one of those who had bribed in the Conservative interest in 1880 and now treasurer of the LVA and of the newly formed North Ward Ratepayers Association. Among the LVA's candidates were Benjamin Wood, then landlord of the Railway Tavern, and James Elson, once the proprietor of the Paragon Music Hall and now a furniture broker and landlord of the Duke of Wellington in Water Street. Votes were cast on 7 November and at 10.00pm amid scenes of boisterous, beer-fuelled disorder ("loud applause, continuous shouts of "Hip, hip hurrah", cries of "order", and great confusion"[67]) both were declared victorious. Wood spoke confidently in thanking his supporters, Elson rather less so:

> "...the speaker appeared to lose himself in the confusion, and stood rubbing his head and laughing, causing much amusement. Voices: "Good old Punch and Judy," and "Speak up." Still he paused, and rubbed his head, causing roars of laughter. (Ald. Hayman: Thank them all for voting for you)..."[68].

The publicans' third preferred candidate for North Ward was also elected, as were all three favoured South Ward candidates. Not surprisingly, the publicans' organised intervention caused anger in some quarters. "Equity", writing to the *Mercury*, considered the attempt to influence the ballot "beyond all reason...if publicans are to rule the affairs of the town, we might just as well convert the Council Chamber into a refreshment bar without any further ceremony"[69]. "An Elector Who Votes" complained that "the contest in the North Ward was left almost entirely to the decision of the working classes, while the voter who was capable of exercising his vote with absolute impartiality stayed at home"[70], and the *Mercury* shared his concern that the success of the publicans in North Ward had come at the expense of two long-serving councillors. At least one publican also strongly disapproved of the LVA's tactics, writing to warn that the Association was "simply abusing the greatest stronghold our trade ever had to fall back upon when in need of a helping hand. I hold up both hands in support of the Axiom that 'Unity is strength' in all matters that pertain to the defence and welfare of our much-abused trade, but I cannot admit that we are justified in exerting our energies in support of certain candidates in a municipal contest"[71].

Perhaps rather chastened, the LVA seems to have retreated from any further direct involvement in annual municipal elections. But it was no doubt very pleased to support, and may behind the scenes have inspired, the candidacies of several other landlords in the years that followed. Although James Elson stood down after a single term of office ("Mr Elson's municipal career has been too uneventful to enable one to pen an encomium on the strength of it"[72], observed the *Mercury* drily) Henry May, William Licence's successor at the Saracen's Head, was elected in 1900 for North Ward and Richard Currie, formerly of the Rose but by then landlord of the Magnet in Middle Deal, represented South Ward between 1904 and 1907. Benjamin Wood, though no longer in the drinks trade, remained on the council for many years as councillor and alderman, serving alongside the LVA's long-serving chairman, William Redsull of the New Plough.

The town council, several of whose members at any one time were also borough magistrates, reflected and helped shape attitudes towards the sale of drink and the existence of large numbers of public houses, but licensing decisions were for the bench alone. It was a source of considerable irritation to the drink trade that teetotallers could serve as magistrates. As John Dunne put it when addressing the LVA in 1896, a man who had taken the magistrate's oath "committed purjury every time he sat on a Licensing Bench, if he had subscribed to a teetotal society"[73]. This was a topical issue in the town, since the previous year teetotal William Ramell had been appointed to the Deal bench. Ramell saw no contradiction in continuing to play a leading role within the Deal and Walmer Temperance Union, and it is not surprising that he was several times invited by lawyers acting for brewers or landlords to stand down from hearing particular licensing cases. His fellow magistrates, whatever they may have felt in private, had no wish to rock the boat: "it was thought that the matter rested with Mr Ramell himself entirely, and as the gentleman could see no reason why, in the absence of a decision on the point, he should not adjudicate, he retained his position on the Bench during the session"[74]. It was certainly the case that there was by now no shortage of licensing work for Ramell and his colleagues to get through.

Magistrates under pressure

The seemingly inexorable stream of public house closures in the twenty-first century flows from decisions taken by brewers, pub companies and freehold licence holders in response to changing patterns in the consumption of alcohol and in the opportunities for the profitable alternative use of pub premises. In Victorian and Edwardian England, unlike today, the possession of a licence was a valuable asset in itself, eagerly sought and given up with great reluctance. The key decision makers were therefore the licensing magistrates. They decided if a new house could open, if an existing house would have to close, if a beerhouse would be permitted to sell beer on as well as off the premises or become a public house through the possession of a spirit licence, and if a landlord could be allowed to keep his house open for longer on a specified day. They also became responsible for awarding the licences which from 1861, to the great displeasure of the publicans, permitted grocers to sell beer, wine and spirits.

Attempts to influence the Deal magistrates' decisions came from a variety of different directions. After 1889, when the county police force took over from the disbanded borough police, the local inspector might find himself required by his superiors to argue against the award or renewal of a licence. Groups of landlords, sometimes with the support of one of the local brewers, not only routinely opposed the award of grocers' licences but might also try to prevent a beerhouse from acquiring a spirit licence. This sometimes meant making common cause with temperance spokesmen in opposing a particular application. But brewers and landlords on the one hand and temperance spokesmen on the other were of course usually to be found on opposite sides.

Clergymen and ministers very often took the lead in presenting temperance memorials and sometimes in speaking on behalf of local residents annoyed at the conduct of a house. In 1875 Reverend Payne, joining forces with the Rector of St Andrew's and the Congregational minister, persuaded the magistrates to close the Bricklayer's Arms. The owners, Thompson's, were caught wrong footed and did not contest the decision. It did not help that public houses and places of worship were often in close proximity. In 1861 Reverend Hammill's complaint that the racket coming from the Park Tavern made it almost impossible to conduct services in his Primitive Methodist chapel directly opposite helped persuade the magistrates not to renew the landlord's licence, and the house closed for a time. In 1878 the Duke of York beerhouse, a short distance from the two chapels of the municipal cemetery, felt the wrath of parishioners of St Andrew's church marshalled by their senior curate. The magistrates refused to grant a spirit licence and the house closed a few years later. On the other hand, the support of the Rector of St Andrew's for those opposing the licensing of a rebuilt Queen's Arms in 1892, to be situated opposite the parish mission room and previously attracting, he said, the "social wreckage of Deal"[75], failed to deter the magistrates, and Hills were able to build their new premises facing Middle Street as they wished.

One did not of course have to be an avowed temperance supporter to find the conduct of a nearby public house objectionable, and indeed it could sometimes be an advantage to disclaim any temperance connection when bringing forward a complaint or objection. Organised temperance interventions, although usually well marshalled, did however tend to be triggered by specific concerns rather than forming part of a sustained strategy for influencing the bench. This changed for a time in the early 1880s as the powerful if transitory impact of the Blue Ribbon movement was felt in the town. In 1881 the Deal Temperance Society lodged a petition, "signed by upwards of 150 respectable inhabitants"[76], asking the bench to refuse any new licence application and to use their best endeavours to reduce the overall number of houses. The Blue Ribbon party were out in force again the following year, and in 1883 wheeled out their big guns in the shape of Reverend Payne and his nonconformist colleagues to present a memorial "to the effect that drunkenness, immorality and pauperism were the result of traffic in intoxicating liquors, and that the licensed houses in Deal were far beyond the requirement of the borough, and urging the Magistrates to reduce their number"[77]. Their efforts had little or no immediate impact, but the temperance lobby was at least beginning to make headway in arguing that Deal simply had too many public houses.

Much less successful were the periodic efforts to persuade the magistrates and the landlords themselves to restrict Sunday drinking. In 1873 Reverend Bartram and his colleagues failed to dissuade the bench from agreeing an extra hour's Sunday drinking time during the summer months, and in June 1881 the council simply refused to entertain a petition in favour of closing all houses on Sunday ("Councillor Kelsey said if carried with effect the people would not be deterred from having their beer, but would get in two gallons on Saturday and get tight on Sunday"[78]). The application by the landlord of the Park Tavern in 1872 for a six-day licence seems to have been unique, and neither Hills nor Thompson's showed any inclination to follow the example of Fremlins, the Maidstone brewers, who were reported in 1878 to have required their tenants to take out six-day licences and close entirely on Sundays. Sabbatarians in Deal do not seem to have been able to raise a head of steam, unlike their colleagues in Dover where in 1875 "one of the largest and most exciting meetings that [the town] has ever seen was held on Tuesday evening, at Wellington Hall; it was called in support of Mr C H Wilson's Sunday Closing Bill..."[79].

The Deal temperance lobby were equally unsuccessful later in the century in pressing the magistrates to clamp down on the serving of beer to young children. The LVA put in a strong counter-memorial, arguing that the question "can only be settled by the parents and guardians of the children ... it is their cooperation which should have been invited..[They] know the ages and characters of the children they send as messengers to licensed premises"[80]. The magistrates were unmoved by evidence from the Reverend McGill that many other benches had taken action, and declared themselves powerless to intervene.

Landlords and brewers, however, had to defend on many fronts. The teetotaller William Ramell for example, on his appointment to the bench in 1895, regularly opposed the granting of early morning licences (a "very great evil"[81]) and occasional licences, sometimes to the considerable irritation of his fellow magistrates. On the other hand it was not unusual for temperance supporters, brewers and landlords to find themselves on the same side in opposing applications to the magistrates. In September 1882, for example, Hills, George Beer and other brewers with houses in the town joined forces to urge the magistrates not to approve any applications for new spirit licences; a memorial from the total abstainers presented later in the meeting argued the same thing.

In practice new spirit licences became almost impossible to obtain after 1870. Thompson's Lifeboat was able to open as a beerhouse in the face of stiff opposition from nearby landlords and the owner of the North End Brewery, but the magistrates repeatedly refused a spirit licence. The Fox was no more successful, and also remained a beerhouse throughout its existence. When the landlord of Hills' rebuilt Roxburgh Castle applied for a spirit licence in 1887 he was successfully opposed by the landlords of the Pier Hotel, New Inn and King's Head and also by Thompson's on the grounds that in a town already boasting some 75 public houses another one in the centre of town was quite unnecessary. The landlords, of course, feared the additional competition, while for brewers there was always the risk that the award of a new licence would tend to depreciate the value of their existing licensed houses.

In the case of the Roxburgh Castle the magistrates finally granted a spirit licence in 1899 on the basis that its particular character and "modern style" deserved special treatment. Two years later they agreed a spirit licence for the Oak and Ivy in Blenheim Road after receiving a petition bearing an "immense number of signatures", facing a barrage of arguments from the lawyer acting for George Beer and securing an undertaking from the Canterbury brewers to rebuild the house. But the Mayor went out of his way to warn that this should not be taken "in any shape or form as a precedent"[82] and the Roxburgh Castle and the Oak and Ivy were in fact the only two beerhouses granted spirit licences between 1870 and 1914.

For some beerhouses the challenge was simply to be allowed to sell beer for consumption on as well as off the premises. Samuel Terry, a market gardener, became landlord of the Yew Tree near Upper Deal mill when granted an off-licence in 1878. He found it much harder, several years later, to secure an on-licence despite pleading the frustrations of his fellow market gardeners unable to take beer when eating at his house and the disappointment of visitors allegedly drawn there to admire the view. The magistrates finally acquiesced in 1886. The newly built Brickmaker's Arms, a grocery store licensed for off sales in 1882, had to wait much longer despite the best efforts of the East Kent Brewery. Success finally came in 1899, but only in the face of stiff opposition from George Beer, in their capacity as owners of the nearby Oak and Ivy. Previous licence holders having fallen foul of the magistrates on several occasions, the brewers had taken care to guard their flank by putting in place a former borough and county police sergeant. The magistrates were nonetheless divided on the issue – William Ramell no doubt opposing – and the Mayor made clear his view that the house should never have been licensed in the first place.

Both the Yew Tree and the Brickmaker's Arms were in developing areas on the outskirts of Deal, and the owners could point to new demand from labourers working in the nearby brickfields, and indeed from the crews of the traction engines needed to transport the bricks. But the unnamed beerhouse at 19 Farrier Street in the centre of Deal had no such special case to plead, and the landlord's account in 1882 of disgruntled customers unable to take a drink with their dinners "even if purchased from another house"[83] failed to sway the magistrates. The police in fact seem to have found it much easier to uphold the letter of the law in relation to houses with an on-licence, and might even – off the record – have agreed with a lawyer acting for the Brickmaker's Arms who suggested that refusing a beerhouse an on-licence amounted to "an inducement for the landlord to break the law"[84]. But even this consideration did not rescue 19 Farrier Street, which had the unwanted distinction of being the only beerhouse in Edwardian Deal unable to serve its customers with beer to drink inside its doors.

The Brickmaker's Arms beerhouse c.1905. At the door is probably the landlord Nathan Everett, a Royal Marine pensioner. The premises were built around 1882 and William Wyborn, "pork butcher and general shop-keeper", secured an off-licence soon afterwards. But it was an uphill struggle, lasting many years, to convert this into an on-licence.

Landlords and brewers might sometimes tussle amongst themselves where on-licence and spirit licence applications were concerned, but they were at one in attempting to limit the number of grocers' licences, in particular the beer off-licences whose numbers, nationally, rose four-fold to almost 12,500 over the ten years to 1881. In 1872, attempting to stem the local tide, David Almond of the Rose presented a memorial to the bench signed by a large number of publicans against the granting of a licence to John Linscott, a Middle Street grocer. Linscott denied any intention of selling beer in draught but did want to follow several other grocers in selling bottled beer ("his prices would always be higher than the publicans', because he would sell Allsopp's and such like beers. He had no desire to turn his house into a public-house..."). Almond protested that the existing beer-retailing grocers had already done great injury to nearby public houses, and when the magistrates decided that they could not refuse Linscott's application complained sarcastically that "it was very hard upon the publicans...he supposed they would soon have the drapers applying for licences"[85]. (He spoke more truly than he knew. John Capeling, who successfully applied for a licence in 1888, was described as a "grocer and draper" of Ark Lane.)

The licensed victuallers were fighting a losing battle but they could sometimes delay the retreat. John Capeling, who had himself been a landlord for a time, was persuaded in the event not to sell bottled beer in addition to wines and spirits, and in 1897 only three of the six licensed grocers in Deal possessed one of the controversial beer off-licences. In that year the LVA chose not to contest an application from a High Street grocer to sell wines and spirits but argued strongly against his being allowed to sell beer. The grocers' lawyer, facing an uphill task in proving the need for another local outlet, claimed that the licence was particularly needed for "the visitors' trade, and more especially for the country trade, in which they covered 150 miles, and called at 150 houses weekly, where brewers' drays absolutely would not call"[86]. The LVA's lawyer argued in turn that the fact that the grocers concerned might lose a few customers was neither here nor there; the Deal magistrates had to consider the interests of Deal, and the town did not need any more licences permitting the sale of bottled beer. Moreover – he threw in for good measure – there was plenty of evidence "that to a certain extent these licences had been a temptation to women to drink at home, and led to increased drinking and other evils"[87]. In this instance the LVA had their way, and the bench refused the application.

The Association also had some success in persuading the bench to hold the line against the award of licences to lodging and boarding houses. This was another issue where licensed victuallers and temperance spokesmen would often find themselves in alliance, and happy to agree on the lamentable consequences of decisions taken around the coast. According to Dr Hardman, acting for the LVA:

> "there was one watering-place on this coast that granted such licenses in particular cases...Margate had the unenviable reputation of having a list of convictions for drunkenness that was increasing by leaps and bounds every year...It was particularly objectionable, because of having a row of boarding-houses where drink could be obtained, it entirely altered the character of a seaside town"[88].

This steady stream of contested licence applications, involving a shifting cast of landlords, brewers, grocers, lodging house keepers, residents and temperance advocates, sometimes appearing in person but more often legally represented, had now placed the magistrates centre stage in the contests for the survival and prosperity of individual public houses. They did so in the context of the now widely held belief that there were far too many public houses for the public good. Sixty years of endeavour by the temperance movement, in so many ways a history of false dawns and unrealised hopes, had at least in this respect helped to shift the centre ground of opinion. For campaigners in Deal the figures seemed particularly compelling. Nationally there were estimated in 1901 to be one on-licence for every 316 people, but according to the police the ratio in Deal was 1:103. The town was also out of step with many other towns in Kent. In Gravesend the ratio in 1908 was 1:187 and the Maidstone 1:211. Folkestone had a population more than three times the size of Deal's but only some 15% more on-licences.

Some nonetheless argued that, in the words of George Beer's lawyer, "it was a great mistake to think that an excessive number of houses led to more drinking. On the contrary, if they drove the trade into a fewer number of houses, a larger number of people would congregate in each, and there would be more treating, and as they all knew, drinking led to drinking"[89]. But there were certainly many who favoured a reduction in licences without at all subscribing to the temperance analysis of the harm caused by the ready availability of drink. The *Mercury*, no friend of radical temperance, clearly reflected the mood of the times and of the leading citizens of the town when it pronounced in 1891 that "the abnormal number of licensed houses in Deal has long been an acknowledged evil, being a grievance in public opinion, and causing astonishment among our visitors..."[90].

In March 1891 the House of Lords upheld a judgment by the Queen's Bench in the case of Sharp v. Wakefield which seemed clearly to establish the right of magistrates, on grounds other than misconduct, to refuse to renew an existing licence. Six months later, emboldened by the judgment, urged on by temperance activists, and applauded by the *Mercury* for their "enlightened action and moral courage"[91], the Deal magistrates refused to renew the licences of two public houses on the grounds that they were not required to meet the needs of the neighbourhood. The Prince of Wales in Middle Street was a former beerhouse now in poor condition and had been shut for several months. On the other hand the old established Sir John Falstaff in Lower Street, owned by the Canterbury brewers Flint & Co, had recently been modernised and also did service as a common lodging house. But the house had also been shut for some time, with a rapid turnover of landlords before that, and the police opposed the application. This was a more difficult case. The magistrates initially divided two and two, and it was only at a second meeting with an extra justice present that the bench decided not to renew the licence. The brewers did not appeal to the county magistrates, and the house closed without fuss.

Four years later the case of the Three Compasses, a public house on Beach Street, would take a very different course. This was triggered by complaints made by Captain Alfred Channer, who lived across the street, and by his landlord James MacIntosh. John Outwin had been declared bankrupt in 1890 when running the Three Compasses, and over the next few years the house was either shut, or open and causing trouble. In June 1895 the magistrates agreed by a majority to yet another transfer of the licence, but the new landlord took to drink and could not cope. Rather late in the day, the owners of the house, George Beer, took pains to find a very presentable replacement. This was John Edwards, who had run the Ship Hotel in Dover for 22 unblemished years and whose referees included the Rector of Holy Trinity.

But the magistrates were losing patience, and inclined to agree with Channer and his solicitor that the house, if properly conducted, simply could not be made to pay. Landlords had come and gone, either losing money or conducting the house in a "loose way". According to Channer, "if he had not exercised the greatest supervision, backed up by the police, the house would have been little less than an immoral one for the use of soldiers"[92]. Moreover there was no evidence that significant inconvenience had been felt during the times when the Three Compasses had been shut – there were in fact four or five other public houses within 150 yards. At the annual licensing meeting in September 1895 these arguments proved decisive and the magistrates decided against the renewal of the licence – though only by a majority – on the grounds that the house was not required by the public. But George Beer, unlike Flint, had no intention of going quietly. They promptly appealed to the East Kent Quarter Sessions, and the resulting hearing took place in Canterbury in October.

Complaints from residents about the conduct of individual public houses had been a regular occurrence over the years, but had never before triggered such a tussle between the magistrates and a brewer. Times had certainly changed. The activities of temperance advocates and of the Licensed Victuallers Association had brought the drink question into the electoral politics of North Deal, while Sharp v Wakefield seemed to clear the ground for a magisterial initiative to tackle what the *Mercury* described as a "super-abundance"[93] of public houses in the town. The balance of view among members of the Deal bench had undoubtedly been affected by the rather surprising appointment earlier in the year of the teetotaller William Ramell, and probably also by the fact that the chairman was now the builder George Cottew, a Liberal and pillar of the Wesleyan church, in his capacity as Mayor.

The *Mercury* was delighted that the Three Compasses "will no longer point in the direction of dissipation...no one who affects to have any regard for the reputation of the town will regret it". "Can it be possible", it asked, "for all the landlords of the eighty-seven ale and beer houses to earn an honest living? We would answer most emphatically in the negative"[94]. But it also worried that the magistrates might be on weak ground having allowed the house to be re-licensed several times before. The magistrates for their part girded themselves for the fight, and indeed raised the stakes by deciding to defend the appeal themselves rather than leaving the task to Channer and MacIntosh as the original instigators of the proceedings.

The case went badly from the start. The county magistrates had, so it transpired, decided two years before that, notwithstanding Sharp v Wakefield, the fact that there were too many licensed houses in a locality would not in itself be considered sufficient reason to refuse a licence to a particular house – a ruling that seems to have escaped the notice of the clerk to the Deal bench. When their counsel attempted nonetheless to draw support from the comments of Mr Justice Lopez during Sharp v Wakefield to the effect that, were he a magistrate, he would apply a "last in, first out" principle – 65 of the 72 public houses in Deal, and all of those nearby having been licensed before the Three Compasses – this cut little ice. Worse was to come when the chairman went out of his way to dismiss the issue of whether or not the house, if properly conducted, could be run at a profit: "they already had that subject under consideration...and came to the conclusion that the question whether the house could be profitably conducted was one for the owners and licensee of the house, and not one which the Magistrates ought to take into consideration"[95]. Nor did it help when the clerk to the Deal bench reluctantly admitted that the decision not to renew the Three Compasses' licence had been reached by a bare majority of four votes to three.

The upshot was that the case turned solely on whether the conduct of the house in the immediate past justified the removal of the licence. Counsel for George Beer therefore did all he could to show that although the house had been badly run at times since 1890, particularly during the tenure of William Wyborn, there had in fact been little or no cause for concern since the house reopened in May 1895. Moreover, although

The builder George Cottew was Mayor of Deal between 1893 and 1895. His was the casting vote, in his capacity as chairman of the borough magistrates, in the decision to close the Three Compasses.

Channner and MacIntosh had complained to the police and to the brewers on many occasions since 1890, no summons had been taken out against the house, and as it happened, the rate of turnover of landlords at the house was no worse than at other nearby houses. The hearing dragged on for a full four and a half hours, and when finally the bench announced their decision it was, by a large majority, to uphold the appeal against closure. Rubbing salt in the wound, the Chairman made clear that the way in which the Three Compasses had been conducted in William Wyborn's time, on the other hand, would have made it "perfectly right, and almost imperative"[96] for the borough magistrates to have shut the house at that point.

The magistrates' attempt to close the Three Compasses in 1895 ended in failure and drew criticism from members of the council. By 1922, the probable date of this picture, four of the five nearby public houses whose existence had helped persuade the bench that the Three Compasses was no longer needed had themselves closed.

The Deal magistrates had certainly missed their chance. Had Ramell joined the bench a year or two before this might have tilted the magistrates towards taking action at an earlier stage on what would have been surer ground. They might have succeeded in 1895, even so, had the owners been one of the two local brewers. Hills, and possibly even Thompson's, might well have decided to roll with the punch for the sake of maintaining good relations with the bench and in the knowledge that much of the business displaced from the Three Compasses would transfer to their other houses. But George Beer were sizeable and ambitious county brewers, with few ties to the town beyond owning a clutch of public houses, and were unlikely to take things lying down. They could certainly be satisfied with the outcome, and with their new tenant. John Edwards remained at the Three Compasses until his death in 1908 and the house itself survived for another hundred years or so before becoming a restaurant. In contrast three of the five neighbouring houses, whose apparently secure existence in 1895 had helped persuade the Deal bench that the licence of the Three Compasses could properly be extinguished, were themselves closed down before the First World War (the Paragon Music Hall, the Horse and Farrier and the Crown) to be followed in 1921 by the Clifton and finally, in 1944, by the Sir Sidney Smith.

In January 1896 the town council discussed the Three Compasses affair. The chairman of the Quarter Sessions, speaking for most of the county magistrates, had roundly condemned the actions of the Deal bench in "sacrificing their judicial position, and placing themselves in the position of partizans...If there ever was a case in which the costs should be given against the Justices, he thought this was such a case"[97]. By a small majority they had decided to stay their hand, but there remained the matter of the magistrates' own costs – £47 3s 0d – which would have to be met by the town council. The Mayor and his colleagues from the bench who were also members of the council faced a good deal of criticism and teasing for the "muddle" they had got themselves into. The Town Clerk was unrepentant ("the present Lord Chancellor, and nine other Justices of the High Court, had told the Magistrates that it was their duty to enquire into the requirements of any place, and if a public-house was not wanted, to take away the licence") while for the Mayor the simple fact of the matter was that "the Borough Magistrates thought, and he still thought, that they were right, and they knew a very great deal more about the merits of the case than the Justices of Canterbury"[98].

Five years later Alderman Cottew was still smarting from the Three Compasses defeat. He and his colleagues – William Ramell now the lone dissenting voice – gave extremely short shrift to a memorial presented in 1900 by teetotallers in the town which asked for a sharp reduction in the number of licences. "A pretty hole they would be in if they followed the advice of these gentlemen" grumbled Cottew who then, though describing himself as a temperance man, went out of his way to ridicule the teetotal position. The Mayor, Alderman Thompson, may have startled the landlords present when he commented that "it was quite the opinion of the Bench that if there were about half the number of licensed houses in the town it would be a great deal better for those who were left, and perhaps in some cases it might stop some of the drunkenness"[99] but went on to make it clear that the bench had no intention of removing licences on their own initiative where houses were conducted responsibly. Whether indignant or chastened – or no doubt, in the case of those who never wanted the contest in the first place, confirmed in their wisdom – the magistrates never again locked horns with a brewer in this way in attempting to close a house.

Managing the closures
John Greenaway, in his recent history of drink and British politics, identifies six Victorian approaches to the "drink problem"[100]. The first, "moral suasion", was evident in Deal throughout the period, particularly during the Blue Ribbon surge in the 1880s, though the increasing tendency was for temperance men and women to talk one to the other rather than to strive for converts. The second approach, which saw intemperance as "a product of a faulty social order", seems in contrast to have had little resonance in the town. Third in Greenaway's list, which this book has discussed at length in the Deal context, comes the "traditional" system of regulation by the magistrates. By the late nineteenth century "as British local government moved in the direction of representative democracy, the licensing position of the magistrates became increasingly uncomfortable, and even anomalous"[101]. But it would be over a century before the responsibility was lifted from them.

The fourth approach, arguably the most radical response to the drink problem, was the application of laissez-faire economic theory through "free licensing". This had found dramatic expression much earlier in the century when the 1830 Beer Act permitted the opening of beerhouses without the need to obtain the approval of the magistrates. The impact in Deal had been less than in many other parts of the country, but significant nonetheless. In contrast, the fifth approach – prohibition, as advocated above all by the United Kingdom Alliance from the 1850s onwards – found relatively little support in Deal and, with the exception of non-conformist ministers, virtually none among leading figures in the town. The impact of the last of Greenaway's six approaches, "progressive temperance restriction" was certainly felt within the town – when, for example, reduced hours of sale were introduced in the 1870s, but above all as the pressures mounted to restrict and to reduce the number of public houses and beerhouses. This issue would overshadow and then dominate the licensing work of the borough magistrates from the 1890s onwards.

If there was one thing that magistrates and councillors of all shades of opinion could happily agree upon it was that senior officers of the county police force had little understanding of the interests of the town and should not interfere in licensing decisions. When in April 1897 the local inspector conveyed the advice of Superintendent Chaney that there was no requirement for certain early morning licences this was brushed aside by Alderman Cottew on the grounds that Chaney was simply not in a position to know. Great then was the indignation when the Superintendent appeared at the 1901 annual licensing meeting to oppose, on the direct instructions of his Chief Constable, the renewal of no fewer that 21 licences "on the ground of close proximity and their not being required by the general public"[102]. These included ten houses in Beach Street, among them the King's Head, the Antwerp and Amelia Kemp's Yarmouth Packet. One of the 21, the Horse and Farrier, should moreover be closed on the additional grounds of being a disorderly house.

The police having served notice on all the houses in question, the meeting chamber was packed with licensed victuallers. A memorial from the LVA was read which argued that the conduct of public houses had noticeably improved year on year; the fact of the matter was that drunkenness was much more likely to be caused by unlicensed secret drinking clubs and, especially among women, by the bottle supply from grocers' shops or provision stores. The Association invited the magistrates to refuse to receive memorials which were "provocative of bad feeling" and which, it added with some calculated provocation of its own, "indicate a want to confidence in your impartiality"[103]. The memorial had probably been prepared in expectation of another intervention by the teetotallers, but did equally good service in encouraging the magistrates to resist the frontal assault by the Chief Constable.

The *Mercury* soon added its penny-worth. The Chief Constable, so it understood, had simply decided that where two houses were within a certain distance of each other, one would have to close. It considered such a "mechanical scheme... Utopian both in principle and practice"[104] and frankly ludicrous. Probably realising the futility of the attempt – or satisfied to have rattled a few cages – the Chief Constable threw in his hand. At the adjourned licensing meeting the following month Superintendent Chaney beat a hasty retreat, withdrawing opposition to the renewal of 20 licences and intimating that the same would apply to the Horse and Farrier if a satisfactory new tenant were found. For the

Mayor, now Councillor Soloman, the original proposals had been a manifestation of "centralisation in the worst and narrowest form"[105] and the Chief Constable had been extremely disrespectful in giving no explanation or written notification of his change of mind. One wonders what approach the county magistrates would have taken had the Deal bench acted upon the recommendations of the county police, and on whom the costs of the brewers' appeals would have fallen. The *Mercury*, for one, had no doubt that "we cannot afford to trifle with the subject, and it is unreasonable that the Kentish taxpayer should be compelled to find the motive power for the unwieldy machinery which any faddist chooses to set in motion"[106].

Unwilling to risk another Three Compasses débâcle, or to be led by the nose by the county police, the Deal magistrates cast around for another way forward. They did have one important point of leverage: brewers might still hope to acquire licences for new premises in developing areas on the outskirts of town. In which case, as the magistrates put it in 1899, "where a brewer was the owner of a number of houses in the town he ought to be prepared, when he asked for a concession in one spot, to give up in another spot"[107]. In agreeing a spirit licence for the Oak and Ivy in 1901 the magistrates repeated their view that brewers should always be ready to make some concession, although in this case it amounted to the rebuilding of the existing beerhouse. Two years later, however, faced with applications from Thompson's for three completely new houses, the magistrates were in a position to engage in some productive bargaining.

News of the brewers' plans quickly spread, and prompted a well-attended temperance meeting at the Blackburn Hall in Middle Street to marshal support against the granting of any new licences. A petition carrying some 300 signatures was then presented to the magistrates by the Wesleyan minister. But also on the table, when the adjourned licensing meeting took place in March, was an offer from Thompson's to close five of their existing houses if allowed to open three new houses on the outskirts of town. Two of these would be built in north Deal, one in North Wall (421 yards from the Jolly Sailor in a working-class district "with every prospect of future development") and the other a larger house on the corner of Harold and Golf Roads (for the particular benefit of "the great many people passing to and from the Golf Club and along the sea front"[108]).

Thompson's were probably not unduly surprised when the magistrates refused these applications, and in fact no such houses were ever built. Their third application was a very different matter. This was for a new house on the corner of Telegraph and Cemetery Roads, near the railway line and close to the boundary with Walmer. Thompson's lawyer vigorously argued the needs of married marines living in the vicinity, of the developing population of the "mechanic class" and – again – of men working in the brickfields. Purchasing beer from the nearest existing house (the Lord Warden) meant a walk of a quarter of a mile ("Mr Mowll: ... it doesn't improve the beer does it? Witness: no, it makes it dead"[109]) while the brewers' "two for one" offer was of course most wonderfully generous.

A modern picture of the Telegraph, built by Thompson's in 1903–4 after trading in the licences of the Empire Theatre of Varieties and the Lord Nelson. According to the *Mercury* the decision of the magistrates, by a majority vote, came as a surprise to most people in the town.

The lawyer acting for the objectors poured scorn on this. Local residents were certainly not of one mind, and in practice such demand as there might be was more likely to come from across the boundary in north Walmer. Yet the Cinque Ports magistrates had just rejected a separate application from Thompson's to build a house in what was effectively the same area, and had been quite unmoved by hints that the brewers would be ready to give up an existing licence in Walmer in return. As for the two old houses in central Deal now being offered for closure, one (the Empire Theatre of Varieties) had been shut for six months and the other (Lord Nelson) had a bad reputation. In short, it was anything but a generous offer.

Yet it was an offer that the Deal bench – William Ramell of course dissenting – decided to accept. The *Mercury* was astonished that the magistrates had approved a provisional licence for a new house for the neighbourhood shortly after the Cinque Ports bench had decided there was no such need; and surely, having so decided, they could have driven a much harder bargain? A further hearing was then required, by a special court consisting of three borough and three county magistrates, to confirm or overturn the provisional order. Notwithstanding the presence of the Chief Constable, and Superintendent Chaney's assertion that if the house were opened he would need to station a special constable in the area, the award of a licence was confirmed. Thompson's planned to invest £1,400 in building and fitting up the new house, which duly opened the following year and was christened the Telegraph. The closure of two of their many central Deal houses was a price easily paid. As counsel for the objectors had dryly observed:

> "was it to be assumed for one moment that this Brewery Company were going to instruct an architect, solicitor and counsel, and pay a number of workmen 10s each to come to Court and give evidence, and to give up two licences into the bargain, if they were not going to see more drink. It was not in the cause of temperance they were doing all this"[110].

Actual temperance supporters were outraged by the outcome. For Reverend Tabraham, the Wesleyan minister, the events "almost made one feel ashamed to be associated with the town"[111]. His bitterness was no doubt exacerbated by his unpleasant experience at the hands of Thompson's solicitor during the preliminary hearing; it was of course the regular fate of witnesses known to be personally teetotal to be deemed incapable of offering worthwhile comment on the patterns of demand for alcoholic refreshment and on the licensing of individual houses.

The magistrates themselves might also have been forgiven for feeling rather jaded. It had been their lot over many years to wrestle with the complexities and uncertainties surrounding the removal of licences, sometimes burning their fingers in the process and often divided among themselves. It was all very well for the licensing authority of a huge area like Birmingham to devise and publish a "tariff" for the award of new licences (in terms of the number and type of houses to be closed in compensation) but that could not work in a small town like Deal. Thompson's, who owned 60% of houses in the town, had been granted a generous "two for one" deal but had now been prevented from expanding in north Deal. It might be years before they had an interest in another exchange. What the borough magistrates and their colleagues across the country therefore wanted above all was a clear statutory framework for managing the closure of public houses within which they could operate. Yet national politicians had been wrestling with this challenge for twenty years or more with little success and much exasperation. It was not simply a question of who should decide on closures and on what basis. Should brewers and landlords be entitled to compensation when a house was closed for reasons other than misconduct (absolutely not, said most temperance organisations) and, if so, where was the money to come from?

Eventually, fortified by a big election victory in 1900 and under heavy fire from brewers and publicans for the number of licences being denied renewal, without compensation, by licensing authorities, the Conservative Government grasped the nettle. In 1904 the Home Secretary, now the local MP Aretas Akers-Douglas, secured the passage of legislation which provided that no licence could be suppressed (other than on grounds of misconduct) without compensation equal to the difference in value in 1904 of the premises with and without the licence. Compensation funds would be created by a levy on brewers and all other licensed property owners, and the number of reductions would be limited by the size of the fund and any money borrowed on its security. Brewers grumbled, but acquiesced. Many did quite well out of the scheme, and were not necessarily disadvantaged by having fewer tied houses. Temperance organisations were of course outraged.

The 1904 Licensing Act put the borough magistrates into the spotlight once again. The process under the legislation had three main stages, the first of which was for the magistrates to draw up a list of houses intended that year for closure and to announce the names at the annual licensing session. Informal conversations with the police must surely have taken place at times, though this was sometimes denied. The criteria adopted by the Deal magistrates were not explicitly stated, but included the size and character of the existing trade, whether the house met a particular need – for example of visitors – the reputation and conduct of the house, its proximity to other premises and the ease or otherwise of police supervision. Magistrates might sometimes visit a house to see for themselves the amount of trade being done. In the first year, 1906, the bench identified six houses for closure. The Hope, Sun, Deal Cutter and Globe were all owned by Thompson's, with whom there may well have been some prior consultation. The other two houses were a small beerhouse owned by George Beer (the Deal Lugger) and the sometimes troublesome Maxton Arms, by this time owned by the West Malling brewer Thomas Phillips.

The next stage was for the magistrates in public session to taken evidence from the local police inspector, to consider any arguments made on behalf of the brewers and landlords concerned, and then to decide whether to recommend the licences to the Quarter Sessions for extinction. In this first year, other than in the case of the Maxton Arms, opposition from the brewers was relatively half-hearted, and all six houses were recommended for closure. The third stage was reached in October when, in accordance with the new legislation, the cases were decided on by the "Compensation Committee" of the East Kent Quarter Sessions in Canterbury. This further involvement of the county magistrates in the affairs of the town was naturally an irritation to the borough council, who considered that the business should be left entirely in the hands of local justices – "a gratuitous insult", in the Town Clerk's view in 1904. It was left to Alderman Thompson to summarise in the time honoured way: "local government is getting more centralised every week"[112].

In the event neither George Beer nor Thompson's challenged the closure of their houses. Arthur Matthews attended nonetheless, explaining rather tortuously that "we have not opposed the application on behalf of the justices because we wish to give the Act a fair chance, but it is not to be taken that we are altogether assenting" (Lord Harris; Assenting to the Act? (Laughter). Counsel for the justices; Passive resistance, my lord (Laughter)"[113]). Counsel for Thomas Phillips did his best to show that the Maxton Arms, properly conducted by a pensioner from the 9th

A gloomy picture of Beach Street looking north. Acacia House, nearest the camera, had long ago been the Red Lion public house. The Fountain, next door, was one of six houses considered for closure in 1907, but the magistrates stayed their hand. At the far end is the Royal Hotel.

Lancers, had a worthwhile trade and provided a useful service as a common lodging house. But his application for a renewal of the licence was refused.

For the brewers, the compensation payments went a long way towards sweetening the pill. Thompson's received a total of £1,761 in respect of their four houses – a good deal more than they had paid to build and fit out the Telegraph three years before – George Beer £548 for the Deal Lugger, and Thomas Phillips £570 for the Maxton Arms. Payments made to the sitting tenants were of a different order. Army pensioner Thomas Latter, the last landlord of the Maxton Arms, received £50. Harry Thomas, landlord of the Hope, who after the closure moved a short distance to the Ship in Middle Street, a mere £5.

The following year the magistrates identified another six houses for closure. At the licensing meeting in March Thompson's lawyer put up a strong defence of the Fountain on the grounds of the accommodation offered to visitors ("there were a couple of very nice verandahs where one could sit and smoke, and thoroughly enjoy the sea breezes, and watch the boats going down the channel"[114]) and extracted helpful support from the police inspector. Ramell's suggestion that a de-licensed Fountain might attract just as much trade was coolly received, and the house was reprieved. The closure of four of Thompson's other houses (the Druid's Arms, and the Crispin, Friendly Port and Lifeboat beerhouses) was allowed to go through almost on the nod. George Beer however stoutly defended the Crown, their large house on the seaward side of Beach Street, and having failed to shift the borough magistrates argued their case before the Compensation Committee in July and won. In two years the magistrates' cull had brought about the closure of six public houses and four beerhouses, with two houses given a reprieve.

It was anything but the case however that the passions so long aroused by the drink question had now been safely channelled into judicious deliberations about the size, location and social value of individual houses being considered for closure. In 1906 the Liberal Party had won a landslide election victory, and two years later the Government introduced a bill which was expected to bring about the elimination of around 30,000 licences (a third of the total) with less generous compensation diminishing over a 14 year period; the full monopoly value of remaining licences would then transfer to the state. There would also be the option of local referenda to prohibit any new licences or, after the 14 years, to close all remaining houses. Brewers and publicans thereupon mounted a huge campaign of opposition, culminating in a massive demonstration in Hyde Park in September. This included contingents from Deal and other towns in east Kent, transported in a special train. As John Greenaway has observed, the "demonstrations on either side in favour of or against the liquor licensing bills of 1904 and 1908 were enormous, on a scale comparable to those of the Campaign for Nuclear Disarmament or Countryside Alliance three generations later"[115]. Men and women in Deal were swept up in the fervour, on both sides of the argument.

The first local public meeting was organised in March by the LVA and held in Eastry. Arthur Matthews of Thompson's, who was to play a leading role in mobilising opposition to the Bill in east Kent, was among the speakers. The temperance lobby responded with a public meeting next month in Walmer, but this was outshone by a large meeting organised by the LVA the following week at the Theatre Royal (the former Oddfellows Hall) in Deal. After a period of waiting "pleasantly occupied in listening to the strains of Mr Goss's bijou orchestra"[116], the platform filled with a large number of local and regional worthies amongst whom were representatives of no fewer than twelve east Kent breweries. The Mayor, ignoring complaints from the temperance lobby, took the chair himself. The main speakers were the organising agent of the National Trade Defence Association and Aretas Akers-Douglas MP, the latter of course being happy to deplore the new legislation in contrast to the admirable 1904 Licensing Act he had seen through as Home Secretary. Reverend Stanley Treanor, long serving chaplain to the Missions to Seaman in Deal, was also given a slot, and in "a characteristic speech...declared himself an abstainer and ardent advocate of temperance, but an equally ardent opponent of injustice"[117]. Councillor Redsull, chairman of the LVA, then presented Akers-Douglas with a petition against the Bill carrying 3,700 signatures.

In September came three open-air meetings in Deal and Walmer (at the first of these however, in Alfred Square, "the sound of a warning gun from a lightship...rather diminished the audience"[118]). The drink trade pinned its hopes on the House of Lords, and with good reason. In November the House threw out the Bill in its entirety. Temperance advocates were bitterly disappointed but it was rather a Pyrrhic victory for the brewers and publicans; Lloyd George's attention was now firmly fixed on raising manufacturing and retailing licences, both to fuel the Government's social reforms and as a back door way of reducing the number of drinking places. Retail licences would now be assessed at a half and beersellers a third of their licensed premises' annual value, raising the yield from some £2m to nearly £6m.

Back in Deal the magistrates pressed on with their task of identifying premises for closure, bringing forward a third tranche of six houses in 1909 (though withdrawing one, the Horse and Farrier, before the licensing day hearing). Of the remaining five, the Crown, back in the frame, had again to be defended by George Beer, while the proposed closure of the Harp was strongly but unsuccessfully resisted on behalf of the East Kent Brewery. There was

Reverend Treanor, most famous as the author of *Heroes of the Goodwin Sands* (1892), promoted temperance among seaman but had no truck with the plans of the 1906 Liberal Government to bring about the closure of large numbers of pubs.

clearly a feeling among the brewers that the slack had now been taken up and that further closures would have a serious impact. Arthur Matthews attended in person to try to stem the tide that had so far washed away eight of Thompson's houses: "... he thought it was time they were left alone. Candidly speaking, they had no houses in the place that were not holding their own, and that, he took it, ought to be the test of the public requirements"[119]. He was able to protect the Anchor in West Street, the magistrates clearly sympathetic to Emily Hall in her efforts to sustain trade at the house following the fatal accident to her husband, but not the Waterman's Arms. By the end of the round the Compensation Committee had closed a further three houses in the town: the Waterman's Arms, the Harp and, its reprieve two years before proving short lived, the Crown.

George Beer fought hard to preserve the Crown on Beach Street but the Compensation Committee decided on closure in 1909. The picture shows the house, boarded up, looking south down Beach Street with the Royal Hotel just visible in the distance.

And so it went on, though at a slower rate. The following year saw a proposal from Thompson's that if allowed to retain one of the two houses notified for closure they would "make a sacrifice" of the other. This may have helped persuade magistrates to refer only the Horse and Farrier, though the landlord of the Sir Sidney Smith clearly won credit for opening at 6.00am to meet the needs of boatmen (among whom "some liked a "little something" in their coffee, but teetotallers had the cocoa"[120]). In the event the Compensation Committee closed only the Tally Ho beerhouse owned by Gardner & Co of Ash. But both Thompson's houses were put back to the Committee in 1911, notwithstanding new evidence from the proprietor of bathing machines that the Sir Sidney Smith had often been of service to people feeling faint after bathing. This time the Horse and Farrier met its end, together with Leney & Co's Napier Tavern, the latter a boatman's house on the seaward side of Beach Street complete with veranda and telescopes. It had frequently been the case, according to the landlord Richard Riley, that "vessels in distress were first sighted from that point of view. That was so on the occasions of the last two launches of the lifeboat"[121]. But the house was closed nonetheless.

Across the country around 1,000 houses were closed each year between 1905 and 1909, two thirds of which were beerhouses, with a further 900 annual closures until 1914. The figures were in fact a good deal lower than expected, but still constituted about 10% of the total. Deal, by common agreement particularly oversupplied, took a significantly larger hit. In all, the magistrates and the Compensation Committee closed 13 public houses and 5 beerhouses between 1906 and 1914. This reduced the number of houses to 68, a reduction of 20%. Thompson's of course bore the brunt, their own eleven closures representing a fifth of their estate in Deal. It was not surprising that all but two of the houses closed down had been situated to the east of Lower Street. Of these, Beach Street lost seven houses and Middle Street a further five. The ratio of houses per head of population, the most important official indicator, had fallen from roughly 1:123 in 1906 to 1:167 in 1914. A comparable ratio today, following the slow and in the last ten years rapid further reduction in the number of houses, and continuing population growth, is in the order of 1:1,000.

The last two houses to be closed before the First World War, the Greyhound and the Liverpool Arms, can stand as fitting representatives of the hundred or so houses which plied their trade in Deal between 1830 and 1914, most of which have long since closed their doors. The humble Greyhound in Middle Street had started life as a beerhouse called the Seven Stars. In 1867 it became one of the many beerhouses during the 1860s allowed to join the ranks of the public houses, only to be repeatedly identified by the police as operating as a brothel when the Contagious Diseases Acts were extended to Deal two years later. Like so many other privately owned houses, the Greyhound was bought in due course by a brewer, in this case Nalder & Collyer of Croydon. Its appearances in the local newspapers almost always came about when something went wrong: a set-to with the Inspector of Nuisances after a brewery wagon blocked the pavement, with the landlord then bound over to keep the peace; a prosecution for serving out of hours (though dismissed on payment of 4s 6d costs); the bankruptcy of a former landlord turned High Street grocer and draper.

The tide turned with the arrival of Ernest Stride as landlord in 1892. The following year he pursued two marines who had stolen various items including a pint and a half of rum and successfully turned them over to the police. Two years later his wife Ada, supported by the LVA, brought about the prosecution of two men who had caused malicious damage after she refused them beer on credit. Under their firm hand the Greyhound achieved a measure of quiet respectability. As seen in Chapter 3, in 1905 it was the venue for the meeting of members of the Hearts of Oak Benefit Society at which the decision was taken to form a local association of members, and in December that year members of a Self Help Society met there to agree the fifth annual distribution of funds. Stride was also able to supplement his income on occasion by supplying refreshment at outdoor events and to Oatridge's restaurant on Beach Street. But when the time came the Greyhound's relatively small size and the limited accommodation it could offer told against it when compared to the four other houses less than 100 yards away. Described by the police as a well-conducted house, with "chiefly working class" trade[122], the Greyhound was closed down in 1913 and Ernest Stride's 20-year tenure as landlord came to an end. In due course the house became a private residence – just as it had been some 60 years earlier.

The Liverpool Arms, previously the King's Head and then the Three Horseshoes but re-named again in 1828 in honour of a former Prime Minister and Lord Warden of the Cinque Ports, was a different kind of public house. Standing opposite St Leonard's church in Upper Deal, it

The Liverpool Arms towards the end of its life. Further up the street, also on the left, is the Admiral Keppel. Out of picture on the right is St Leonard's, the parish church for Upper Deal.

was one of the 39 houses in existence in 1830 and dated from the late seventeenth century. Becoming part of the Hills estate in mid-century, when it passed to Thompson's in 1901 it included a coffee room as well as a bar and two sitting rooms on the ground floor. Successive landlords worked as master carpenters, making use of the spacious yard and outbuildings that formed part of the property. They were followed from 1884 until his death in 1898 by the builder George Burton.

Whereas the Greyhound sat within the tight network of streets dominated for most of the century by the activities and habits of the Deal boatmen, the Liverpool Arms stood with its back to the sea at the heart of Upper Deal and its rural hinterland: a venue for harvest suppers and the sale of rabbits, for meetings of the Mongeham and District Sparrow Club, the local Horticultural Society and the Upper Deal Bell Ringers. It also played a civic role as a place in which to hold inquests and election meetings. In September 1868, for example, following the extension of the franchise to many working men the year before, the two Conservative candidates addressed a packed meeting at the house. The Liberal candidates spoke there soon afterwards at a large gathering convened by the Liberal Workingmen's Association (during which, reported the *Telegram*, "the chairman, though a working man, acquitted himself with great tact and ability.."[123]).

But the two houses also had much in common. Both were patronised predominantly or overwhelmingly by working men, to whom they provided alcoholic refreshment and a place to meet, relax and do business. Both felt the impact of the presence nearby of large numbers of marines, whether in their capacity as customers or miscreants or both (the deserter found drinking in the tap room of the Liverpool Arms in 1891 still dressed in full uniform had certainly pushed his luck). Both played a part in helping to bring into being and to sustain the remarkable array of clubs and societies that had become such a feature of life in Deal by late Victorian times – as Thompson's lawyer argued in attempting to stave off closure "there was something more in a public-house-keeper's duty than the mere selling of beer and spirits"[124]. The two landlords operated within a common framework of regulation and control, and they had to keep in the good books of the brewers from whom they rented their houses. They also had to cope with the sheer awkwardness of keeping their houses supplied with barrels of beer, be it the difficulty in making deliveries to the Greyhound in narrow Middle Street or the dangers when lowering barrels into the cellars, which cost a Hills drayman a broken leg at the Liverpool Arms in 1894.

Like many of his colleagues during the Edwardian period, the last landlord of the Liverpool Arms, Arthur Skinner, had a military background, in his case as a Company Sergeant Major in the Royal Garrison Artillery and instructor for the local volunteer artillery. Skinner had given the impression when the magistrates had visited his house that he would not have been able to make a living were it not for his pension, and although Thompson's manager produced an optimistic forecast ("advent of coal might bring a greater population") Skinner's ten year tenancy ended in June 1913 and the house closed down. Under the hammer in January 1914 went an impressive collection of household furnishings, from easy, Austrian and Windsor bentwood chairs to an upright pianoforte in a rosewood case by W H Wilkie and a mahogany folding portable bagatelle table. Some of the domestic items may have remained in the property with its new owners. But there would be no further need for the:

> "three-pull metal lined beer engine and fittings, mahogany top and grained return front bar counter, mahogany glazed screens with Muranese and mirror panels...stoneware spirit barrels, pewter measures, beer, wine and spirit glasses, balance scales, [and] automatic game machines"[125].

The high summer of public houses in Deal had been relatively short lived. The magistrates' mid-century response to the efflorescence of beerhouses had helped to create an ample sufficiency of public houses. But sufficiency soon began to be widely perceived as an unhealthy surfeit, and by the 1890s the clouds had gathered over brewers and landlords alike. Yet despite the attentions of both central government and the local magistrates, the persistent campaigning of the temperance lobby and the development of alternative venues and attractions, many public houses still functioned or even prospered as small – overwhelmingly male – worlds of relaxation and association. They continued to meet most of the needs of visitors, travellers and others seeking refreshment and accommodation. East Kent breweries still brewed and delivered most of the beer drunk by the men and women of the town, in public houses or at home, as they had done since the eighteenth century. On

Outside the Prince Albert, 3 August 1914. The landlord, George "Cash" Erridge, sits fourth from the right in the middle row. The following day the country was at war.

the other hand the later Victorian and Edwardian periods had seen a steady improvement in the conduct of public houses the brewers supplied, and a decline in rowdy drunkenness. But there would be no reprieve for good behaviour; the First World War would instead bring previously unthinkable restrictions on the brewing, retailing and consumption of beer.

1. B. Harrison, *Drink and the Victorians: The Temperance Question in England, 1815–1872* (London, 1971) p 58
2. *Telegram* 11 July 1860
3. *Telegram* 25 February 1865
4. *Telegram* 2 October 1869
5. *Mercury* 22 January 1870
6. Quoted in L. L. Shiman, *Crusade against Drink in Victorian England* (Basingstoke, 1988) p 178
7. Shiman p 112
8. *Mercury* 19 May 1883
9. *Mercury* 27 November 1909
10. *Mercury* 29 April 1911
11. *Mercury* 24 April 1912
12. Quoted in *Telegram* 20 August 1887
13. T. Stanley Treanor, *The Log of a Sky-Pilot* (London, 1894) pp 217–18
14. G. Holyoake, *Deal: All in the Downs* (Seaford, 2008) p 301
15. Shiman p 97
16. R. Highet, *Rechabite History: A Record of the Origin, Rise and Progress of the Independent Order of Rechabites (Salford Unity) Temperance Friendly Society* (Manchester. 1936) p 15

17. *Mercury* 23 March 1895
18. *Mercury* 15 March 1890
19. Obituary of Reverend Payne in *Mercury* 14 June 1913
20. *Mercury* 6 April 1907
21. Shiman p 178
22. *Mercury* 24 May 1890
23. *Telegram* 16 June 1858
24. *Illustrated and Historical Deal, Walmer and Sandwich* (Deal, 1890)
25. Advertisement in *Telegram* 20 January 1883
26. *Report of the Commissioners into the Existence of Corrupt Practices in the Borough of Sandwich* (1881) p 104
27. *Mercury* 19 October 1901
28. Ibid
29. *Telegram* 21 March 1860
30. *Telegram* 26 September 1868
31. *Telegram* 6 September 1873
32. *Telegram* 24 November 1888
33. *Mercury* 24 February 1894
34. *Mercury* 13 June 1896
35. D. W. Gutzke, *Protecting the Pub: Brewers and Publicans Against Temperance* (Woodbridge, 1989) p 110
36. *Mercury* 30 March 1895
37. T. J. Chander at the Association's second annual dinner *Mercury* 28 March 1896
38. *Mercury* 6 March 1909
39. *Mercury* 3 February 1912
40. *Mercury* 5 July 1902
41. Gutzke p 153
42. *Mercury* 8 March 1913
43. *Mercury* 15 January 1881
44. *Mercury* 19 June 1875
45. *Telegram* 14 May 1864
46. *Telegram* 3 May 1873
47. *Telegram* 28 November 1874
48. *Telegram* 13 March 1880
49. *Mercury* 20 June 1874
50. Harrison p 263
51. Letter to the *Telegram* 7 December 1872
52. *Mercury* 21 June 1873
53. *Telegram* 28 June 1873
54. *Mercury* 20 September 1873
55. *Mercury* 24 April 1875
56. *Hansard* 16 June 1875 col 59
57. *Mercury* 22 May 1880
58. *Mercury* 13 January 1906
59. Quoted in J. Laker, *History of Deal* (2nd ed, Deal 1921) p 248
60. *Mercury* 3 December 1881
61. *Mercury* 5 November 1881
62. Obituary in *Mercury* 15 October 1910
63. *Mercury* 7 November 1891
64. *Mercury* 5 November 1892
65. *Mercury* 28 October 1893
66. Ibid
67. *Mercury* 9 November 1895
68. Ibid
69. Ibid
70. Ibid
71. Ibid
72. *Mercury* 22 October 1898
73. *Mercury* 28 March 1896
74. *Mercury* 30 September 1899
75. *Mercury* 24 September 1892
76. *Telegram* 10 September 1881
77. *Telegram* 8 September 1883
78. *Telegram* 4 June 1881
79. *Telegram* 3 April 1875
80. *Mercury* 3 September 1898
81. *Mercury* 17 April 1897
82. *Mercury* 28 September 1901
83. *Telegram* 30 September 1882
84. *Mercury* 22 September 1888
85. *Mercury* 28 September 1872
86. *Mercury* 25 September 1897
87. Ibid
88. Ibid

89. *Mercury* 21 September 1895
90. *Mercury* 26 September 1891
91. Ibid
92. *Mercury* 1 June 1895
93. *Mercury* 7 September 1895
94. Ibid
95. *Mercury* 19 October 1895
96. Ibid
97. Ibid
98. *Mercury* 4 January 1896
99. *Mercury* 8 September 1900
100. J. Greenaway, *Drink and British Politics since 1830: A Study in Policy-Making* (Basingstoke, 2003) pp 7–19
101. Greenaway p 13
102. *Mercury* 31 August 1901
103. Ibid
104. *Mercury* 24 August 1901
105. *Mercury* 28 September 1901
106. *Mercury* 24 August 1901
107. *Mercury* 30 September 1899
108. *Mercury* 14 March 1903
109. Ibid
110. Ibid
111. *Mercury* 13 June 1903
112. *Mercury* 4 June 1904
113. *Mercury* 6 October 1906
114. *Mercury* 9 March 1907
115. Greenaway p 1
116. *Mercury* 18 April 1908
117. Ibid
118. *Mercury* 12 September 1908
119. *Mercury* 6 March 1909
120. *Mercury* 5 March 1910
121. *Mercury* 11 March 1911
122. *Mercury* 15 March 1913
123. *Telegram* 3 October 1868
124. *Mercury* 15 March 1913
125. S. Glover and M. Rogers, *The Old Pubs of Deal and Walmer (with Kingsdown and Mongeham)* (Whitstable, 2010) p 105

Deal Public Houses and Beerhouses Mentioned in the Text

For the detailed histories of individual houses see Steve Glover and Michael Rogers, *The Old Pubs of Deal and Walmer (with Kingsdown and Mongeham)* (Whitstable, 2010). This notes variations in the names of the streets where houses were situated. Some streets were renamed by the town council, the most significant change being the elevation of Lower Street to High Street in 1879. The names given below are those in use *c.*1870.

19 Farrier Street	Farrier Street	became Deal Lugger (2)
Admiral Keppel	Upper Deal Road	
Admiral Rodney	Beach Street	
Albion	Beach Street	
Alhambra	Robert Street	
Alma	West Street	
Anchor	West Street	
Antwerp	Beach Street	previously Lord Keith
Beehive	Upper Queen Street	became Eagle
Bell	Robert Street	
Black Bull	Lower Street	
Black Horse	Lower Street	
Bowling Green	Church Walk	previously Gun Inn
Bricklayer's Arms	West Street	
Brickmaker's Arms	Mill Road	
Castle	Sandown Road	previously Good Intent, became Sandown Castle
Chequers	Middle Street	
Cinque Port Arms	Market Street	became Druid's Arms
Clarendon Hotel	Beach Street	previously Ship (1)
Clarendon Tap	Middle Street	became Old Victory
Clifton	Middle Street	previously Redan
Crispin	Middle Street	
Crown	Beach Street	
Deal Castle	Prospect Place	
Deal Cutter	Beach Street	

Deal Hoy	Duke Street	
Deal Lugger (1)	Beach Street	
Deal Lugger (2)	Farrier Street	previously 19 Farrier Street
Dover Castle	Middle Street	
Druid's Arms	Market Street	previously Cinque Port Arms
Duke of Wellington	Water Street	
Duke of York	Cemetery Road	
Eagle	Upper Queen Street	previously Beehive
East India Arms	Beach Street	became India Arms
Empire Theatre of Varieties	Middle Street	previously Star and Paragon Music Hall
Fawn	Lower Street	
Fishing Boat	Middle Street	became Shah
Five Bells	Middle Street	
Five Ringers	Church Walk	
Fleur de Lis	Union Row	
Forester	Beach Street	
Fountain	Beach Street	
Fox	Beach Street	
Frederick William	Middle Street	very briefly the name of the Tally Ho
Friendly Port	New Street	briefly the Oddfellow's Arms
Globe	Beach Street	previously Scarborough Cat
Good Intent	Sandown Road	became Castle and Sandown Castle
Greyhound	Middle Street	previously Seven Stars
Gun Inn	Church Walk	became Bowling Green
Hare and Hounds	North Sandy Lane	
Harp	Middle Street	
Hoop and Griffin	Beach Street	
Hope	Middle Street	
Horse and Farrier	Farrier Street	
Hovelling Boat	Silver Street	
India Arms	Beach Street	previously East India Arms
Jolly Butcher	Beach Street	
Jolly Gardener	North Sandy Lane	
Jolly Sailor	West Street	for a time Norfolk Arms
Just Reproach	King Street	
King's Arms	Beach Street	
King's Head	Beach Street	
Laurel Tree	Lower Street	became Phoenix (2)
Lifeboat	Beach Street	

Liverpool Arms	Upper Deal Road	
Locomotive	West Street	
Lord Keith	Beach Street	became Antwerp
Lord Nelson	Short Street	
Lord Warden	Cemetery Road	previously Sydenham Green
Magnet	Church Walk	
Maxton Arms	Western Road	
Napier Tavern	Beach Street	
New Inn	Lower Street	previously Three Compasses (1)
New Plough/Plough	Middle Deal Road	
Noah's Ark	Ark Lane	
Norfolk Arms	West Street	previously and later Jolly Sailor
North Star	Beach Street	
Oak and Ivy	Blenheim Road	
Oddfellow's Arms	New Street	briefly the name of the Friendly Port
Old Victory	Middle Street	previously Clarendon Tap
Paragon Music Hall	Middle Street	previously Star, later Empire Theatre of Varieties
Park Tavern	Park Street	
Pelican (1)	Beach Street	
Pelican (2)	Beach Street	
Phoenix (1)	Lower Street	became Queen's Arms
Phoenix (2)	Lower Street	previously Laurel Tree
Pier Hotel	Beach Street	previously Sandwich Arms
Pier Refreshment Rooms	Pier	
Port Arms	Beach Street	
Prince Albert	Middle Street	
Prince Alfred	Lower Street	
Prince of Wales	Middle Street	
Providence	King Street	
Queen's Arms	Lower Street	previously Phoenix (1)
Queen's Head	Bridge Row, then Middle Street	
Railway Tavern	Upper Queen Street	
Redan	Middle Street	became Clifton
Rose	Lower Street	
Rose and Crown	Beach Street	
Roxburgh Castle	Broad Street	
Royal Exchange	Beach Street	

Royal George	Lower Street	
Royal Hotel	Beach Street	
Royal Marine	Gladstone Road	
Royal Oak	Middle Street	
Sandown Castle	Sandown Road	previously Castle and Good Intent
Sandwich Arms	Beach Street	became Pier Hotel
Saracen's Head	Alfred Square	
Scarborough Cat	Beach Street	became Globe
Seven Stars	Middle Street	became Greyhound
Shah	Middle Street	previously Fishing Boat
Ship (1)	Middle Street	became Clarendon Hotel
Ship (2)	Middle Street	
Ship and Castle	Lower Street	became Sir John Falstaff
Sir John Falstaff	Lower Street	previously Ship and Castle
Sir Norman Wisdom	Queen Street	
Sir Sidney Smith	Beach Street	
South Foreland	Beach Street	
Star	Middle Street	became Paragon Music Hall and Empire Theatre of Varieties
Star and Garter	Beach Street	
Sun/Rising Sun	George Street	
Swan (1)	Beach Street	
Swan (2)	Queen Street	
Sydenham Green	Cemetery Road	became Lord Warden
Tally Ho	Middle Street	very briefly Frederick William
Telegraph	Cemetery Road	
Three Compasses (1)	Lower Street	became New Inn
Three Compasses (2)	Beach Street	
Two Brewers	Middle Street	became Star (etc)
Victoria	Gladstone Road	previously Wheatsheaf
Walmer Castle	Lower Street, then South Street	
Waterman's Arms	Beach Street	
Wheatsheaf	Gladstone Road	became Victoria
White Horse	Upper Queen Street	
Windsor Castle	Lower Street	
Wine Shades	Beach Street	
Yarmouth Packet	Beach Street	
Yew Tree	Mill Road	

SELECT BIBLIOGRAPHY

Deal and Walmer
G. Appleton, "Deal Luggers", *Mariner's Mirror*, Vol 45 (1959), No 2, pp 145–153
J. Bower, "Deal and the Deal Boatmen *c.* 1840–*c.* 1880", Unpublished PhD thesis, University of Kent, 1990
H. S. Chapman, *Deal: Past and Present* (London, 1890)
E. B. V. Christian, *Edmund Brown: A Deal Worthy* (Canterbury, 1931)
E. W. Clark, *Reminiscences of Old Deal* (Deal, 1949)
B. Collins, *Discovering Deal (Historic Guide)* (Deal, 1969)
D. G. Collyer, "The Walmer Brewery 1816–1978: Part One: "Bread, beer and "baccy"", in *Bygone Kent*, Vol 24 (2003), pp 613–20; Part Two: "Bright and airy buildings, lit by smiling faces", in *Bygone Kent*, Vol 24 (2003), pp 635–9
J. Deller, "Death in the Druid's Arms", in *Bygone Kent*, Vol 15 (1994), pp 613–17
C. R. S. Elvin, *Records of Walmer* (London, 1890)
J. M. Fells, *The Origin of the Deal and Walmer Carter Institute* (Deal, 1921)
W. H. Gillespie, "An Old Force", in *The Police Journal*, Vol 27 (1954), pp 306–17
S. Glover and M. Rogers, *The Old Pubs of Deal and Walmer (with Kingsdown and Mongeham)* (Whitstable, 2010)
I. Green, *The Book of Deal and Walmer* (Buckingham, 1983)
G. Holyoake, *Wellington at Walmer* (London, 1996)
G. Holyoake, *Deal: Sad Smuggling Town* (Seaford, 2001)
G. Holyoake, *Deal: All in the Downs* (Seaford, 2008)
J. Laker, *History of Deal* (2nd ed, Deal, 1921)
A. Lane, *Royal Marines Deal: A Pictorial History* (Bodmin, 2000)
A. L. Macfie, "Dover and Deal Police, 1836–1886", in *Bygone Kent*, Vol 5 (1984), pp 402–7
A. L. Macfie, "The Boatmen of Dover and Deal: The Report of the House of Commons Select Committee on the Cinque-Port Pilots, 1833", in *Archaeolgia Cantiana* , Vol 101 (1984), pp 131–6
A. L. Minter, *Deal Railway Station: A History, 1847–1995* (Sandwich, 1995)
G. Nunns, "The Ship Inn: Middle Street, Deal", in *Deal Society Magazine* (1995), pp 3–5
G. Nunns, *A History of Deal* (Canterbury, 2006)
E. C. Pain, *The Last of Our Luggers and the Men Who Sailed Them* (Deal, 1929)
S. Pritchard, *The History of Deal* (Deal, 1864)

P.E. Robinson, "The Queen's Arms Inn, High Street, Deal" (Unpublished article in Deal Library)
J.L. Roget, *Sketches of Deal, Walmer and Sandwich* (London, 1911)
J. Roy and T. Thompson, *Picture Palaces Remembered: An affectionate look at the cinema theatres of Dover, Deal and Folkestone* (Dover, 1987)
W. Clark Russell, *Betwixt the Forelands* (London, 1889)
W. H. Stanton, *The Journal of William Stanton, Pilot of Deal* (Portsmouth, 1929)
W. P. D. Stebbing, *The Invader's Shore: Some Observations on the Physiography, Archaeology, History and Sociology of Deal and Walmer* (Deal, 1937)
Thompson & Son, Ltd, *The Walmer Brewery, Kent: A Guide to the Brewery and to the District where Walmer Ales are Sold* (London, 1950)
T. Stanley Treanor, *Heroes of the Goodwin Sands* (London, 1892)
T. Stanley Treanor, *The Log of a Sky-Pilot* (London, 1894)
T. Stanley Treanor, *The Cry From the Sea and the Answer from the Shore* (London, 1899)
J. Whyman, "Rise and Decline: Dover and Deal in the Nineteenth Century", in *Archaeologia Cantiana*, Vol 84 (1969), pp 107–37

General
O. Anderson, *Suicide in Victorian and Edwardian England* (Oxford, 1987)
F.W.G. Andrews, "The Road Services in Kent in the Nineteenth Century", in *Archaeologia Cantiana*, Vol 127 (2007), pp 213–35
A. Armstrong (ed), *The Economy of Kent, 1640–1914* (Woodbridge, 1995)
N. Barber, *A Century of British Brewers Plus, 1890 to 2004* (Longfield, 2005)
T. Barker, *Shepherd Neame: A Story That's Been Brewing for 300 Years* (Chesterton, 1998)
A. Barnard, *The Noted Breweries of Great Britain and Ireland* (London, 1889–90)
A. Bateman, *Victorian Canterbury: A Close Look at Day-to-Day Life in the Cathedral City, 1837–1901* (Buckingham, 1991)
J. S. Blocker Jnr, D. M. Fahey and I. R. Tyrrell (eds), *Alcohol and Temperance in Modern History: An International Encyclopedia*, 2 Vols (Santa Barbara, 2003)
G. Brandwood, A. Davison and M. Slaughter, *Licensed to Sell: The History and Heritage of the Public House* (London, 2004)
J. Burnett, *Liquid Pleasures: A Social History of Drinks in Modern Britain* (London, 1999)
I. A. Burney, *Bodies of Evidence: Medicine and the Politics of the English Inquest, 1830–1926* (Baltimore, 2000)
R. Campbell, *Rechabite History: A Record of the Origin, Rise, and Progress of the Independent Order of Rechabites* (Manchester, 1911)
J. A. Chandler, *Explaining Local Government: Local Government in Britain since 1800* (Manchester, 2007)
P. Chaplin, *Darts in England, 1900–39: A Social History* (Manchester, 2009)
C. Clark, *The British Malting Industry Since 1830* (London, 1998)

P. Clark, *The English Alehouse: A Social History, 1200–1830* (Harlow, 1983)

P. Clark (ed), *The Cambridge Urban History of Britain* Vol. 2 *1540–1840* (Cambridge, 2000)

C. A. Conley, *The Unwritten Law: Criminal Justice in Victorian Kent* (Oxford, 1991)

S. Cordery, *British Friendly Societies, 1750–1914* (Basingstoke, 2003)

M. Cornell, *Beer: The Story of the Pint. The History of Britain's Most Popular Drink* (London, 2003)

W. R. Cornish et al, *Crime and Law in Nineteenth Century Britain* (Dublin, 1978)

V. S. Dennis, *Discovering Friendly and Fraternal Societies: Their Badges and Regalia* (Buckinghamshire, 2005)

A. E. Dingle, "Drink and Working-class Living Standards in Britain, 1870–1914", in D. J. Oddy and D.S. Miller, *The Making of the Modern British Diet* (London, 1976), pp 117–33

A. E. Dingle, *The Campaign for Prohibition in Victorian England* (London, 1980)

R. Donovan, "Drinking in Victorian Norwich" in *Brewery History*, No 130, pp 18–64; No 132, pp 67–133; No 134, pp 87–139; No 137, pp 73–165

C. Emsley, *The English Police: A Political and Social History* (2nd ed, Harlow 1996)

C. Emsley, *Crime and Society in England, 1750–1900* (4th ed, London 2010)

M. Girouard, *Victorian Pubs* (New Haven, 1984)

P. H. J. H. Gosden, *The Friendly Societies in England, 1815–1875* (Manchester, 1961)

T. R. Gourvish and R. G. Wilson, *The British Brewing Industry, 1830–1980* (Cambridge, 1994)

J. Greenaway, *Drink and British Politics since 1830: A Study in Policy-Making* (Basingstoke, 2003)

C. Greenwood, *An Epitome of County History*, Vol 1, *County of Kent* (London, 1838)

G. M. Grover (ed), *The Royal Marines: History of the Royal Marine Divisions* (Portsmouth, 1931)

D. W. Gutzke, *Protecting the Pub: Brewers and Publicans Against Temperance* (Woodbridge, 1989)

D. W. Gutzke, *Pubs and Progressives: Reinventing the Public House in England, 1896–1960* (Northern Illinois, 2006)

W. B. Gwyn, *Democracy and the Cost of Politics in Britain* (London, 1962)

H. J. Hanham, *Elections and Party Management: Politics in the Time of Disraeli and Gladstone* (London, 1959)

D. Harper, *Whitbread: The Inn Behind the Signs* (The Author, 2005)

B. Harrison, *Drink and the Victorians: The Temperance Question in England, 1815–1872* (London, 1971)

J. Hart, "Reform of the Borough Police 1835–1856", *English Historical Review*, Vol LXX (1955), pp 411–427

E. Hasted, *The History and Topographical Survey of the County of Kent*, Vol X

Select Bibliography

(Canterbury, 1800)

R. Highet, *Rechabite History: A Record of the Origin, Rise and Progress of the Independent Order of Rechabites (Salford Unity) Temperance Friendly Society* (Manchester, 1936)

M. Hilton, *Smoking in British Popular Culture, 1800–2000: Perfect Pleasures* (Manchester, 2000)

R. Ingleton, *Policing Kent: Guarding the Garden of England, 1800–2000* (Chichester, 2002)

P. Jennings, *The Public House in Bradford, 1770–1970* (Keele, 1995)

P. Jennings, *The Local: A History of the English Pub* (Stroud, 2007)

F. Lansberry (ed), *Government and Politics in Kent, 1640–1914* (Woodbridge, 2001)

T. Lawson and D Killingray (eds), *An Historical Atlas of Kent* (Chichester, 2004)

A.J. Lee, *The Origins of the Popular Press in England, 1855–1914* (London, 1976)

C. Lee, *Policing Prostitution, 1856–1886: Deviance, Surveillance and Morality* (London, 2013)

W. L. M. Lee, *A History of Police in England* (New Jersey, 1971 ed)

P. Mathias, *The Brewing Industry in England, 1700–1830* (Cambridge, 1959)

P. Moynihan, *Kentish Brewers and the Brewers of Kent* (Longfield, 2011)

J. Nicholls, *The Politics of Alcohol: A History of the Drink Question in England* (Manchester, 2009)

K. Osborne, *Bygone Breweries* (Whitstable, 1982)

L. Pearson, *British Breweries: An Architectural History* (London, 1999)

D. Philips and R. D. Storch, *Policing Provincial England, 1829–1856: The Politics of Reform* (Leicester, 1999)

J. Preston, *Malting and Malthouses in Kent* (Stroud, 2015)

J. Redlich and F. Hirst, *The History of Local Government in England* (London, 1958 ed)

R. C. Riley and P. Eley, "Public Houses and Beerhouses in Nineteenth Century Portsmouth", *The Portsmouth Papers*, No 38 (Portsmouth, 1983)

M. Roake (ed), *Religious Worship in Kent: The Census of 1851* (Maidstone, 1999)

A. Rootes, "Canterbury: A City Too Corrupt for Parliament" in *Bygone Kent*, Vol 35, No 5, pp 28–33

R. Seth, *The Specials: The Story of the Special Constabulary in England, Wales and Scotland* (London, 1961)

H. Shaw, "A Croydon Brewery" [Nalder and Collyer], in *Brewery History* (No 131), pp 2–18

L. L. Shiman, *Crusade Against Drink in Victorian England* (Basingstoke, 1988)

A. R. Skelley, *The Victorian Army at Home: The Recruitment and Terms and Conditions of the British Regular, 1859–1899* (London, 1977)

T. Skyrme, *History of the Justice of the Peace* Vol 2 *1689–1989* (Chichester, 1991)

E. M. Spiers, *The Army and Society, 1815–1914* (London, 1980)

E. M. Spiers, *The Late Victorian Army 1868–1902* (Manchester, 1992)

F. Stafford and N. Yates, *The Later Kentish Seaside (1840–1974)* (Gloucester, 1985)

C. Steedman, *Policing the Victorian Community: the Formation of English Provincial Police Forces, 1856–80* (London, 1984)

A. Taylor, *Played at the Pub: the Pub Games of Britain* (Swindon, 2009)

F. M. L. Thompson (ed), *The Cambridge Social History of Britain, 1750–1950* (Cambridge, 1990)

J. R. Walkowitz, *Prostitution and Victorian Society: Women, Class and the State* (Cambridge, 1980)

S. and B. Webb, *The History of Liquor Licensing in England Principally from 1700 to 1830* (London, 1903)

D. Weinbren, *The Oddfellows 1810–2010: 200 Years of Making Friends and Helping People* (Lancaster, 2010)

R. A. Whitehead, "Kentish Brewers' Steam Wagons (Part Two: Users of Overtypes)", in *Bygone Kent*, No 14 (1993), pp 163–7

J. Whyman, *The Early Kentish Seaside (1736–1840)* (Gloucester, 1985)

G. B. Wilson, *Alcohol and the Nation* (London, 1940)

R. G. Wilson, "The Changing Taste for Beer in Victorian Britain", in R. G. Wilson and T. R. Gourvish, *The Dynamics of the International Brewing Industry since 1800* (London, 1998), pp 93–104

M. Winstanley, "The Rural Publican and His Business in East Kent before 1914", in *Oral History*, Vol 4 (1976), No 2, pp 63–78

N. Yates, R. Hume and P. Hastings, *Religion and Society in Kent, 1640–1914* (Woodbridge, 1994)

INDEX

Public houses in Deal are shown in **bold**

19 Farrier Street 70, 246

Abrahams, Alf 120–1
Abrahams, Horace 120–1
Acacia House 260
Adams, James 119
Adamson, Thomas 175
Admiral Keppel 65, 70, 88, 93, **95**, 119, 124, 142, 172, 198, **266**
Admiral Rodney 70, 78
Adulteration Acts 159
adulteration of spirits 200–1
AFS Bird wine merchants 36
AK light bitter 28
Akers-Douglas, Aretas 237, **237**, 259, 262
Albert Victor lugger 208
Albion 34, 87–8, 166
Alcazar music hall 120
Alfred Leney & Co, brewers **17**, 38, 44–5, 75, 122, 264
Alhambra 68, 120
Allen, Alice 94
Allen, Amos 190
Allen, Robert 71, 75, 84–5, 94, 146, 238
Alma 36, **37**, 62, 70, 116, 119, 138, 238
Almond, David 87, 133, 136, 247
Anchor 79, 80, 82, 90, 101, 122, 123, 147, 263
Anchor Brewery 26
Ancient Order of Druids 71, 134
Ancient Order of Foresters 132–4, 136
Ancient Order of Oddfellows 134
Andrews, Albert 86
angling clubs 138
Anglo-Lager Beer 36
Annall, PC John 167
The Anti-Adulteration Review 29
Antwerp 14, 77, 82, 116, 127, 175, 208, 255
Apollo Harmony Society 118
Appleton, William 207
Astor Community Theatre 54, **54**
auctions 144

bagatelle 123
Bailey, Thomas 170
Baker, Mary 200
Baker, Samuel 92
Bands of Hope 221–2, 223
Banfield, Arthur 84
Bank Holiday Act (1871) 115
Banks, Mary 125
Baptist Total Abstinence Society 221
Barnard, Alfred 28, 29, 30, 38, 40
Bartram, Rev James **222**, 244
Bass beer 30, 36
Bass brewery 39
bathing machines 264
Bayly, Thomas Steed 52–3
Beach House Temperance Hotel 138, 223, **227**
Beach Street brewery (Oakley) 23
Beale, James 162
beer: bottled beer 30, 36, 55, 247; consumption 15, 139; cost of 126; production 28, 52; quality 29; sales 30, 89; sales to children 199–200; transportation 36; types produced 28–9
Beer Act (1830) 9, 60–1, 254
Beer, Albert 34
beerhouses 9–10, 18, 60–65; *see also* public houses
Bell 56, 93, 123, 128, 130
bell ringing 138, 267
Bell, Virginia 183
Bell's birthday club 128
billiards 123
Bingham, Thomas 85, 97
Bird, Alexander 59, 228
Bishop, John 89
Black Bull 70, 94, **155**
Black Horse 53, 59, 70, 72, 74, 84, 88, 91, 114, 123, 135, 136, 138, 144, 147, 186
Blue Ribbon Army Brain Restorative 225
Blue Ribbon Gospel Temperance movement 218–19, 227, 243, 254
Boakes, Elizabeth 93
boatmen: as customers 101–2; fights and 169; hardship and 59, 102; as landlords 81, 104; as lodgers 114; and marines 110; numbers of 102–3; and salvage 102–4; voting by 208
Boatmen's Benefit Society 131–2
borough council status/reform 14, 152–4
borough magistrates 14, 16, 17, 151–68; *see also* licensing
Bower, Jacqueline 81
bowling 122–3
Bowling Green 34, **35**, 87, 122, 140, 178
Boyd, Sgt 158, 160
Boys, Edward 102
Bradley, Eliza 125
Brassey, Henry 203, 234, 236
Brassington, Arthur 90
breweries: in 1875 **11**; cooling equipment 29; employment 39–40; and licensing 242–5; management 40–2; trade organisations 228–42; brewers, as prominent figures 47
brewery off-licences 30
brewery purchase consolidation 49–56
Bricklayer's Arms 125, 177, 180, 184, 242–3
Bricklayers' Union 137
Brickmaker's Arms 89, 94, 95, 97, 167, 197, 199–200, 245, 246, **246**
British Women's Temperance Association 222
brothels 179–87
Brown, Edmund 203
Brown, John 191
Brown, Tom 172–3
Browning, PC 157
Browning, William 84, 93
Bruce, Henry 234
Buckland Brewery 34, 37
Burdett-Coutts, Angela 146
Burns, Sgt 162
Burton, George 82, 121, 267
Burville, Henry 86
Bush Hotel (Southsea) 89
by-election (1880) 203–11

Cambridge Arms (Walmer) 93, **111**
CAMRA 15
Candalet, George 234, 236
Canterbury Barley Wine 35
Cantis' pale beer 29
Capeling, John 247

281

Capon, Jonathan 165, 185
Capps, Superintendent Helder Ben 162, 163–4, 167, 191, 194–5
card playing **124**
Carpenters' and Joiners' Union 137
Carter, Walter 35
Castle 72, 75, 78, 82, 83, 86–7, 97, 122, 171, 178
Castle, Mary 94
Cattermole, Mrs 98
Cattermole, Thomas 78, 83, 178
Cawthorne, George 189
Central Association for Stopping the Sale of Intoxicating Liquors on Sundays 226
Chamber of Commerce 137
Chambers, Albert 98–9
Chambers, Jane 98–9
Chandler, Edward 93
Chaney, Supt 255, 258
Channer, Capt Alfred 249–52
Chapman, PC 86, 151, 184, 197
charabanc outings 129, 145
Charrington's brewery 55, 56
Chequers 172
chess 138
Chitty, Edward 218, 238
Christy, Thomas 113
Church of England Temperance Society (CETS) 219–20, 221, 224, 227
Church, John 43
Church Temperance Chronicle 227
churches 14
cigarette smoking 126–7
cinemas 139
Cinque Port Arms 71, 73, 134
Cinque Ports Artillery Volunteers 25, 47
civic functions 139–45
Clarence coach **146**
Clarendon Hotel 71, 75, 76, 78, 84, 85, 90, 91, 92, 107, 116, 117, 123, 151, 206
Clarendon Tap 77, 86, 91, 135, 190
Clark, Peter 139
clay pipes 126
Clayton, William 85, 171
Clements, John 77
Clifton 36, 71, **121**, 122, 123, 230, 253
clubs and societies 128–39
Cobb & Co, brewers 30–1, 49,

51, 73, 74
Cobb, Francis 21
cock fighting 121
coffee rooms 73
coinage 126
Coleman, John Noakes 23
Collins, Barbara 52
Collins, William 75, 90
community services, by brewers 46–7
Compensation Committee 260–1, 263, 264, 265
Conley, William 77
Contagious Diseases (CD) Acts 179–84, 265
conviviality 117–28
Cooper, Edward 97–8
Cooper, Sarah 97–8
Corrupt Practices Act (1883) 211
Corrupt Practices Prevention Act (1854) 204
corruption trials 204–11
Cottew, George 25
Cottew, George (jnr) 83, 250, **251**, 253, 255
County Police Act (1839) 157
courts 154–6
Cox, PC James Shelvey 158, **158**, 160
cricket 124
Crispin 73, 86, 90, 261
Crown 35, 62, 70, 78, 79, 81, 85, 93, 106, **115**, 118, 124, 135, 138, 171, 229, 253, 263, **264**
curiosities 123
Curling, George 84
Currie, Richard 241
Curtis, Sgt 164
cycling clubs 138

Daily News 209–10
Darby, Edward 102
Darby, Henry 166
Dartford Brewery Company 49, 51
darts 124
Davidson, Archbishop Randall 220
Davies, WH 24
Dawes, Edwin 53–4, 86
Dawes, Richard 172
Deal beach **9**
Deal Boatmen's Friendly Soci-

ety 132
Deal Castle 74, 82, 135, **137**
Deal Catch Club 118, 120
Deal Chronicle, Sandwich Express and Walmer Gazette 12
Deal Commercial Association 136–7
Deal Cutter 70, 82, 90, 91, 95, 259
Deal fire brigade **76**
Deal Friendly Society 131
Deal Hoy 70, 76, 122, 123, 126, 136, 142, 178
Deal Hoy Working Men's Club outing 129
Deal Improvement Act (1791) 162
Deal lifeboat house 32, **32**
Deal Lugger 35, 63, 70, 101, 190, 195, 198, 260, 261
Deal navy yard 13, 21, 75, 115
Deal Pale Ale 29
Deal pier 91, **103**, 106
Deal regattas 20, 46
Deal Temperance Society 216–17, 223, 243
Deal Town Hall **155**
Deal United Friendly Association (DUFA) 130–1
Deal and Walmer Amalgamated Friendly Societies 134
Deal and Walmer Burial Society 132
Deal and Walmer (Carter) Institute 55, 117
Deal and Walmer Friendly Association 135
Deal and Walmer Mutual Provident Life Association 132
Deal, Walmer and Sandwich Licensed Victuallers Protection Association (LVA) 96, 170, 199, 229–41, 244, 247–8, 250, 255, 262, 265
Deal, Walmer and Sandwich Licensed Victuallers Protection Society 61, 192, 229, 230
Deal, Walmer and Sandwich Mercury, Downs Reporter and Cinque Ports Messenger 12
Deal, Walmer and Sandwich Telegram 12
Deal and Walmer Temperance Union (DWTU) 224, 229, 241
Deal and Walmer Trade Protec-

INDEX

tion Association 137
Deal and Walmer Tradesmen's Friendly Society 132
Denne, Charles 62, 201, 225
Denne, Elizabeth 201
Denne, William 32
Denton, Henry 169–70
Denton, John 169–70
Desormeaux, Thomas 63, 83
Diamond Brewery 54
Dickens, Charles 146
Diggerson, Annie 96
disorderly behaviour 16, 155–7, 168–79, 186
Dog (Wingham) 129, 232
domestic violence 97
Donoghue, Charlotte 94
Dover Brewery Company 95
Dover Castle 125, 183
Dover Express 49, 220–1
Downs naval anchorage 106–9
draymen, injuries to 42–3, 45–6, 112, 268
drays 44–6, **45**
Druid's Arms 32, 71, 76, 84, 86, 93, 94, 134, 261
drunkenness 16, 168–79; among police 161–3
Duke of Connaught (Dover) 99
Duke of Wellington 17, 93, 240
Duke of York 31, 184, 243
Dunne, John 230, 241
Duttson, WH 49

Eagle 134, **134**, 136, 147, 188, 198, 199, 208
East India Arms 114
East India Pale Ale 29
East Kent breweries 34
East Kent Brewery 63, 119, 245, 263
Eastes, Benjamin 186
Eastry Workhouse 46
economic depression 59
Edwards, James Barber 209
Edwards, John 249
elections 201–11
electoral corruption 204–11
Elkins, George 24
Elson, James 120, 183–4, 240, 241
Emmerson, Richard 202
Empire Theatre of Varieties 120–1, 257

employees: annual dinners 119; outings **39**; and paternalist management 40–1; recreation 41, 118–19
Endeavour (Shatterling) **33**
entertainment: at marine barracks 111–12; in public houses 117–28
Erridge, Edward 106
Erridge, Frederick 169
Erridge, George 35, 91, **91**, 125, 269
Erridge, John 46
Erridge, Lucy 169
Erridge, Ralph 91
Evans, Charles 71, 77
Everett, Eliza 94
Everett, Nathan **246**
excise office 143, 144

Fawn 50, 88
Finnis, Mary 95
Finnis, Thomas 82, 90, 208
fire brigade 46, 75–7, 144
Fisher, John 81, 115, 138
fishing 116, 117, 138
Fishing Boat 70
Five Bells 33, 97, **124**
Five Ringers 64, 73, 77, 82, 123, 137
Flint & Co, brewers 99, 249–50
flooding 77–8
Foden steam wagons 44
food sales 116
Forester 32, **32**, 201
Foresters Hall 132–3
Fountain 79, 81, 92, 94, 101, 104, 111, 114, 116, 123, 136, 137, 142, 144, 171, 195, 208, 260, 261
Fountain (Canterbury) 146
Fox 35, 79, 82, 196, 197, 208
Fraternal masonic lodge 135
Frederick William 71
free houses 30–1
free licensing 254
freemasonry 135
Fremlins brewery 244
Friend, George 220
Friend, John 120
Friendly Port 71, 80, 101, 133, 261
friendly societies 130–1
frog-marching 178–9
Frost, Percy 118
function rooms 119
Funnell, Mark 97

Galatea lugger 93
gambling 127–8
Gaming Act (1845) 123
gaming machines 127–8
gardening clubs 37, 138, 267
Gardner & Co, brewers 264
gas explosion 74, 75
general election (1874) 202, 203; (1880) 203; (1892) 229; (1895) 230; (1906) 237, 261
George Beer, brewers 10, 34, 35, 37, 62, 74, 75, 80, 92, 188, 195, 197, 199, 244, 245, 248, 249–50, 251, 252, 260, 261, 263, 264
George and Dragon (Walmer) 56
Gillow, Captain 229
Gimber, Thomas 160
Globe 79, 198, 259
Glover, Steve 137, 144
Gloucester Arms (Bayswater) 189
Goldsmid, Sir Julian 204, **205**, 236
Goldup, John 90
Good Intent 78, 122
Goodchild, William 90, 147
Goodwin Light Good Templars 217–18, 223, 225
Goodwin Sands 13, 103
Gould, Thomas 89
Gourvish, T.R. 60
Grand Shadow Pantomime 120
Graves, James 90–1
Great Mongeham brewery 23, 43, 49
Green Man (Covent Garden) 84
Greenaway, John 156, 254, 262
Greyhound 36, 71, 89, 90, 95, 128, 136, 169–70, 265–6, 267
Greyhound Self Help society 130
Grigg, Edward Galley 87, 88, **88**, 166
Grigg, John Galley 88
Grigg, Philip 88
grocers' licences 193, 242, 247
Guinness bottled beer 36
gun clubs 138
Gun Inn 122
Gunner, Emma 95, 197
Gunter, Philip 89
Gutzke, David 33, 230, 232

habitual drunkenness 172
Hall, Edward 80
Hall, Emily 80, 263

283

Hall, Henry 80
Halliday, Edward 40
Halliday, William 42
Hamilton, Charles 190
Hammill, Rev 243
Hammond, George 62
Hanger, Edward 82, **82**
Hare and Hounds 75, 122, **122**, 167, 198
Harp 63, 83, 119, 263
Harris, Patrick 207
Harrison, Brian 215, 226, 234
Harrison, Francis 126
Harvey, Alexander 90, 177
Hasted, Edward 114
Hatton, John 24, 32
Haunch of Mutton supper 136
Hayman, William 41, 238
Hayward, George 71
Hayward, William 112
Hearts of Oak Benefit Society 136, 266
Heroes of the Goodwin Sands 220
Hight, Thomas 20, 23, 47, 238
Hight, Thomas Tapley 23–4
Hills Brewery 22–3, 30, 31, 33, 34, 37, **38**, 40, 44, **45**, 49, 52–6, 72, 74, 88, 243, 244, 252
Hills, Charles 20, 22, 31, 38, 48
Hills, Charles (Jr.) 22
Hills, Daniel 22, 41, 47, 48, 49, 52, 191, 238
Hills, Edwin 22, 39, 49, 91, 238
Hills' fire engine 46
Hills, John 62, 147
Hills' public houses, distribution of **51**
Hills and Thompson's breweries 20–30, 38, 80
HMS *Bulldog* 107
HMS *Mars* 107
Hodges, shipping agents 106
Hoile, Inspector George 157, 158
holiday making 114–17, **115**
Holness, Richard 84
Holt, George 111, 178–9
Holtum, George 25
Holtum, John 25
Homer, John 234–5
Hoop and Griffin 131
Hope 259, 261
Horse and Farrier 82, 96, 97, 101, 108, 123, 253, 255, 263, 264

House of Commons Select Committee 59, 102
houses of ill-repute 179–87
Hovelling Boat 70
Hughes, Edwin 203, 207
Hurst, George 206

Iggulden, Edward 20, 21–2, 31, 38, 39, 47, 48, 52, 102
Iggulden, John 20, 21–2, 31, 38
Independent Order of Friends 134
Independent Order of Good Templars 217–19, 223, 225, 236
Independent Order of Oddfellows 71, 132–4, 136
Independent Order of Rechabites 135, 222–3
India Arms 36–7, 59, **59**, 72, 75, 84, 135, 136
indoor games 123–4, 267
industrial accidents 42–3
Ingleton, Roy 158
inquests 141–2
Inspector of Nuisances 44, 159, 265
Iron Crown salvage 103

Jefferson, Samuel 223
Jennings, Mary 94
Jennings, Paul 125
Jewitt, William 75, 145
Jolly Gardener 15, 42, 73, 83, 127, 164, 195, 198, 200, 207
Jolly Sailor 71, 90, 110, 111, 112, 113, 177, 178, **179**, 256
Jones, Harry 86
Jubilee celebrations **39**
Just Reproach 15
Justices of the Peace 154; brewers as 47
JW Court & Son 225

Karslake & Co 27
Kelsey, William 238, 244
Kemp, Amelia 93–4, 96, 97, 105, 112, 255
Kemp, Ellen 97
Kemp, Mariner 93, 97, 171
Kemp, Thomas **64**
Kentish Gazette 22, 29, 130, 135, 144
Kentish Observer 210
Kentish Post 114

Kewell, Supt 164
Kidner, Thomas 87
King's Arms 68, 70, 72, 73, 82, 93
King's Head 70, 93, 95, 143, 175, 245, 255
King's Head (Dover) 86
Knatchbull-Hugessen, Edward 48, 203, 234–6, **235**, 239
Knight, Thomas 40

Labourers' Union 137
Laird, Thomas 143
Lambert, William 93
landladies *see* landlords
landlords 11, 15, 35, 81–93; absentee licensees 97; ages of 84; bankruptcy/insolvency of 89–92; boatmen as 81; character of 61; and electoral corruption 204–11; ex-servicemen as 85–6; landladies 11, 15, 35, 93–9; LVA social activities 232; and military police 177–9; on municipal council 238–42; murders 92; part-time 97; places of birth 84; previous experience of 84–7; rapid turnover of 87; representations by 228–42; second occupations of 81–3, 88; suicides 42, 92–3; tenant rents 88–9; trade organisations 228–42; tradesmen as 82
Langley, Morris 41, 144, 238
Langley, Thomas 165
Larkins, Robert 112
Latter, Thomas 261
lawn tennis 122
Lawson, Sir Wilfred 236
Licence, Sarah **98**
Licence, William 87, 98, 240, **240**
Licensed Victuallers Protection Society of London 228, 229
licensing 9, 10, 16, 31–3, 38, 54, 58, 60–5, 68–70, 80–1, 97, 104, 120, 127, 140, 156–7, 184, 185, 186, 242–57; assessment 263; beer sales to children 199–200; bowling greens 122: contested applications 242–69; enforcement 127, 187–201; free licensing 254; grocers' licences 193, 242, 247; licence issue referendum 262–3; licence transfers

INDEX

86–7, 92–5, 183, 191; magistrates' decisions 242–69; occasional licenses 199, 231; permitted hours 192–9; reduction of licences 248–9; *Sharp* v. *Wakefield* licensing judgement 249, 250, 251; and structural alterations 200; Sunday closing 226, 237, 244; trading-in 257; two-for-one deal 257, 258
Licensing Acts: (1872) 180–1, 188, 192–3, 195, 197, 229; (1874) 193, 195; (1902) 80, 142; (1904) 54, 80, 87, 232, 237, 259, 262
Licensing Bill (1908) 232, 235, 261–2
Lifeboat 32, **32**, 70, 97, 163, 208, 245, 261
Line Regiments, in Deal 109–10
Lines, James 189
Linscott, John 247
Liquor Traffic Control Bill 230
live-in servants 96–7
Liverpool Arms 43, 65, 82, 86, **95**, 121, 138, 265, 266–7, **266**, 268
Lloyd George, David 262–3
Local Veto Bill 233
Locomotive 70, 147
lodging houses 112–14
London breweries 36
London Cooper Stout 36
long pull 200
Lord Keith 70
Lord Nelson 70, 73, 94, 97, 129, 183, 185, 257
Lord Warden 31, 123, 207, 257
Lord Warden (Walmer) 133, 136,
Lord Warden masonic lodge 135
Lovegrove, Thomas 84
Lower Deal 13, 14
Lower Street brewery 20, 21–2
Lush, Justice 204
LVA (Deal, Walmer and Sandwich Licensed Victuallers Protection Association) 229–41, 244, 247–8, 250, 255, 262, 265

McCarroll, Lieutenant 92
Macey, Ann 97, 180, 184
McGill, Rev 244
MacIntosh, James 249–52
Mackenzie, Eliza 183
Mackeson & Co, brewers 36

Mackie, Henry 97
Mackie, Robert 82
Mackins, John 209, **211**
Macnamara, Patrick 179
Macready, Major Edward 175
magistrates, and police 151–68
Magnet 73, 74, 123, 241
mail coaches 144–5
Maltby, Charles 136
malting 23, 27, 28
Mancini, John 127
Mangilli, Achille 128
Manisty, Justice 204
Manor of Chamberlain's Fee 31
Maori chief's head 123
Marine Mutiny Act 178
Marsh, George 86
Marsh, James 95
Marsh, Simon 82
Marsh, Susannah 93, 95, 119
masonic lodges 135
Massachusetts Anti-Saloon League 16
Mathias, Peter 21
Matthews, Arthur 39–40, 41, 47, 50, 55, 101, 260, 262, 263
Matthews & Canning 26, 28, 30
Matthews, Jessie 50
Matthews, John 26, 27, 28, 29–30, 38, 39, 41, 47, 48–9, 50, 55
Matthews, Mary 50
Matthews, Willie 41, 47, 50, 137
Maxted, Joseph 185
Maxton Arms 86, 88, 89, 101, 110, 112, 113, 163, 177, 180, 184, 185, 189, 200, 260, 261
Maxton Brewery 88, 189
May, Henry 118, 241
mayoral dinners 119
Mayors 154–5
Meakins, Harry 81, 119
Mercer, PC 151
Merchant Navy Act 156
Mercury 12, 36, 43, 48, 49, 52, 53, 107, 108, 116, 120, 138, 141, 143, 151, 156, 164, 170, 172, 175, 176, 193, 203, 204, 209, 210, 217, 218, 220, 223, 227, 230, 233, 236, 238, 239, 249, 250, 255, 257
Mild and Brilliant ale 29
military drunkenness 174–7
military police, and landlords 177–9

military service 109
Mockett, George 238
Morgan, Eugene 113
Morning Star 115
Morrah, Major 144
mortuary, public houses as 142
Mote, George 143
Municipal Corporations Act (1835) 153–4, 157
murders 92, 112
Murray, Percy 92

Nalder & Collyer, brewers 36, 37, 119, 121, 265
Napier Tavern 38, 62, 70, 72, 79, 81, 104, 116, 132, 138, 169, 198, 264
National Insurance Act (1911) 223
National Temperance League 223
National Trade Defence Association 262
National Trade Defence Fund 230
naval shore leave 106–9
Neale, Robert 84
New Inn 72, 87, 90, **143**, 144, 245
New Plough 74, 123, 232, 241
Newcastle programme 229
Nicholas, Mrs 97
No 1 Ale 29
No 1 Stout 29
No 2 Ale 29
No 2 Stout 29
Noah's Ark 97, 111, 112, 190
Noah's Ark Sick Benefit Club 130
Norfolk Arms 71, 88, 112, **179**, 180, 184, 207
Norris, George 63, 76, 195
North Deal 14, **32**
North Deal Bowling Club 129
North Deal lifeboat 82, 87
North End Brewery 20, 23–4, 29, 31, 32, 33, 245
North Star 24, 31, 32, **32**, 59, 82, 91, 97, 118, 196, 208
North Ward Ratepayers Association 240

Oak and Ivy 123, 195, 198, 245, 256
Oakley, Thomas 21, 23, 47, 135
Oakley, Thomas Parker 21
Oakley's Stout Ale 29
Oatridge, William 127, 128

285

Oatridge's restaurant **127**, 128
Obree, Thomas 169
occasional licenses 199, 231
Oddfellow's Arms 71, 133
Oddfellows Hall 199, 262
Old Victory 144, 190
Olds, Samuel 146, 206, 207, 208, 209
Omer, John 31
Ommaney, Frederick 47–8, 49, 50
omnibus transport 145–7
O'Neil, Percy 169
Orange Institution 135
Order of Enlightened Cottages 131
Orrick, Richard 104
outdoor activities 121–4, 267
Outwin, John 71, 91–2, 107, 117, 163, 192, 206, **206**, 208, 229, 231, 238, 249

Pain, Arthur 129
Pain, Edward 87
Pain, George 162
Paragon Music Hall 71, 120, 170, 184, 240, 253
Park Street public rooms 117
Park Street Sale Rooms 49
Park Tavern 32, 62, 97, 110, 125, 172, 175, 183, 186, **187**, 198, 243, 244
Parker, Supt Thomas 160, 162, 185, 186, 194
Parker, Supt William 162–3, 165, 167
Parliamentary Commissioners 59, 115, 152–3, 204–5
Parrett, James 71
Pavement Commissioners 14, 75, 78–9, 153
Payne, Rev Bruce 209–10, 217, 219–20, **219**, 221, 223–4, 242–3
Pearce, Robert 92
Pelican 31, 59, 74, 95
Pettet, Isabella 94
Pettet, William 82
Phillips, Thomas 260, 261
Philpott, Mrs 171
Philpott, Sgt Joshua 52, 163, 165, **167**
Pier Hotel 32, 70, 109, 198, 245
Pier Refreshment Rooms 37
Pierce, Hetty 111–12
Piercy, William 92–3

pigeon shoots 121
pilots 104–5, 112
Pilots Mutual Benefit Society 132
ping pong 124
Piper, Richard 137
Pittock, William 181–2
Pleasant Sunday Afternoon (PSA) Brotherhood 226
Plough 175
police court missionaries 220
policing 14, 16, 127, 147, 151–79, 242, 255; and licensing decisions 255, 258; licensing enforcement 127, 187–201, 246
political activities, by brewers 48–9
political corruption 204–11
political party meetings 141
pool 123
population 13, 59, 60, 65, 70
Port Arms 34, 81, 105, 119, 131, 227
Porter, George 81, 171
Powell, Thomas 237
Prince Albert 10, 34, 35, 62, 70, 73, 86, 91, 125, 166, 200, 208, **269**
Prince Alfred 144
Prince of Wales 68, 82, 249
Pritchard, Stephen (historian) 60, 62, 155
Pritchard, Stephen (landlord) 87, 136, 147, 208
private and public-house brewing, decline of 30, 33–4
private limited companies, breweries as 50
prohibitionists 233, 236, 239, 254
prosecutions, by LVA 231
prostitution 125, 170, 179–87
Providence 32, 76, 93, 166, 198
Provident Benefit Society 136
Provincial Licensed Victuallers Defence League 228, 234
Pryor, Charles 187
public functions 139–45
Public Health Act (1872) 193
public houses: at election times 201–11; beer sales 30, 89; billeting in 141, 228; changing appearance of 80; civic meetings in 140–1; closures 14, 242–69; Deal (1870) 66–70, **66–70**; dinners for non-commissioned of-

ficers 111; and electoral corruption 204–11; entertainment in 117–28; as excise office 143, 144; extra activities by 144; fires/explosions 74–7, 119, 126; flooding 77–8; internal design/usages 72–3; licensing see licensing; and mail coaches 144–5; as mortuaries 142; names of 70–1; numbers of 15, 17, 31, 58–99, 248; open plan 73; opening hours 192–9; ownership of 31, 52; public auctions in 144; public bodies using 144; public inquests in 141–2; public/political meetings in 141, 152, 201; ratings valuations 72; reduction programme 70, 259–65; refurbishment/rebuilding 74–9, 261; regulation of 9, 10, 16, 31, 32–3, 54, 80–1, 140, 147, 151–68, 192; see also licensing; rents 88–9; role of 16; sale prices of 73–4, 79; and ship-wrecked crews 63, 143; signs on 80–1; stabling 145; as staging posts 144–5, **146**; Sunday closing 226, 237, 244; and travellers 147, 195–6; unfair competition between 231–2; users of 101–47; women customers 125; see also beer, individual public houses
public order 16, 155–7
public service, by brewers 47–8
publicans see landlords
Puckeridge, Oswald 147
Punch and Cake Festival 136
pyramids 123

Queen's Arms 70, 77, 89, 107, 112, 114, 243
Queen's Hall Picture Palace (cinema) 54, **54**
Queen's Head 31, 70, 77, 119, 123
Queen's Head (Walmer) 132
quoits 122

rail transport 145–7
railway houses 36
Railway Tavern 62, 70, 105, 114, 147, **196**, 240
Ralph, PC George 163, 167, 208

Index

Ramell, William 238, 239, 241–2, 244, 250, 253, 257, 261
Ramsden, George 86–7
Ramsey, PC 163
Randall, Eliza 97
Randall, Thomas 97
Randolph, Francesco 113
Ratcliffe, PC 167
Rea, Edward 208, 209
Red Lion 260
Red Lion (Minster) 129
Redan 62, 70, 71
Redlich, Josef 154
Redman, Charles 198, 207
Redman, James 197
Redman, William 206
Redsull, Edward 42, 83, 88
Redsull, Elizabeth 88
Redsull, Henry 158, 162, 169
Redsull, James 171
Redsull, Louise 160
Redsull, Robert 88, 123
Redsull, Thomas 169
Redsull, William 88, 241
Reform Act (1832) 203
Reform Act (1867) 141
Reform lugger 82, 93
refractory seamen 106
Richardson, Thomas 39
Ricketts, Benjamin 97
Riley, Richard 10, **10**, 264
Riley, William 10, 62, 166, 208
road transport 145–7
"Roaring Thompson" beer 124
Roberts, Crompton 203–4
Roberts, Frederick "Flint" **85**, **198**
Roberts, John (**Albion**) 87
Roberts, John (**Fox**) 35
Robin Hood shipwreck 23
Rogers, Michael 137, 144
Rose 22, 70, 72, 74, 84, 87, 118, 123, **133**, 135, 136, 199, 241, 247
Rose and Crown 70, 85, 104, 143, 144, 171, 197, 198, **198**, 200, 207
Rose Inn (Broadstairs) 84
Roxburgh Castle 74, 163, **182**, 245
Royal Antediluvian Order of Buffaloes 134, **134**, 136
Royal Cafe Restaurant 128
Royal Clarendon Hotel 71
Royal Exchange 84, 94, 104, **105**, 114, 134, 135, 137, 239
Royal George 76, 238

Royal Hotel 37, 59, 71, 72, 75, 76, 79, 84–5, 90, 94, 114, 119, 123, 136, 137, 146, 206, 238, 260
Royal Marine 32
Royal Marine Depot Band of Hope 223
Royal Marines 109–11, **111**, 117, 175, **176**, 178
Royal Naval Temperance Society 223
Royal Navy, as visitors 106–9, **108**
Royal Navy masonic lodge 135
Royal Oak 118, 120, 123, 131, 135, 144, 145
Royal Standard (Walmer) 132
Ruxton, Capt John Hay 168

St George's Hall 117, 136
salvage 102–4
Salvation Army 226
Sandown Castle 75, **79**, 122
Sandown Castle 141
Sandwich Arms 71
Sandwich brewery 32
Sandwich Gaol 160–1, **161**
Saracen's Head 62, 87, 98, 118, **129**, 171, 175, 240, 241
savings clubs 129, 130
Sawford, Alfred 189
Sayers, Herbert 35, 87
Scarborough Cat 70, 74, 79, 85
Scorched Bean Society 132
Scott, Private 111
sea bathing 114–17, **115**
sea transport 145–7
Self Help societies 130
Seven Stars 71, 180, 183, 265
Shah 88, 113
Sharp v. *Wakefield* licensing judgement 249, 250, 251
Shelvey, Edward 199–200
Shelvey, Frederick 122
Shepherd Neame, brewers 15
Shiman, Lilian 222
"Shinny Hilly" beer 124
Ship 31, 70, 88, 92, 261
Ship and Castle 112, 113
ship-wrecked crews 63, 143
Shipley, Henry 62, 138
shore leave 106–9
Signor Angelici's Troupe of Mandolinists 118

Simmons, Frank 41, 126
Simmons, PC 197
Simpson, David 189
Sir John Falstaff 79, 97, 99, 112, 168, 249
Sir Norman Wisdom 15
Sir Sidney Smith 70, 89, 117, 132, 165, 180, 185, **186**, 253, 264
skating rink 119
Skinner, Arthur 86, 268
Skinner, George 190–1
Skinner, John 198, 207
skittles 123
Slate Clubs 130
Slawson, Charles 199
slot machines 128
Smith, Charles 207
Smith, George 178
Smith, James 110
Smith, John 99
Smith, Sydney 61
smoking 126–7
smoking concerts 118, 124, 199
smoking rooms 73
smuggling 102
Sneller, Onesiphorus 37–8, 81, 169
Society for the Protection of Fire and Life 76
soft drinks 225
South Barracks 111
South Deal 14
South Eastern Hotel 115–16
South Foreland 78, 88
Sparkes, Alfred 95
Sparkes, Esther 95–6
sparrow shoots 121
Spears, Henry 208, 209
Spears, William 82
special constables 166
Spicer, William 177
Spinner, William 40
sporting/leisure clubs 137–8
stabling 145
Stacey, William 86
Stag (Walmer) 209
staging posts 144–5
Stanhope Hall 54, **54**
Stanhope Road **53**, 54, **54**, 55
Stanton, William 105
Star 71, 89, 120, 169, 170, **170**, 177, 180, 183, 184
Star and Garter 37, 62, 72, 114, 128, 201, **201**, 206

Startup, George 198
steam wagons **44**
Steed, Ernest 86
Stephen Parker 225
Stoddart, Daniel 29
Stoke Hotel (Guildford) 84
storms 77–8, 105
Strathclyde shipwreck 143
Stride, Ada 265–6
Stride, Ernest 265–6
structural alterations 200
Success lugger 82
suicides 42, 92–3
Sun 72, 101, 180, 259
Sunday closing 226, 237, 244
Swan 74, 94, 121, 130, 145, 146
Sydenham Green 174, 185

Tabraham, Rev 258
Tally Ho 71, 264
Tandy, John 82, **83**
Taylor, Henry 86, 135
teetotallers *see* temperance movement
Telegram 12, 20, 25, 40, 43, 62, 67, 75, 78, 104, 108, 118, 123, 130, 131, 132, 141, 142, 143, 162, 165, 171, 174, 177, 179, 193, 202, 203, 216, 223–4, 225, 229, 233, 234, 235, 267
Telegraph (public house) 136, 257–8, **257**, 260
temperance movement 11, 16, 68, 215–27, 228, 229–30, 233, 237–9, 241, 243–4, 249, 250, 254, 256, 258, 262; temperance referendum proposal 230
Temperance Refreshment Room 225
tenant publicans 30, 35
tenant/brewery relationships 35
Theatre Royal 262
Theobald, Thomas 209
Thomas, Harry 261
Thompson, Edmund 20, 24–5, 32, 38, 39, 40, 47, 48
Thompson employees' outings **39**
Thompson, Harriet 183
Thompson, Morris 25, 26–7, 40, 42, 47, 48, 132
Thompson, Richard 24
Thompson and Son's Brewery 25–8, 32, 33, 37, 40, 44, 49, 50–2, 54, 55, 79, 80, 243, 244, 245, 252, 256, 258, 259, 260, 261, 263, 267; *see also* Walmer brewery
Thompsons and Matthews family tree **26**
Thompson's Bell (Walmer) 56
Thompson's steam wagons **44**
Three Compasses 17, 63, 92, 105, 110, 133, 157, 207, 249–53, **252**, 256
Three Compasses affair 157
Three Jolly Butchers (Tottenham) 85
tied houses 30–1
tobacco 126–7
town life, and brewing 38–49
trade unions 137
tradesmen 82, 113
Trafalgar Hotel (Ramsgate) 90
transport 145–7
travellers 147, 195–6
Treanor, Rev T Stanley 220–1, **221**, 262, **263**
Tringrove, Maria 172
Trott, Edward 82, 93
Trott, Sarah 93
Trott, Thomas 131
Two of Ale 200
Two Brewers 120, 121

Union masonic lodge 135, 137
United Kingdom Alliance 216, 226, 230, 236, 239, 254
United Services Magazine 174–5
Upper Deal 13, 14, **95**
Upper Deal Bowling Club 123

venereal disease 180–1
Verrier, George 140
Verrier, Richard 87, 122
Victoria 32, 70, 164, 206
voting rights 153

Walmer ales 28
Walmer barracks 75, 109
Walmer brewery 20, 25, **25**, 26, 27, **27**, 28, 30, 40, 44, **55**, 56; *see also* Thompson & Sons
Walmer Castle 53, 59, 71, 72, 74, 75, 79, 87, 88, 89, 91, 114, 118, 119, 120, 123, 129, 132, 135, 137, 144, 145, 146, **146**, 162–3, 189, 228, 238; Christmas Goose and Spirit Club 129
Walmer Castle affair 162–3
watch committee *see* policing
water closets 73
water quality 23
water supply 24
Waterman's Arms 62, 86, 263
Webb, Henry 187
Weller, George 89
Wellington, Arthur Wellesley, 1st Duke of 9, 17, 146
Wellington masonic lodge 135–6
Wells, Henry 197
West, Henry 87
Weston, Alfred 238
Weston, John 177, 183
Wheelhouse, William 233
Whitbread, brewers 30
White, Edwin 42
White, Henry 43
White Horse 32, 70, 87, 101, 124, 126, 206
White Horse (Bridge) 230
White Post Brewery 32
Whitlaw, Herman 90
Wilds, Robert 82, 97, 208
Wilkinson, Elizabeth 183
Willis, Capt 159
Wilson, R.G. 60
Windsor Castle 32
Wine and Beerhouse Act (1869) 64
Wine Shades 91
Winstanley, M. 83
Wise, Arthur 52–3
women customers 125
Wood, Benjamin 240, 241
Woodward, Sarah 183
Wooten, Jane 125
working men's clubs 139
Workmen's Union 137
Wraight, George 45
Wyborn, Bethel 82
Wyborn, William 246, 251
Wylde, Frederick 118

X, XX and XXX ales 28–9, 35

Yarmouth Packet 70, 77, 87, 93–4, **96**, 97, 104, 105, 112, 255
Ye Olde Bowling Club 123
Yew Tree 246
Young, Caroline 94
Young, Horace 94